NEW MEETING POINT 2de

Anglais A2 / B1

DIRECTRICE D'OUVRAGE ET AUTEUR :

Josette STARCK
Lycée Richelieu, Rueil-Malmaison (92)

AUTEURS :

Cynthia BENREY
Lycée International, Saint-Germain-en-Laye (78)

Pascale CAMPS-VAQUER
Collège Les Vallées, La Garenne-Colombes (92)

Pryscilla HEBEL
Lycée Evariste Galois, Sartrouville (78)

Véronique JAUBERT
Lycée Jacques Prévert, Longjumeau (91)

Maël JOYEUX
LTG François Villon, Les Mureaux (78)

Paul LARREYA
Professeur en linguistique

Lucile MENU
Lycée Richelieu, Rueil-Malmaison (92)

Laurence PEYRESSATRE-GILLOT
Lycée Richelieu, Rueil-Malmaison (92)

Dominique SANTONI
Collège-lycée Buffon, Paris (75)

Hatier

Les auteurs tiennent à remercier profondément leurs familles qui les ont soutenus dans cette belle aventure, ainsi que leurs élèves, et tous ceux qui ont pu contribuer par leurs remarques à l'élaboration de *New Meeting Point.*

Conception graphique :
Marc Henry
Massimo Miola
Studio Favre & Lhaïk
Gudrun Challe

Réalisation :
Studio Favre & Lhaïk
Gudrun Challe

Illustrations :
Juliette Baily
Vincent Landrin

Infographie :
Johanna Crainmark

Iconographie :
Nadine Gudimard

Édition :
Cécilia Paymon

Achevé d'imprimer en Italie par L.E.G.O. S.p. A., Lavis (TN) - Dépôt légal n° 96198-4/01 - Avril 2014

© Hatier - Paris, 2014 - ISBN : 978-2-218- 96198-4

Discovering the world through English!

Apprendre une langue étrangère, c'est voyager dans le temps et dans l'espace, s'initier à d'autres modes de vie et découvrir de nouveaux auteurs et artistes...

***New Meeting Point* 2de est LE lieu de rencontre avec le monde anglophone. Votre manuel vous accompagne, toute l'année, en classe et en dehors de la classe, dans la découverte de la culture anglo-saxonne.**

Travelling broadens the mind.

Avec ***New Meeting Point* 2de**, vous êtes **acteur de votre apprentissage** :

- Les pages *YOUR TASK* vous aideront à mobiliser vos connaissances et à réinvestir les acquis des cours précédents. Elles sont présentes à la fin de chaque unité et vous permettront d'être créatifs et de prendre la parole.
- Les encadrés *HELP* et les doubles-pages *LANGUAGE AT WORK* vous permettront d'enrichir votre lexique et de consolider vos acquis grammaticaux.
- Les rubriques *IMPROVE YOUR SKILLS* vous aideront à acquérir les stratégies nécessaires pour devenir autonome.

Try, and you will achieve!

Avec ***New Meeting Point* 2de**, **de nouveaux horizons s'ouvrent à vous** :

- Le choix des thèmes et des documents (textes, audio, images, vidéos) originaux et de difficultés variées vous permettra de travailler quel que soit votre niveau. Toutes les unités ont été testées dans nos classes.
- Les doubles-pages *READING / SPEAKING / SONG CORNER* sont aussi l'occasion de découvrir des textes, des œuvres d'art et des chansons qui apportent un éclairage différent sur le thème de l'unité.
- Les *FAST FACTS* donnent un accès visuel rapide aux repères culturels essentiels pour mieux comprendre le Royaume-Uni, les États-Unis et l'Afrique du Sud.

Avec ***New Meeting Point* 2de**, **vous mesurerez vos progrès tout au long de l'année** :

- Une évaluation diagnostique vous aidera en début d'année à connaître votre niveau d'anglais par rapport aux critères du Cadre Européen Commun de Références pour les Langues.
- Des évaluations sommatives clôturent chaque grande partie et permettront de mesurer vos progrès dans chaque activité langagière.

Get help when you're not sure.

Speak, and don't let others speak for you!

LES SUPPORTS DE LA COLLECTION SONT PENSÉS POUR VOUS :

- Le *Workbook* propose **15 fiches « Apprendre à apprendre »**, pour vous entraîner à travailler individuellement.
- Le **site compagnon** **www.editions-hatier.fr/meetingpoint/** vous propose les enregistrements sous format MP3 de la méthode à télécharger.

Teachers open the door, but you must enter by yourself!

La structure des unités

Le manuel est divisé en cinq modules qui permettent un travail équilibré des cinq activités langagières.

Découvrir

Ouverture

Les notions du programme et l'annonce de la tâche finale

Introduction de la thématique et du champ lexical de l'unité

Deux nouvelles rubriques « *Play with words* » et « *Song Corner* »

Les documents

Selon les unités, nous travaillerons ensuite sur 5 à 7 pages. L'objectif est de construire une **pratique communicative**, de donner de vraies raisons de lire, communiquer, prendre la parole, écrire.

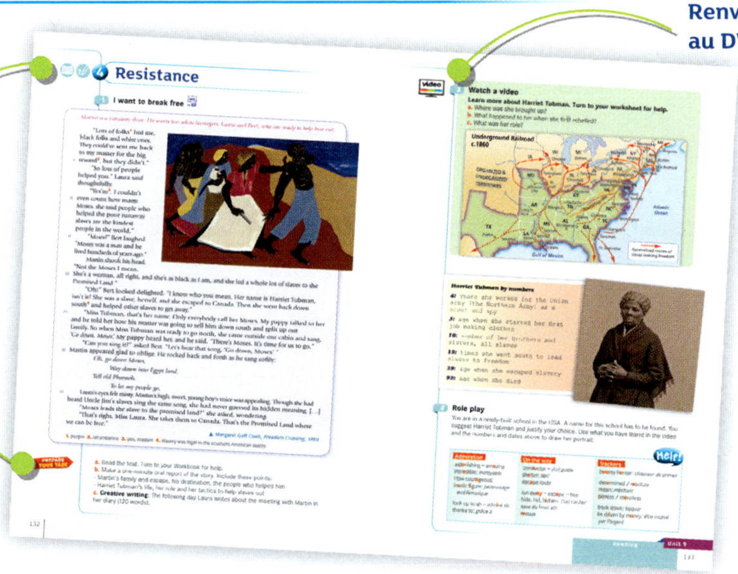

La ou les compétences langagières travaillées

Tâche intermédiaire préparant la tâche finale

Renvoi au DVD

Aides lexicales

Help!

Champ lexical

Nom

Adjectifs

Verbes

Who? What?

former big executive: *ex cadre supérieur*
corporation /firm /fɜːm/: *société, compagnie*
philanthropist: someone who freely gives money and help to people in need
committed to V-ING: *engagé*
destitute: *démuni*
deprived of: *privé de*
disadvantaged
quit, (quit, quit) one's job

Goals

inequalities
literacy rate: *taux d'alphabétisation*
be on an equal footing with: *être sur un pied d'égalité avec*
give equal opportunities
bridge the gap: *combler le fossé*
get a fair deal: *être traité de façon équitable*
take measures /ˈmeʒəz/

Voyelle accentuée

Traduction

Phonétique

votre manuel

Travail de la langue

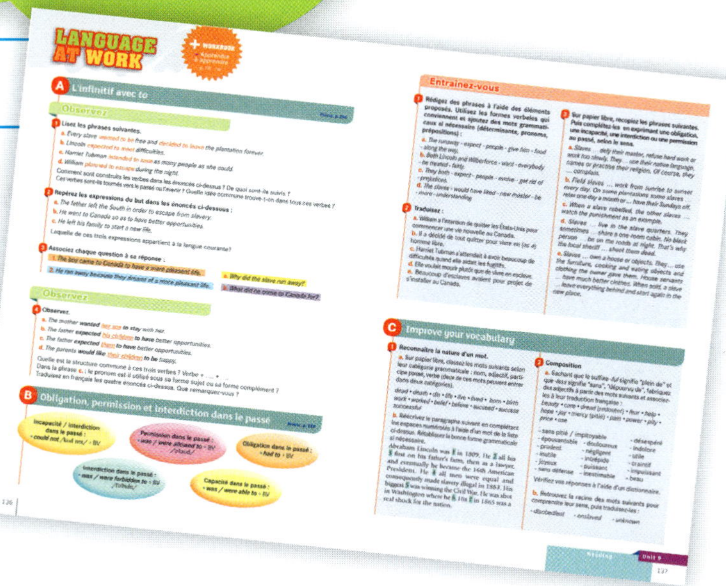

La réflexion sur la langue est en contexte, l'élève est actif, il observe, compare, déduit et s'entraîne : **Observez / Déduisez / Entraînez-vous**.
La rubrique *« Improve your Vocabulary »* prolonge le renforcement lexical.
« On your own » permet de consolider les acquis et développer l'autonomie de l'élève en rebrassant les faits de langue et/ou le lexique vu dans l'unité dans un contexte différent.

Stratégies à développer

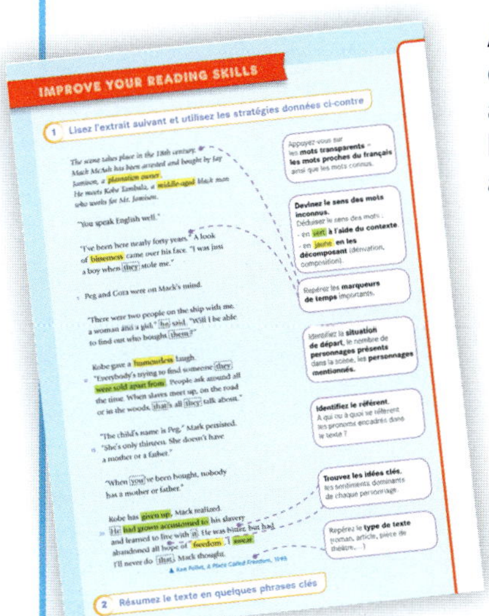

Aide méthodologique *« Improve Your Skills »* : cette page dans l'activité langagière visée a pour but d'aider les élèves à acquérir les savoir-faire nécessaires pour devenir autonome.

Tâche finale

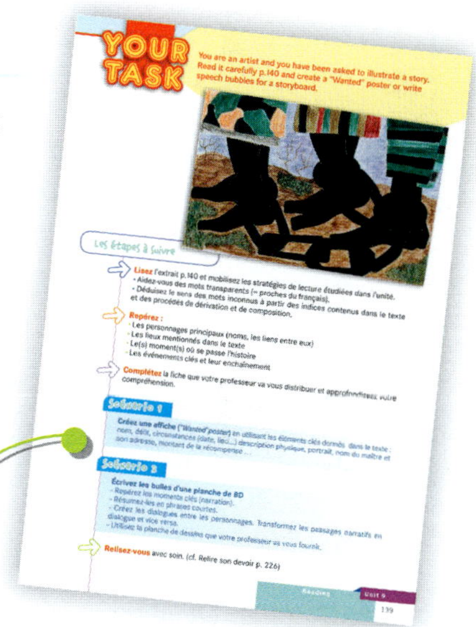

Mise en œuvre concrète et guidée de la tâche finale.

En autonomie

Développement de l'autonomie de l'élève lecture, prise de parole orale, œuvres d'art, chansons… qui permettent à l'élève de **découvrir de nouveaux horizons** en classe ou en autonomie.

Évaluations : mode d'emploi

> Évaluations diagnostiques

Le but de l'évaluation diagnostique

Grille des compétences évaluées sur le CECRL

Entrée dans le thème des évaluations

Déroulement des évaluations

> Évaluations sommatives

La compétence testée dans cette évaluation

Grille d'évaluation du CECRL pour faire le point et prendre conscience des progrès à accomplir

Déroulement des évaluations

Que signifient les pictos du manuel ?

ACTIVITÉ LANGAGIÈRE TRAVAILLÉE

- Lire
- Écouter
- Parler en continu
- Parler en interaction
- Écrire

AUTRES INDICATIONS

- PREPARE YOUR TASK — Étapes de préparation / entraînement à la tâche
- WB P.000 — Renvoi au *Workbook*
- CD1 PISTE 1 — Renvoi aux CD classe
- MP3 PISTE 1 — Renvoi aux MP3 élève
- video — Renvoi au DVD et à la fiche d'aide

À la découverte des pages « Apprendre à apprendre »

Ces fiches détachables clairement identifiables par un bandeau dans le cahier présentent un parcours clair qui va de la mémorisation du mot à la construction de phrase en passant par la révision du point de grammaire clé. Des conseils et des aides ponctuelles facilitent le travail autonome.

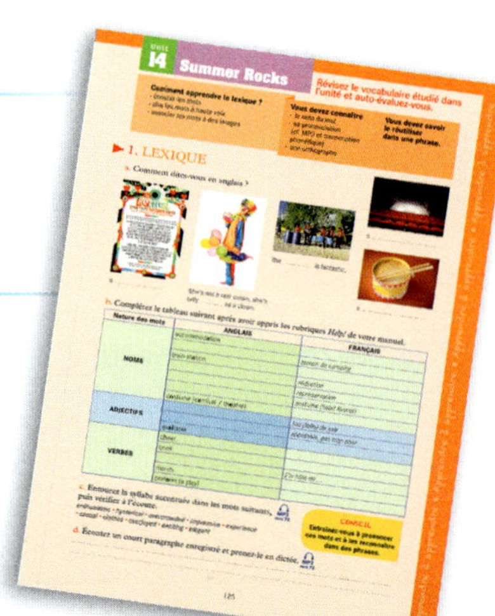

Les annexes du manuel : des outils pour réussir

Aide méthodo-logique

Des outils pour relire son devoir, lire les consignes, commenter une image fixe et animée et enrichir sa prise de parole.

Pour mieux parler

Si la phonétique est présente tout au long du manuel, cette page propose de reprendre les points essentiels qui vous permettront d'améliorer votre prise de parole.

Anglais GB et anglais US

Américains et Britanniques parlent la même langue, quoique… Découvrez les différences essentielles pour faciliter votre compréhension de l'oral.

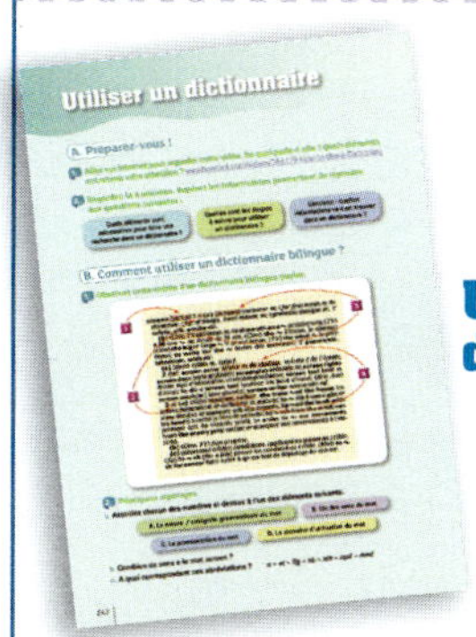

Utiliser un dictionnaire

Apprendre à se servir d'un dictionnaire papier ou en ligne pour trouver les différents sens d'un mot, découvrir sa prononciation.

Fast Facts (UK, US, South Africa)

Des repères historiques et culturels clés pour mieux appréhender le Royaume-Uni, les Etats-Unis et l'Afrique du Sud.

Précis grammatical

Pour vous aider à mieux comprendre et mémoriser les points de grammaire essentiels du niveau B1.

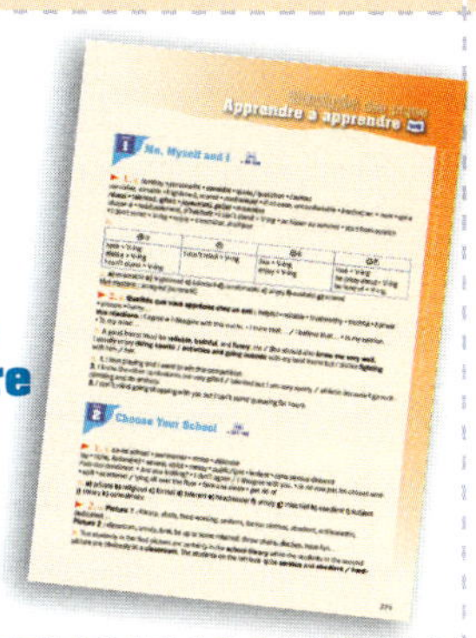

Corrigés apprendre à apprendre

Ces pages situées dans le cahier peuvent être travaillées en autonomie. Retrouvez ici les corrigés qui vous aideront à mesurer vos acquis.

Classroom English

Toujours pour aider votre travail en classe, vous trouverez ici tous les outils dont vous avez besoin pour participer à la vie de la classe, prendre la parole et travailler en groupe.

Conseils de lecture

Quelques conseils pour vous aider à choisir un livre et vous lancer dans la lecture seul(e).

Sommaire

Listening

Unit 4 Destination UK
MÉMOIRE • SENTIMENT D'APPARTENANCE

Unit 5 Over the Rainbow
MÉMOIRE • VISION D'AVENIR

Unit 6 Beyond Limits
VISION D'AVENIR • SENTIMENT D'APPARTENANCE

Reading

Sommaire

Speaking interaction

Writing

Unit 13 City in the Sky

MÉMOIRE • SENTIMENT D'APPARTENANCE

Unit 14 Summer Rocks

SENTIMENT D'APPARTENANCE • MÉMOIRE

Unit 15 Masters of Suspense

SENTIMENT D'APPARTENANCE • MÉMOIRE

Annexes

Évaluation diagnostique à l'entrée en seconde

Une évaluation pour repérer mes points faibles et mes points forts

En cours de langue on s'entraîne dans cinq activités langagières : compréhension écrite, compréhension orale, expression orale en continu ou expression orale en interaction et expression écrite.
L'évaluation diagnostique de début d'année n'est pas un examen.
Elle sert uniquement à faire le bilan de vos acquis du collège.
Chacune de ces évaluations nécessite toute votre attention et votre sérieux.
Grâce à ces évaluations, votre professeur pourra établir quel palier vous avez atteint dans chacune des évaluations en s'appuyant sue le **Cadre Européen Commun de Référence pour les Langues (CECRL)**.
Le **CECRL** a été adopté en 1998 par le Conseil de l'Europe. Il est devenu la référence pour les programmes de langues vivantes en Europe.
A la fin de la classe de troisième, vous devez avoir atteint le niveau B1. En classe de seconde, votre objectif est de consolider le palier B1. Pour le baccalauréat, selon les séries vous devez viser le palier B2 ou C1 pour les LV1. Le tableau ci-dessous résume les compétences pour les niveaux A1, A2 et B1.
Relisez ce tableau de temps à autres afin de garder en mémoire les objectifs à atteindre.

		A1	A2	B1
Parler	S'exprimer en continu	Je peux parler de moi et de sujets familiers brièvement et très simplement, je fais beaucoup de pauses.	Je peux décrire simplement mon environnement (famille, autres gens, quotidien, études et stages).	Je peux raconter une histoire, des expériences, des événements, mes rêves, mes espoirs ou mes buts de manière simple. Je peux réagir brièvement, expliquer mes opinions ou projets.
Parler	Prendre part à une conversation	Je peux échanger simplement et en faisant de nombreuses pauses si mon interlocuteur répète lentement ou reformule ses idées.	Je peux échanger brièvement des informations sur des sujets ou des activités familiers lors de tâches simples et habituelles.	Je peux faire face à de nombreuses situations rencontrées lors d'un voyage dans un pays anglophone. Je peux prendre part, sans préparation, à une conversation sur des sujets familiers (famille, loisirs, travail, voyage et actualité).
Comprendre	Ecouter	Je peux comprendre des consignes et des instructions courtes et simples. Je peux reconnaître des mots et expressions courants si la personne parle lentement et clairement.	Je peux comprendre un message oral sur un sujet familier. Je peux saisir l'essentiel d'annonces et de messages simples et clairs.	Je peux comprendre un message clair donné dans un langage standard s'il concerne des sujets familiers. Je peux saisir l'essentiel de nombreuses émissions (radio, télévision) sur l'actualité ou sur des sujets courants si l'on parle lentement et distinctement.

Comprendre	Lire	Je peux cerner l'idée principale d'un texte très court de façon approximative.	Je peux lire des textes courts et des lettres personnelles très simples. Je peux trouver une information particulière dans des documents courants (publicités, prospectus, menus et horaires).	Je peux comprendre des textes rédigés dans une langue courante. Je peux comprendre la description d'événements, l'expression de sentiments et de souhaits dans des lettres personnelles.
Écrire	Rédiger	Je peux écrire des phrases très courtes avec des mots simples à partir d'un modèle.	Je peux écrire des notes et messages simples et courts.	Je peux écrire un texte simple et cohérent sur des sujets familiers ou qui m'intéressent personnellement.

Je m'entraîne avant l'évaluation

Dans l'évaluation diagnostique proposée, vous retrouverez des sujets qui vous sont familiers. Afin de vous entraîner avant de commencer, réagissez au dessin humoristique suivant :

1. essay assignment: *sujet de rédaction* 2. vacation: *vacances (US)*

1. Faites une liste de mots qui vous seront utiles pour parler du professeur, des élèves, de la situation et classez-les.

2. A partir de votre liste, faites une présentation de la situation : Où ? Quand ? Que se passe-t-il ?

3. Trouvez-vous ce dessin amusant ou non ? Pourquoi ?

4. Vous êtes un/e élève de la classe, vous racontez le soir à vos parents ce qui s'est passé le matin.

ATTENTION !
Quelles formes verbales vous seront utiles pour présenter la situation ?

Evaluation

Votre professeur va vous fournir les différentes fiches d'évaluation. Une fois les évaluations terminées, il/elle pourra déterminer à quel palier vous vous situez par rapport à la grille d'évaluation du Cadre Européen Commun de Référence pour les Langues.

▲ *Country Strong*, Shana Feste, 2010 (starring Leighton Meester)

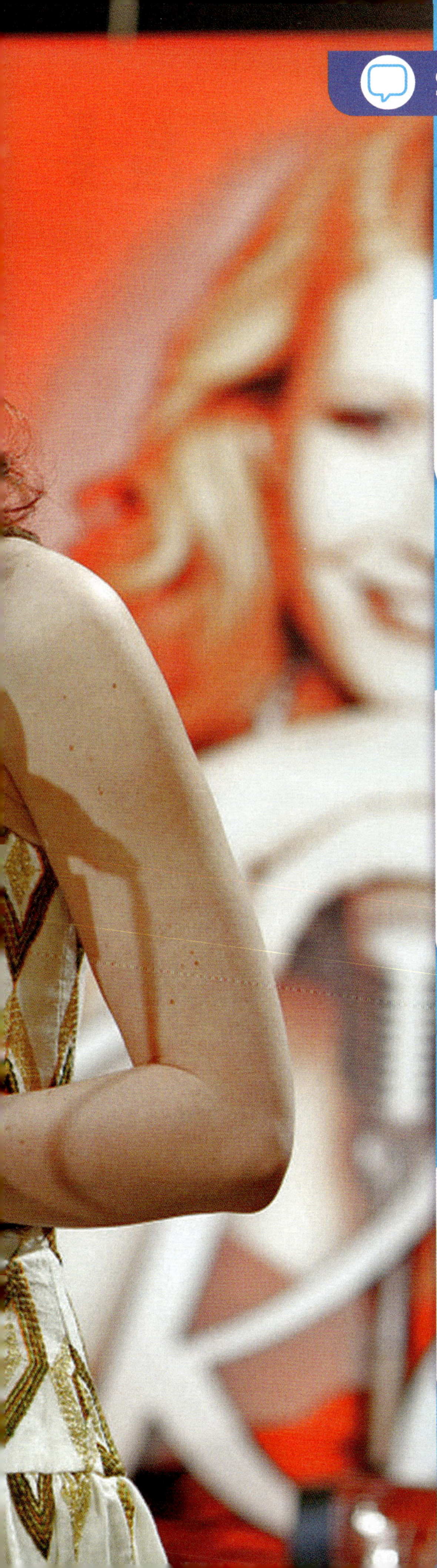

Spoken production

Unit 1 — Me, Myself & I

SENTIMENT D'APPARTENANCE

- **Introduce yourself.**
- **Discover new facets of your personality.**
- **Speak about your likes and dislikes.**
- **Learn more about some reality TV programmes and influential celebrities from the US and the UK.**

YOUR TASK You are entering a casting for a reality TV programme. Prepare your audition

p. 27

Unit 2 — Choose Your School

SENTIMENT D'APPARTENANCE • MÉMOIRE

- **Learn about the different school systems in the US and the UK.**
- **Discover alternative forms of education.**
- **Decide if you would prefer to go to a mixed or a single-sex school.**

YOUR TASK You are the headmaster, or a teacher, or a student representative of a school. You will present the school to your classmates, who will play the part of the parents of future students. At the end of the presentations, they will choose the school they like best.

p. 39

Unit 3 — Change the World

VISION D'AVENIR

- **Discover why John Wood has opened libraries all over the world.**
- **Learn more about the fight of girls to have access to education.**
- **Work on *Imagine*, John Lennon's iconic song.**

YOUR TASK You are taking part in a poetry contest. Choose a poem or a song you like or write your own. Recite it in front of the audience and explain your choice.

p. 51

Unit 1

SENTIMENT D'APPARTENANCE

Me, Myself & I

YOUR TASK AT THE END OF THIS UNIT

You are entering a casting for a reality TV programme. Prepare your audition. p. 27

1 Tune In!

Fiona SCOTT

Family: 13

Brother

Mother

Friends: 469

Mark

Megan

John

Age: 16 years old

Hometown: Calgary, Alberta (Canada)

School: Bowness High School

Birthplace: Dublin (Ireland)

Favorite quotations

- *"I'm a tomboy and I know it!"*
- *"Your favorite quote says more about who you are than about the people or stories you're quoting..."*

Likes

Bowness High School

Calgary Rowing Club

Calgary Hockey Team

Adele

Post

Vacation is over! Can't wait to see you all, guys! ♥

Places

New York (NY, USA) last spring break
Sydney (Australia) next summer hopefully ☺

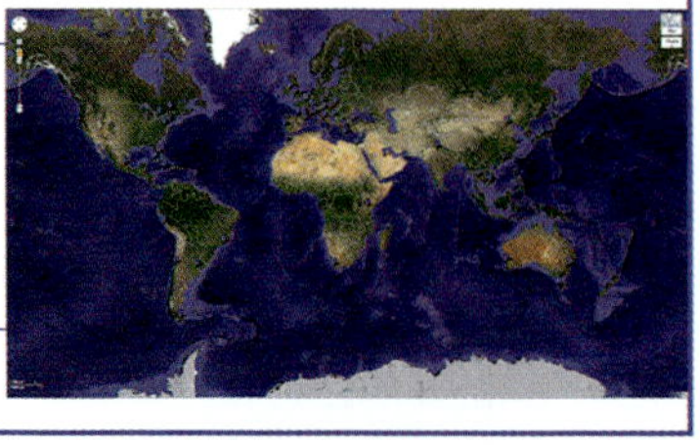

1 Get ready

Observe the profile page opposite.

a. What immediately strikes you?

b. Pick out as many elements as possible to compare Fiona to you.

2 Play with words

WB p. 5

Turn to your Workbook to improve your vocabulary.

3 A new friend?

CD1 PISTE 3

a. Listen to a teenager. Pick out as many key words as you can to present him.

b. Decide if he could become Fiona's friend. Why? Why not?

4 Over to you!

WB p. 6

Fill in your own profile page in your Workbook.

Help!

Canada (Canadian)
(be of) Irish origin
South Africa
Australia
tomboy: *garçon manqué*
rock climbing /ˈklaɪmɪŋ/: *escalade*
rowing /ˈrəʊɪŋ/: *aviron*
archery: *tir à l'arc*
fencing: *escrime*

2 Making New Friends

1 Personality quiz

a. Answer the questions in this quiz.

Are you a lone wolf or a party animal?

1. In general, I prefer:

○ being alone.
△ one-to-one conversations.
□ group activities.

2. What type of student are you?

□ I love taking part in class discussions and being active.
○ I feel embarrassed to speak in front of my classmates, I prefer listening.
△ I don't really pay attention to what is going on in class, I am a daydreamer!

3. What are your plans for next Saturday night?

△ I already have the choice between two parties on Saturday night.
○ I'll stay home. I hate going out.
□ I have no idea what I will be doing on Saturday night but I will go out for sure!

4. Your cell phone rings and you don't recognise the number. What do you do?

○ I don't have a cell phone.
□ I immediately answer.
△ I don't answer; I'll call back if the person leaves a message.

5. Do your friends think you are…

△ calm and reliable?
□ crazy and funny?
○ mysterious and secretive?

6. How easy is it to know who you really are?

○ Difficult, I don't show the real me to my friends.
△ Easy, but I need to get to know the other person first.
□ Very easy! I'm an outgoing person and I trust people easily.

b. Examine your answers. What do they reveal about your personality?
c. Your teacher will give you the results of this quiz. Do they correspond to what you expected? Why? Why not?

PREPARE YOUR TASK

2 Speed meeting

a. Learn more about some of your new classmates. Prepare some questions to get to know them better (name, age, date of birth, hobbies…). Be ready to answer theirs!
b. Write an account of your meetings. Who would you like to know better? Why?

Help!

What talent do you have?
What type of …?
How + (adjective) are you?
What are you good at?
If you were a …,
what would you be?

love V-ING / to + BV
like V-ING / to + BV
enjoy V-ING
prefer V-ING
dislike V-ING
hate V-ING / to + BV

3 I Am Who I Am

1 Inspirational quotes

a. Read these quotes. Which one do you prefer? Why?

"Whatever you want to do, the only secret is to believe in it and satisfy yourself. Don't do it for anyone else."
Keith Haring

BE YOURSELF; EVERYONE ELSE IS ALREADY TAKEN.
Oscar Wilde

The future belongs to those who believe in the beauty of their dreams.
Eleanor Roosevelt

If you don't like something, change it. If you can't change it, change your attitude. Don't complain.
Maya Angelou

A good head and a good heart are always a formidable combination.
Nelson Mandela

b. Look at this word cloud for a minute, then close your book. How many words can you remember?

c. Group work: Decide which adjective(s) could describe the personality of the author of each quote. Explain your choice to the class. Use a dictionary if necessary.

PREPARE YOUR TASK

d. Pick out the adjectives that best represent your personality. Add others and create your own word cloud about your personality. Turn to your Workbook for help. WB p.7

2 "I am" poem

Read the following poems and explain what they are about.

"I am Lazy and Zen"

I like sleeping until noon
I like to stretch out[1] on my bed
I like to stay sitting on a seat
I hate cleaning the house
I am lazy and zen

I rarely get angry
I'm rarely hyperactive
I don't like going outside
I don't have a mobile phone
I am lazy and zen

I don't like doing homework
I wouldn't go to school if I didn't have to
I like discussing with friends
I am lazy and zen

▲ Luc Kalshoven, 2013

1. *m'étendre*

"Myself"

I am who I am
I do not pretend to be someone I'm not
I do like broccoli, and I don't care.
I like to wear what I want, and
I ignore people's stares[2].
I am myself and I will never change.

I must live my life, ignoring the obstacles.
I need to see the bright side of things[3].
I can't give up, you never know how close you are.
I can't, however, always imagine happy endings,
I am myself and I will never change.

I'd like to be stronger though.
I'd like to show no feelings of mine,
I'd like to never feel low.
I'd like to say no, but
I am who I am, and I will never change.

▲ Juliette Thiriet, 2013

2. *regards insistants* 3. *le bon côté des choses*

3 It's your turn

CD1 PISTE 4-5

WB p. 7

a. Listen to the poems and work on rhythm and intonation in your Workbook.
b. Choose the poem you prefer and explain your choice.
c. Get ready to read your favourite poem in front of the class.

4 Meet Marianne

video

Watch the presentation of a teenager who is speaking about herself.

a. What are your reactions?
b. Write your own "I am" poem.
c. Create your own presentation of your "I am" poem (text, video…).

PREPARE YOUR TASK

Help!

happy, cheerful ≠ sad
miserable /ˈmɪzrəbəl/ = unhappy
ecstatic = very happy
embarrassed, ill at ease ≠ comfortable
annoyed: *contrarié*
frustrated
angry = cross
frightened = scared = afraid
ashamed: *honteux*
confused

be crazy about V-ING
be fond of V-ING
I don't mind V-ING : *cela ne me gêne pas de*
I can't stand V-ING : *je ne supporte pas de*

4 Reality TV

1 Read and match

a. Read these descriptions of TV programmes and match each of them with the corresponding title. Justify your answers with key words from the texts.
b. Which TV programme would you like to watch? Why?
c. In groups, decide which qualities the contestants must have to apply to these TV shows. Give an account of your findings to the class.
The contestants must be… / They should…

A An American reality TV singing competition where the contestants sing during blind[1] auditions. If a coach is interested in the performance[2] of the contestant, he/she presses a button which turns his/her chair towards the aspiring singer.
1. *aveugle* **2.** *prestation*

1

2

3

B A cooking competition open to amateur cooks and home chefs. At the end of each round, a panel of judges tastes the contestants' dishes and decides who is out of the competition.

C A show where contestants have to take up different challenges while being completely in the dark.

4

D Teams of two or three contestants go on a worldwide treasure hunt to win a cash prize[1]. Their travels are filmed for entertainment purposes and viewers can watch as teams make key decisions and are progressively eliminated.
1. *money*

video

2 Watch a video

THE SWAP

a. Watch the trailer for a reality show. Turn to your worksheet for help.
b. Do you feel like watching the show? Why or why not?
c. Role play. You are producing the next season of *The Swap*. Suggest two contrasting celebrities to the class: present their personalities, their lifestyles and their likes and dislikes. The class will choose the best suggestions.

PREPARE YOUR TASK

5 Choose Your Coach!

CD1 PISTE 6

1 Five influential celebrities WB p. 8

a. Look at the photographs and say what you know about these people.
b. Turn to your Workbook to learn more about them.
c. Listen to two recordings presenting the two hidden celebrities. Find who they are, and justify your answer with key words or phrases you have heard.
d. Which celebrity could be your coach for a reality TV show? Why?

PREPARE YOUR TASK

2 Writing workshop

We are in 2050, and you are one of the most influential people in the world. Write an article explaining why you are famous and what makes you influential.

Help!

Fame	Success
famous for + *nom* / V-ING	start from scratch: *partir de rien*
well-known: *connu*	make it to the top: *se hisser au sommet*
talented, gifted: *doué*	succeed in V-ING: *réussir à*
successful: *qui a réussi*	be in the limelight /ˈlaɪmlaɪt/: *être sous les feux des projecteurs*
considered + *adj* / *nom*: *considéré*	

LANGUAGE AT WORK

+ WORKBOOK
→ Apprendre à apprendre
p. 99 - 100

A La place des adjectifs en anglais

Précis, p.249

Observez

Repérez les adjectifs dans les phrases ci-dessous :

a. *She has a funny brother and a sporty sister.*

b. *Her mother drives an old red car.*

c. *Kate is athletic.*

d. *She loves good old songs.*

Déduisez

Déduisez la règle concernant la place des adjectifs en anglais :

Quand l'adjectif est épithète, il est placé ...... le nom.
Quand l'adjectif est attribut, il est placé ...... le verbe d'état (*be, look, seem, feel, sound*...).

B Le présent simple

Précis, p.264

Observez

1 Formation

Tous les verbes soulignés des phrases ci-dessous sont au présent. Quelles sont les phrases affirmatives, négatives, interrogatives ? Recopiez le tableau ci-dessous et complétez-le. Déduisez-en la formation du présent simple :

a. *"Where __do__ you __come__ from?" "I __come__ from the United States."*

b. *"What sports __do__ you __do__?" "I __don't do__ any sports."*

c. *"She __does not__ like watching movies and she __hates__ going to the theatre."*

d. *"__Does__ she __like__ reading?" "No, she __doesn't read__ much but she __plays__ the guitar."*

Formes	Affirmative	...	...
Exemples	• *I come* • ... • ...	• *Do you come ...?* • *Do you do...?* • *Does she like ...?*	• ... • ... *She does not like*
Formation	• Sujet (3e personne du singulier) + ... + ... • Sujet (autres personnes) + ...	• ....+ sujet à la 3e personne du singulier + ... • ....+ sujet (aux autres personnes) + ...	• Sujet (3e personne du singulier) + ... + ... • Sujet (autres personnes) + ...

2 Valeurs

a. ***She goes*** *to the cinema every week.*

b. ***She looks*** *very pretty.*

c. ***They love*** *playing golf.*

d. ***He*** *always* ***cycles*** *to school.*

Dans quels énoncés y a-t-il une indication de temps ? Qu'exprime le présent simple dans ces phrases ? Dans les autres énoncés il n'y a pas d'indication explicite de temps. Pourquoi ?

Déduisez

On utilise le présent simple pour faire le portrait de quelqu'un, pour parler de ses ..., de son ..., de tout ce qui le ...
On emploie aussi le présent simple pour parler d'une ....

Rappel : Les adverbes de fréquence (cf. précis grammatical p. 249)

never → rarely / seldom → sometimes / occasionally → usually → often → always

Entraînez-vous

1 **Remettez les phrases suivantes dans l'ordre, attention à la place des adjectifs et des adverbes !**

1. *Many* *have* *often* *artistic* *pupils* *hobbies.*
2. *motivated.* *looks* *She* *her* *very* *does* *rarely* *she* *never* *homework,*
3. *big* *hates* *but* *loves* *Paris.* *he* *usually* *cities* *Mark*
4. *never* *the* *shy.* *chats* *Internet.* *He* *too* *on* *because* *is* *he*
5. *often* *for* *drinks* *coffee* *black* *He* *breakfast.*

2 **Lisez la légende de ce cartoon puis continuez le récit d'une journée type du maître et de la maîtresse des deux animaux.**

"Everything is automatic. The coffee turns on at 7:00. The coffee smell goes upstairs at 7:10. They come down at 7:20. They go to work at 7:25 and we go up and get in their bed."

3 **Are you a couch potato, a helpful son or daughter or a hyperactive teenager?**

À partir de la liste d'activités proposées ci-contre, créez votre propre *personality quiz* pour vos camarades. Préparez les questions et les réponses possibles sous forme de phrases complètes. A partir des réponses de vos camarades, déterminez à quelle catégorie ils appartiennent (*couch potato, helpful, hyperactive*)

do the dishes - tidy your room - do sports - look after your little brother or sister - go out after school

4 **Who is it?**

Un élève sort dans le couloir pendant que ses camarades choisissent le nom d'une personne connue de tous (célèbre ou non). A son retour, il leur pose des *Yes/No questions* pour découvrir de qui il s'agit.

IMPROVE YOUR SPEAKING SKILLS

1 Vous allez écouter une interview, lisez ces passages du script

CD1 PISTE 7 — MP3 PISTE 1

A "Sebastian, what are your hobbies?"

"My greatest hobby is soccer, I absolutely love this sport and I've been involved in it for a long time. In Canada and in France, I referee soccer games. I enjoy watching games on TV. Lyon and Monaco are my favorite French teams."

B "Do you like hockey?"

"Surprisingly, even though I'm Canadian, I don't really like hockey."

C "What else do you like?"

"I like to travel and have visited many parts of Europe and North America. It's fun to see new places and experience different cultures and languages. I like going to the movies and when I go, I usually watch comedies or action movies."

2 Repérez et écoutez

a. Recopiez l'extrait A.
Soulignez les mots qui, à votre avis, seront accentués. Vérifiez à l'écoute.

b. Que remarquez-vous sur la prononciation des mots surlignés en bleu ? A quelles catégories grammaticales appartiennent-ils ?

c. A l'écoute, **repérez les mots accentués** dans l'extrait B. A votre avis, pourquoi sont-ils accentués ?

d. Réécoutez l'extrait C.
Repérez les liaisons consonne-voyelle et les pauses que le jeune garçon marque lorsqu'il s'exprime. Ces pauses délimitent les groupes de sens.

3 Lisez à haute voix la fin de l'interview

CD1 PISTE 8 — MP3 PISTE 2

Repérez les formes qui seront réduites, respectez les liaisons consonne-voyelle et les groupes de sens. N'oubliez pas de parler lentement, haut et fort !

"When I'm not watching soccer on TV, I like to watch crime shows like *CSI: Las Vegas*. My other guilty pleasure is video games. I've always loved playing console games with friends or playing computer games on my own."

4 Enrichissez votre prise de parole

Pour dire les choses différemment :
- *In other words*
- *…, I mean …*

Pour vérifier que l'on vous a compris :
- *Do you know / see what I mean?*
- *…, if you see what I mean.*

Pour demander la permission de commencer :
- *Shall I start? / Can I start?*
- *Do you mind if I start?*

Pour changer de sujet ou ajouter une information :
- *By the way…*
- *Before I forget…*
- *I nearly forgot…*

Pour conclure :
- *In conclusion, …*
- *To conclude …*

YOUR TASK

You are entering a casting for a reality TV programme. Prepare your audition based on the scenario your teacher has chosen.

Scenario 1

You want to enter the casting for a reality TV show entitled *Your Class Has Got Talent*. Audition in front of your classmates. Be ready to explain who you are (likes and dislikes, qualities and talents), and why you should be selected for the show. The class will decide who the most talented student is.

Scenario 2

Your teacher will give you a role.

- **You are a contestant**. Choose one of the reality TV shows presented on p.22. Audition in front of a real jury. Introduce yourself (likes and dislikes, qualities and talents), then explain why you want to take part in this show and why you are the best contestant. Be ready to answer the jury's questions!
- **You are a member of the jury.** Introduce yourself and explain what you are famous for and why you were chosen. Prepare questions for the contestant. Then you will select the best candidate for the show you represent.

Conseils pour votre audition !

Vocabulaire :

Utilisez des adjectifs précis pour nuancer et enrichir votre description :
- **good at** → *excellent at, clever at, brilliant at, gifted in*
- **nice** → *kind, friendly, helpful*
- **intelligent** → *clever, smart, quick, sharp, bright…*

Grammaire :

- Faites des phrases courtes.
- Utilisez le présent simple : *can* + BV, *be good at* + *V-ing* et la forme verbale adaptée après les verbes ou expressions de goût (ex. : *be fond of* V-ING).

Prononciation :

- Accentuez les mots porteurs de sens.
*I **stand** before you to **promote** myself as a **potential candidate** for the **show.***
- Veillez à la syllabe accentuée dans les mots de 2 syllabes ou plus :
candidate, ideal, talented, personality…
- Veillez aux liaisons consonne-voyelle et aux groupes de souffle.
I'm friendly and always in a good mood.

Attitude lors d'une prise de parole devant un auditoire :

- Regardez votre auditoire, évitez les gestes inutiles.
- Parlez distinctement et adaptez votre débit (ni trop lent, ni trop rapide).
- Parlez suffisamment fort pour être entendu(e) même au fond de la classe.
- Utilisez des *gap fillers* si vous hésitez.

Gap fillers

Vous hésitez :
- *Um…/ Er…*
- *Let me see/ think …*
- *…, you know …*
- *…, now what's the word for…?*
- *Actually…/ in fact…*

> Sticks and Stones will break my bones
> But words will never harm me.
>
> (Nursery Rhyme)

Wonder

I know I'm not an ordinary ten-year-old kid. I mean, sure, I do ordinary things. I eat ice cream. I ride my bike. I play ball. I have an Xbox. Stuff like that makes me ordinary. I guess. And I feel ordinary. Inside. But I know ordinary kids don't make other ordinary kids run away screaming in the playground. I know ordinary kids don't get stared at wherever they go.

If I found a magic lamp and I could have one wish, I would wish that I had a normal face that no one ever noticed at all. I would wish that I could walk down the street without people seeing me and then doing that look-away thing. Here's what I think: the only reason I'm not ordinary is that no one else sees me that way.

But I'm kind of used to know how I look by now. I know how to pretend I don't see the faces people make. We've all gotten pretty good at that sort of thing: me, Mom and Dad, Via. Actually, I take that back: Via's not good at it. She can get really annoyed when people do something rude. Like, for instance, one time in the playground some older kids made some noises. I don't even know what the noises were exactly because I didn't hear them myself, but Via heard and she just started yelling at the kids. That's the way she is. I'm not that way.

Via doesn't see me as ordinary. She says she does, but if I were ordinary, she wouldn't feel like she needs to protect me as much. And Mom and Dad don't see me as ordinary, either. They see me as extraordinary. I think the only person in the world who realizes how ordinary I am is me.

My name is August, by the way. I won't describe what I look like. Whatever you're thinking, it's probably worse.

▲ R. J. Palacio, *Wonder*, 2012

Beautiful

Don't look at me

Every day is so wonderful
Then suddenly it's hard to breathe.
Now and then I get insecure
From all the pain, I'm so ashamed.

I am beautiful no matter what they say.
Words can't bring me down.
I am beautiful in every single way.
Yes, words can't bring me down... Oh no.
So don't you bring me down today.

To all your friends you're delirious,
So consumed in all your doom.
Trying hard to fill the emptiness.
The pieces gone, left the puzzle undone.
Is that the way it is?

You are beautiful no matter what they say
Words can't bring you down....oh no
You are beautiful in every single way
Yes, words can't bring you down, oh, no
So don't you bring me down today...

No matter what we do
(no matter what we do)
No matter what we say
(no matter what we say)
We're the song inside the tune
Full of beautiful mistakes

And everywhere we go
(and everywhere we go)
The sun will always shine
(the sun will always, always shine)
And tomorrow we might wake on the other side

We are beautiful no matter what they say
Yes, words won't bring us down, no, no
We are beautiful in every single way
Yes, words can't bring us down, oh, no
So don't you bring me down today

Oh, yeah, don't you bring me down today, yeah, ooh
Don't you bring me down ooh... today

▲ Christina Aguilera, *Stripped,* 2004

Unit 2

SENTIMENT D'APPARTENANCE • MÉMOIRE

Choose Your School

YOUR TASK AT THE END OF THIS UNIT

You are the headmaster, or a teacher, or a student representative of a school. Present the school to your classmates, who will play the part of the parents of future students. At the end of the presentations, they will choose the school they like best. *p. 39*

1 Tune In!

1 Get ready

a. Observe the cartoon below: what immediately strikes you about the room?
b. You are the little girl and you answer the boy's question.
c. Your teacher will now show you the complete cartoon. What is your first reaction? Do you think it is funny? Why? Why not?

Help!

Children
- little brats: *sales gosses*
- slice /slaɪs/: *part, tranche*
- unruly: *turbulent*
- be up to mischief: *faire des bêtises*

Mother
- take a nap: *faire la sieste*
- get rid of: *se débarrasser*
- would like to + BV
- dream of V-ING

House
- messy / in a mess: *en désordre*
- upside down: *sens dessus dessous*
- spill, spilt, spilt: *renverser*
- scattered / lying all over the floor: *éparpillé, qui traîne par terre*

A New School Year

1 Play with words

WB p. 9

Turn to your Workbook to improve your vocabulary on school.

2 Welcome to high school

a. School blues?

Choose the expression that best describes how you feel about going back to school and explain your choice.

So excited!

I have mixed feelings

I feel miserable (= very unhappy)

I really don't want to go!

I am enthusiastic

b. How do you feel about high school? Do you like it better than your school last year? Why? Why not? What is different?

3 Different countries, different schools

a. Look at the report card opposite and compare it to a French one. What differences can you see?

CD1 PISTE 9

b. Listen to a student speaking about her high school.
Pick out as many elements as you can about the American school system.
Turn to your Workbook for help.

WB p. 10

c. Go to resources.woodlands-junior.kent.sch.uk/ourschool/ to learn more about the school system in England. Find information about:

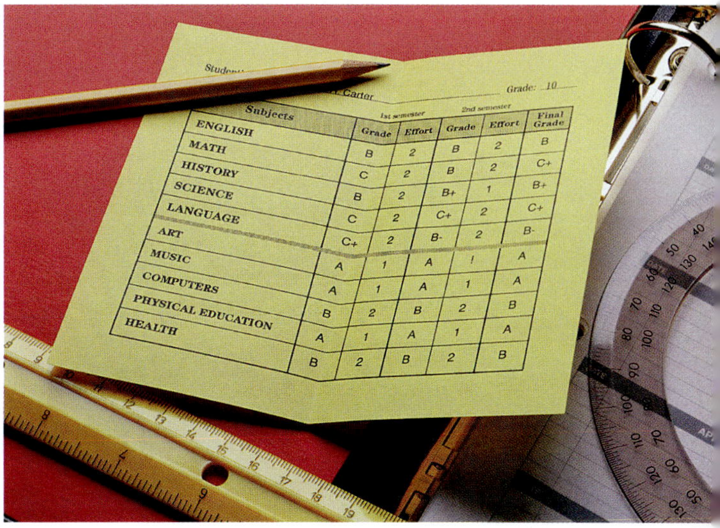
Grade: 10

Subjects	1st semester Grade	1st semester Effort	2nd semester Grade	2nd semester Effort	Final Grade
ENGLISH	B	2	B	2	B
MATH	C	2	B	2	C+
HISTORY	B	2	B+	1	B+
SCIENCE	C	2	C+	2	C+
LANGUAGE	C+	2	B-	2	B-
ART	A	1	A	!	A
MUSIC	A	1	A	1	A
COMPUTERS	B	2	B	2	B
PHYSICAL EDUCATION	A	1	A	1	A
HEALTH	B	2	B	2	B

School hours

Grammar schools vs. comprehensive schools

Mandatory subjects

Dress code

Equivalents of *Seconde* and of the *baccalauréat*

d. Now that you know more about the two school systems, would you prefer to do an exchange with a school in England or in the US? Justify.

PREPARE YOUR TASK

4 On Skype

You are Skyping with Mathilda's high school. Prepare an oral account to present your high school to Mathilda's schoolmates. In groups, you will introduce yourselves and speak in turns about different aspects of your school.
Include the following information:

- Name and location, size, number of students
- Dress code and school rules
- A typical day (daily routine)
- Subjects taught
- Different buildings: library, cafeteria
- General atmosphere

3 Welcome to Welton Academy!

1 Meet the headmaster

a. Watch the trailer of *Dead Poets Society*. Focus on the beginning and pick out the main information: where? When? Who? What?
b. What differences can you see between Welton Academy, its students, its teachers and your high school?

◀ Welton Academy, class of 1959

Help!

single-sex school (= all boys school or all girls school)
≠ co-ed school (mixed schools)
boarding school: *pensionnat*
headmaster (UK) = principal (US)
motto: *devise*

private = public (UK) ≠ state school
religious school ≠ lay = secular school
formal ≠ casual /ˈkæʒjuəl/: *décontracté*
lenient = tolerant
stern: *austère*
well-off = wealthy = rich

CD1 PISTE 10

c. Listen to the headmaster's speech welcoming students back to school. Write down the words you can understand. What does the headmaster want to prove to the pupils and their parents?
d. Listen again. Which words are stressed? WB p. 12

PREPARE YOUR TASK

e. You are the headmaster of Welton Academy: read the speech out loud in front of your classmates.
f. Would you like to enroll at Welton Academy? Why? Why not?

2 Writing workshop

You are a new student at Welton Academy. You write a letter to your best friend who is in a different school. You tell him about your first impressions of the school, your teachers and new classmates. Write the letter. (100 words)

3 The Ivy League

a. Look at the pictures below: what are they?
b. Do you recognise some of these names? Find the common point between all of them.
c. Choose two names and find information about them in an encyclopaedia or on the Internet, then report your findings to the class.

4 Alternative Schools

1 A school for everyone!

Read the following articles and match each extract with its title and illustration. Justify your choice with key words from the text.

Attending a virtual school

That's really the school of the air!

There's no place like home!

1

A It must be the biggest school in the world - its classrooms are spread over 1.3 million square kilometres, yet it only has 120 students and 14 teachers. It's the extraordinary outback Alice Springs School of the Air (ASSOA) and it's been running now for 59 years.
ASSOA and its short-wave radio link was once the only way for kids who lived a day's drive or more from the nearest school to get an education.

▲ www.australiangeographic.com.au

2

3

B Homeschooling is a progressive movement […] in which parents choose to educate their children at home instead of sending them to a traditional public or private school. Families choose to homeschool for a variety of reasons, including dissatisfaction with the educational options available, different religious beliefs or educational philosophies. […] According to the National Home Education Research Institute, there are now more than two million children being homeschooled in the U.S, with the percentage rapidly increasing by 7 percent to 15 percent each year. Homeschooling is legal in all 50 states.

▲ www.parents.com

C Six-year-old Jayden Carter (who lives in Kamuela, Hawaii) spends his school day like most elementary school children. He wakes up early in the morning, gets dressed, and heads to school. But to get to school, Jayden doesn't hop on a bus or in a car. Instead, he logs on to a computer in his kitchen to attend an online school. He attends a live lecture every Tuesday that he views using a webcam and he speaks to the teacher using a microphone. He can even see his classmates, located on other Hawaiian islands, when they speak. The rest of the time, he completes schoolwork in his family's garage or kitchen. He scans and submits work to his teacher via email.

▲ www.parents.com

PREPARE YOUR TASK

2 Give your opinion: which "school" would you like best? Why?

5 Single-Sex Schools Today

http://www.I-Debate.org/opinions/are-single-sex-schools-a-good-idea

Sign In / Log out

I-Debate.org

SEARCH

DEBATES ▼ OPINIONS ▼ FORUMS ▼

Are single-sex schools a good idea?

YES OR NO

Brooklynmum3 Posted on Mon. 5th 6.13 pm	In real life, especially in the workplace, women and men do not live separated. So why should kids be separated at school? To me it's nonsense. In a mixed school you get to socialize and interact with new people and consequently you get to understand how different people think. It's a very enriching experience for children.
LovingDad Posted on Mon. 5th 6.27 pm	I get your point Brooklynmum3, but it has been proved that in single sex schools students learn better because boys and girls learn differently. We all know that boys distract girls and vice versa. I think that at such a young age, kids should focus on learning, not on flirting.
Lizzie&Tom Posted on Mon. 5th 6.48 pm	Come on LovingDad! Don't be so 'old school' ☺! Co-ed schools are much more fun for kids and flirting is not something negative! That's part of growing up[1]! Besides, in a mixed school you meet different people. It broadens our kids' horizons!
EnglishRose Posted on Mon.5th 7.03 pm	I quite agree with Brooklynmum3. Single-sex schools are not good for the development of social skills[2]. If our kids only interact with people of the same gender, they will not be used to interacting with the other sex. It is not a natural thing because, yes, believe it or not, in real life boys and girls mix, they do not live in separate worlds! In the end, I think it may alter their relationships with the opposite sex or make them more difficult later.
BradThompson Posted on Mon. 5th 7.23 pm	I completely disagree with LovingDad because some studies show that boys have better results in co-ed schools than in single-sex schools. The atmosphere in single-sex schools tends to be either 'bitchy' (we know girls tend to have catfights) or aggressive because of the competition between the boys. This is not a healthy[3] learning environment for our kids!
Mummydearest Posted on Mon. 5th 7.52 pm	Yes, but it appears that girls have better results in single-sex schools than in mixed schools. They don't feel limited to choosing so called "girls' subjects". They are not afraid to choose math or sciences as major[4]. They feel more self-confident and more comfortable in the classroom as they have no need to impress boys! They don't have to worry about their looks and make-up! What's more, children become too competitive in co-ed schools which can be detrimental to their studies in the long run[5].

1. *grandir* **2.** *(ici) socialisation* **3.** *sain* **4.** *matière principale* **5.** *sur le long terme*

1 Parents know best… or so they think!

a. What is this forum about?

Group work:

b. Each group will read one post and decide if the author of the post is in favour of or opposed to single-sex education. Justify with elements from the posts.
Classify the parents' arguments in two columns.

c. Which argument(s) do you find particularly convincing?

d. Has your opinion on single-sex education changed? Explain.

2 Sharing views on education

Cheltenham Ladies' College ►

◄ Eton College

PREPARE YOUR TASK

Mini-task 1: FAMILY AFFAIRS
Your parents have decided to enroll you in one of the single-sex schools presented above. Act out the scene.

Mini-task 2: DEBATE CORNER
Your parents are thinking about giving you a different type of education. You discuss with them what type of education suits you best.

Convaincre

- *Trust me / believe me*
- *I know for sure that …*
- *I can assure you that …*
- *Don't forget that …*

Exprimer son désaccord

- *I don't agree / I disagree with you*
- *I don't see things that way!*
- *I don't share your opinion!*
- *Are you kidding?*
- *Certainly not!*
- *No way!*

LANGUAGE AT WORK

+ WORKBOOK
→ Apprendre à apprendre p. 101

A Le comparatif

Précis, p.251

Observez

1 Les phrases d'exemple ci-dessous comportent toutes au moins un comparatif. Repérez-le(s), observez leur formation et complétez les fiches de rappel sur papier libre.

a. *Teachers at Welton Academy looked much more severe than our teachers today.*

b. *Students at Welton Academy were far less disobedient than students today but they were as fun-loving as we are.*

c. *School rules were stricter in the past.*

d. *I like high school better than middle school.*

e. *I am worse at English than at chemistry.*

Déduisez

Le comparatif d'INFÉRIORITÉ

- ...... + **adjectif** + ...

ex : ....

Le comparatif d'ÉGALITÉ

- ...... + **adjectif** + ...

ex : ....

Le comparatif de SUPÉRIORITÉ

- ...... + **adjectif long** + ...

ex : ....

- **Adjectif court** + ... + ...

ex : ....

- **Exceptions/Modifications**

Good → .... → *ex :* ....

Bad → .... → *ex :* ....

B Opposition et concession

Observez

Lisez les énoncés ci-dessous et choisissez la traduction qui vous paraît la plus appropriée pour les mots en gras :

a. *My parents think that attending a single-sex school is a very good idea* ***whereas*** *I am strongly opposed to this type of education.*

alors que — à cause de — malgré

b. ***Although*** *I think there are too many distractions in mixed schools, I am not in favour of single-sex schools.*

donc — par conséquent — bien que

c. *The students worked very hard* ***and yet*** *they failed their exams.*

et pourtant — afin de — pourvu que

d. *Many co-ed schools have an excellent reputation;* ***however*** *students get better results in single-sex schools.*

afin que — cependant — de plus

Déduisez

Quels mots expriment l'opposition? Lesquels expriment la concession ?

Whereas permet d'exprimer une " ... ", on le traduit par " ... " en français.

Although, however, and yet permettent d'exprimer une " ... " (fait d'accorder un point - surtout dans une discussion - à un adversaire) on les traduit respectivement par " ... ", " ... ", " ... " en français.

Entraînez-vous

1 **Comparez l'école de Bart Simpson, ses élèves et ses professeurs à la Welton Academy en utilisant les éléments donnés. A vous de choisir le comparatif qui convient.**

a) *Bart / hard-working / the boys at Welton.*

b) *Bart's headmaster / authoritative / Welton Academy's headmaster.*

c) *Lisa Simpson / obedient / the boys at Welton.*

d) *Life at Bart's school / exciting / life at Welton.*

e) *The dress code at Welton / formal / the dress code at Bart's school.*

f) *Bart's teachers / lenient* (indulgents) */ teachers at Welton.*

2 **Regardez l'image ci-contre et expliquez pourquoi Lisa semble aussi surprise. Pensez à utiliser au moins 4 comparatifs dans votre réponse.**

3 **Traduisez les phrases suivantes en anglais :**

a. Il travaille dur, cependant il n'obtient pas de bons résultats.

b. Mon amie anglaise est inscrite dans un pensionnat de jeunes filles alors que je fréquente une école publique mixte.

c. Bien que les cours se terminent plus tôt dans les écoles américaines, les élèves n'ont pas beaucoup de temps libre car ils ont souvent un petit boulot (*part-time job*).

d. Les professeurs à Welton Academy sont plus sévères que dans mon lycée et pourtant les élèves font autant de bêtises.

4 **Let's play bingo!**

Votre professeur va vous donner une carte avec des comparatifs. Il va ensuite vous proposer des comparaisons dans lesquelles l'adjectif devra être mis au comparatif. Si vous avez la bonne réponse sur votre grille, cochez la case. Dès que vous avez coché 5 cases, annoncez Bingo !

5 **Regardez l'emploi du temps de Mathilda et comparez-le au vôtre. Faites autant de phrases que possible en utilisant des comparatifs ainsi que des mots de liaison.**

Miami High School Class Schedule (10th grade)

	Monday	Tuesday	Wednesday	Thursday	Friday
8:00-8:55 AM	Math	Math	Math	Math	Math
9:00-9:55 AM	Science	Science	Science	Science	Science
10:00-10:55 AM	History	History	History	History	History
11:00-11:55 AM	English	English	English	English	English
12:00-12:30 PM	*Lunch*	*Lunch*	*Lunch*	*Lunch*	*Lunch*
12:35-1:30 PM	Spanish	Spanish	Spanish	Spanish	Spanish
1:35-2:30 PM	Art	Art	Art	Art	Art

IMPROVE YOUR SPEAKING SKILLS

1 Lisez le discours de rentrée ci-dessous

MP3 PISTE 4 CD1 PISTE 12

Dear Students,

It gives me great pleasure to welcome you [...] to Brooklyn Technical High School.

I congratulate[1] you on your achievement in gaining admission to Brooklyn Tech and wish you much success as you embark on what is just the beginning of a lifetime[2] of learning. In addition to being recognized by the U. S. News and World Report as an outstanding[3] high school in the United States, [...] Brooklyn Tech boasts[4] among[5] its graduates Nobel Prize laureates, [...] city and state elected officials, university recognized scientists, engineers, and architects, as well as noted leaders in business, finance, industry [...].

William Shakespeare once said, "We all know what we are but not what we can be." Your Brooklyn Tech education will give you a significant foundation in determining your success and achieving your lifetime goals. [...] Once again, I extend my sincerest wishes for a productive school year at Brooklyn Technical High School.

▲ Randy Asher, Brooklyn Technical High School Principal, *Student Handbook*, 2007-2008

1. *félicite* **2.** *de toute une vie* **3.** *exceptionnelle* **4.** *compte avec fierté* **5.** *parmi*

2 Analysez

a. Quels sont les deux objectifs du proviseur de Brooklyn Tech dans ce discours ?

b. Quelles expressions / groupes de mots lui permettent de mettre en avant les points forts de son école.

c. Second paragraphe : Quels sont les mots que vous choisiriez d'accentuer particulièrement si vous deviez faire ce discours ? Comparez vos réponses avec vos camarades.

d. Comment appelle-t-on ces mots ?

3 Écoutez l'enregistrement de ce discours

Repérez les mots accentués. Comparez avec vos choix.

4 Lisez à haute voix le dernier paragraphe du discours

MP3 PISTE 5 CD1 PISTE 13

Respectez l'accentuation des mots porteurs de sens (en gras), les liaisons consonne-voyelle (‿) et les groupes de souffle (/).

William Shakespeare once said,/ "We **all know what** we are/ but **not what** we **can** be."/ Your **Brooklyn Tech**‿**education** will **give** you a **significant foundation**‿in **determining** your **success**/ and‿**achieving** your **lifetime goals**./ **Once**‿**again**,/ I **extend** my **sincerest wishes**/ for‿a **productive school year**‿at **Brooklyn Technical High School**.

YOUR TASK

You are the headmaster, or a teacher, or a student representative of a school (real or imaginary). Present the school to your classmates, who will play the part of the parents of future students. At the end of the presentations, they will choose the school they like best.

Scenario 1

Create your school. Use the guidelines below. Present it to the parents, who will choose which school they prefer.

Scenario 2

Find information on the website of the school your teacher has assigned you. Present the school. At the end of your presentation the parents will ask you questions, then they will choose the school they like best for their children.

Points to include

- Name of the school, its location (city and country), and the school motto.
- Name of the headmaster (invent names for the teacher and student representative).
- Type of school and a detailed description of the school.
- Dress code.
- Subjects taught and school results.
- Reasons why parents should choose this school.

You may create a slideshow to illustrate your presentation.

Quelques conseils pour votre présentation

Passer la parole
- Now over to you…
- Now, I hand over to …
- You have the floor, over to …
- Now let's listen to …

Vocabulaire
- Réutilisez le vocabulaire lié à l'école étudié dans cette unité.
- Utilisez des adjectifs précis pour décrire votre école et ses élèves.

Grammaire
- Pensez aux mots de liaison pour organiser votre présentation.
- Utilisez les comparatifs pour bien mettre en évidence les points forts de votre école.

Prononciation
- Mettez en valeur les atouts de votre école en accentuant les mots porteurs de sens.
ex : *Our school helps its students to fulfill their dreams.*

Attitude lors d'une prise de parole devant un auditoire :
- Regardez votre auditoire, parlez distinctement (ni trop lentement, ni trop vite) et suffisamment fort pour être entendu(e) même au fond de la classe.
- En cas d'hésitation ou de pause, pensez aux *gap fillers* (cf. p. 27).
- Si vous avez préparé un diaporama, pointez des éléments du doigt afin d'illustrer ce que vous dites.

Reading Corner

Kidnapped!

CD1 PISTE 14

This morning I got kidnapped
By three masked men.
They stopped me on the sidewalk,
And offered me some candy,
And when I wouldn't take it
They grabbed me by the collar,
And pinned my arms behind me,
And shoved me in the backseat
Of this big black limousine and
Tied my hands behind my back
With sharp and rusty wire[1].
Then they put a blindfold on me
So I couldn't see where they took me,
And plugged up my ears with cotton
So I couldn't hear their voices.
And drove for 20 miles or
At least for 20 minutes, and then
Dragged me from the car down to
Some cold and moldy[2] basement,
Where they stuck me in a corner
And went off to get the ransom
Leaving one of them to guard me
With a shotgun pointed at me,
Tied up sitting on a stool[3]...
That's why I'm late for school!

▲ Shel Silverstein, *A Light in the Attic*, 1980

1. *fil de fer* **2.** *moisi* **3.** *tabouret*

Better late than never!

Here are the top three funniest excuses for being late for school. Which one do you like best? Why? Invent your own funny excuse.

I am late for class because it was foggy this morning and I couldn't find my way to school.

I refuse to say anything until my lawyer is present.

My dog ate my homework then flushed it down the toilet. I had to do it all over again.

Once You're an Exchange Student, You're Never the Same

I can't even count how many times I've been asked "How does it feel to be an exchange student?", and how many different answers I've been giving out without finding the one that could express what it is really about.

During my months as an Italian exchange student in Michigan I've been smiling and crying, wishing to go home and wishing I could stay longer.

I've been feeling as if I couldn't get through this experience, and feeling on the top of the world.

I'm not going to tell you where I come from, if I miss my family, or if it's hard speaking another language, if I like my school or how I find American food so far. I want to let you know what this experience really is.

[...] You don't want to be an exchange student just to learn another language or because it's cool to live in the United States or in China. You want to be an exchange student because you dream of it, because you want to grow up and make yourself a better person. [...]

You have to face difficulties before leaving. Your school may not want you to leave and you may not want to leave your family, friends and boyfriend.

You have to face difficulties when you're away, a new house to live in, a new family to deal with, a new language, a computer screen between you and your family back at home, when all you want is just to hug them.

You have to face difficulties when you go back to your country, when you find that many of your friends had a great time even if you weren't there, when you realize that you're grown up and people around you are not, when you realize you left your heart kilometers away.

Each of these situations requires strength and that is what being an exchange student is all about. [...] Stefano, exchange student from Italy, currently in Quebec said, "[...] Taking a plane with the purpose to come back ten months later, many people were crying. I didn't, my mother neither. We both knew that that was the beginning of a huge opportunity and a life-time experience," he said.

I remember when I left, tears falling down my face, kissing and hugging everyone I could.

I can imagine my departure from Michigan, tears falling down my face, kissing and hugging everyone I can.

You're going to have the best time of your life and you're gonna break your heart and leave each half in a different country [...]. You're going to end up having two families, two best friends, two houses that you will both call home, you're going to get the best of both worlds.

So this morning when I was asked by a friend if I was happy to be going home in two months, I told her that I'm already home.

▲ Vittoria Meloni, November 30, 2011
www.chscommunicator.com op-ed/2011/11/30/exchange/

Unit 3

Change the World

YOUR TASK AT THE END OF THIS UNIT

You are taking part in a poetry contest. Choose a poem or a song you like or write your own. Recite it in front of the audience and explain your choice. p. 51

1 Tune In!

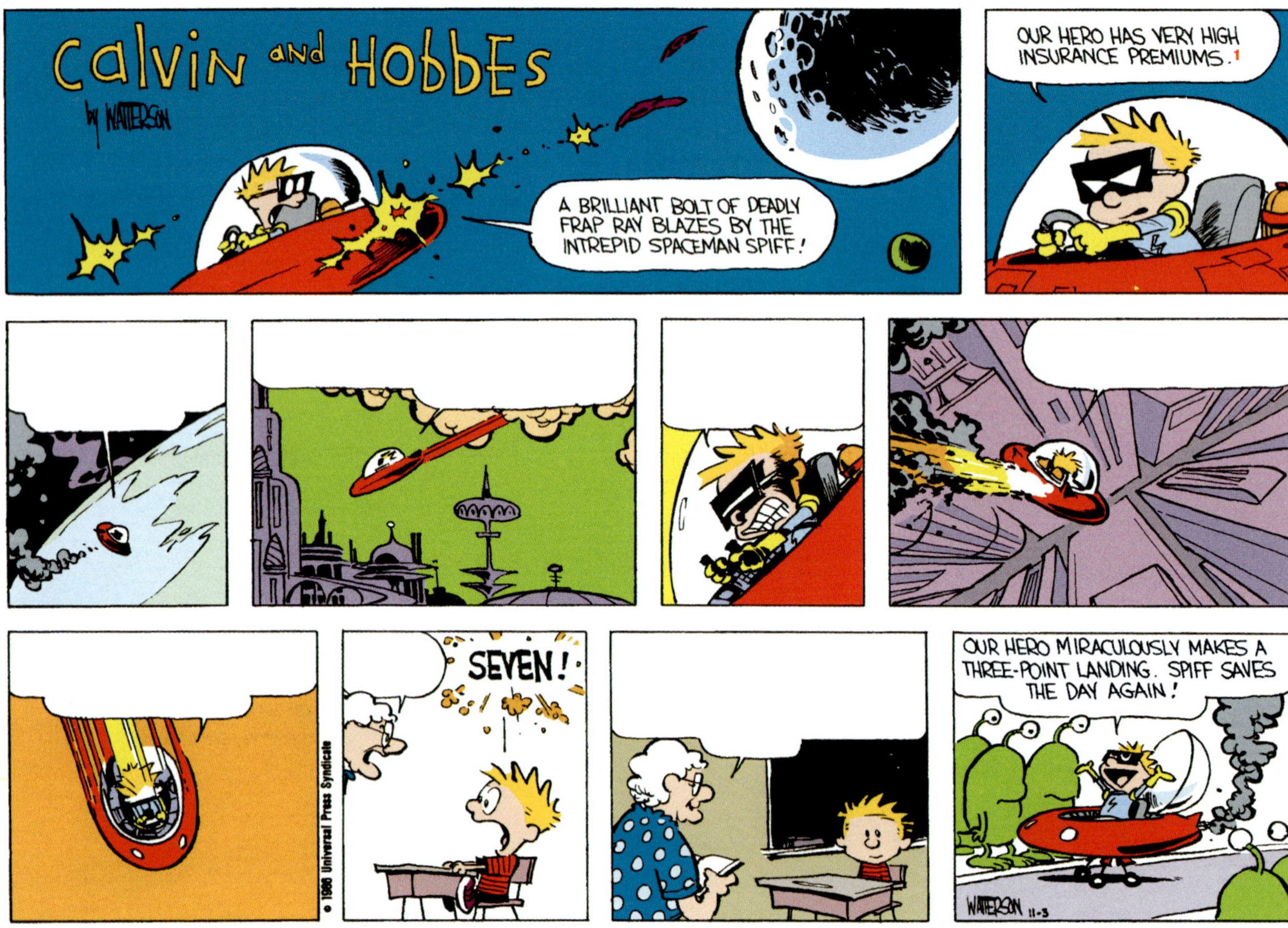

1. insurance premium: *prime d'assurance*

▲ Bill Watterson, *Something Under the Bed is Drooling*, 1988

1 Understanding the comic strip

a. Look at the comic strip carefully, then observe frames 1 and 10. Where does the scene take place? Who are the main characters? Describe the situation in each frame.
b. What is happening to Calvin? Briefly sum up the main events briefly.

2 Matching game

a. In groups, re-order the text: match each sentence with the corresponding balloon. Use the pictures and the key words in the text to help you.

A. Very good, Calvin. Ten minus three equals seven. I didn't think you were paying attention. That question was worth[1] three points.
1. *valait*

B. Spiff wrestles the uncooperative controls! More Preem drive to the thruster blasters[2]!
2. *(ici) plein gaz*

D. Breaking through the cloud layer[3], he careens over an alien city! There's no place to land!
3. *couche nuageuse*

E. The courageous spaceman is hit! He plummets[4] toward Planet Zog!
4. *plonge*

C. Too much stress! The fuel explodes in flame!

F. "Well, Calvin??"

G. The situation is grim[5]! Ten seconds to impact! Nine... Eight...
5. *(ici) horrible*

b. Class work: check your results and justify the order orally.

PREPARE YOUR TASK

3 Role play

Calvin explains to his friend Hobbes why he is always daydreaming. Use the vocabulary below to make as many sentences as you can.

Help!

Calvin's dream	In class
astronaut	bored
emergency landing	absent-minded
thrilling = exciting	caught by surprise
brave = courageous /kəˈreɪdʒəs/	be fed up with sth / V-ING: *en avoir ras le bol de*
bold /bəʊld/: *intrépide*	can't stand / bear V-ING: *ne pas supporter de*
fearless	give the right answer
fly a spaceship	hate V-ING
crash	pay attention to = focus
manage to: *réussir à*	daydream
have a close shave: *l'échapper belle*	it is difficult for me to
I wish I was / were / could....	I find it hard to
take risks	get real: *revenir à la réalité*

4 Play with words

WB p. 13

Turn to your Workbook to improve your vocabulary.

2 His Libraries Change Lives

World Change Starts with Educated Children

Room to Read Celebrates 'Year of Tens'

10 Years, 10,000 Libraries, 1,000 Schools, 10,000 Girls Educated

Part 1

I came here to Vietnam to see John Wood hand out his 10 millionth book at a library[1] that his team founded in this village in the Mekong Delta – as hundreds of local children cheered and embraced the books he brought as if they were the rarest of treasures. Wood's charity, Room to Read, has opened 12,000 of these libraries around the world, along with 1,500 schools. Yes, you read that right. [...] Room to Read is one of America's fastest-growing charities and is now opening new libraries at an astonishing clip[2] of six a day. In contrast, McDonald's opens one new outlet every 1.08 days.

It all began in 1998 when Wood, then a Microsoft marketing director, chanced upon a remote school in Nepal serving 450 children. Only one problem: it had no books to speak of. Wood blithely[3] offered to help and eventually delivered a mountain of books by a caravan of donkeys[4]. The local children were deliriously happy, and Wood said he felt such exhilaration[5] that he quit Microsoft, left his live-in girlfriend (who pretty much thought he had gone insane), and founded Room to Read in 2000. [...]

Part 2

It also supports 13,500 impoverished girls who might otherwise drop out of school. [...]

"If you can change a girl's life forever, and the cost is so low, then why are there so many girls still out of school?" he mused.

"I get frustrated that there are 793 million illiterate people, when the solution is so inexpensive," Wood told me outside one of his libraries in the Mekong. "If we provide this, it's no guarantee that every child will take advantage of it. But if we don't provide it[6], we pretty much guarantee that we perpetuate poverty."

"In 20 years," Wood told me, "I'd like to have 100,000 libraries, reaching 50 million kids. Our 50-year goal is to reverse the notion that any child can be told 'you were born in the wrong place at the wrong time and so you will not get educated.'"

▲ Nicholas D. Kristof,
The New York Times, November 5, 2011

1. *bibliothèque* **2.** *rythme* **3.** *allègrement* **4.** *ânes* **5.** *exaltation / euphorie* **6.** *fournissons*

1 Key facts WB P. 14

Group work: Each group will work on one part. Turn to your Workbook for help. Be ready to sum up what you have learnt.

PREPARE YOUR TASK

2 Action!

Choose one role.

a. The schoolmaster describes his first meeting with Wood, then Wood's second visit when he came back to the village with books.

b. A girl tells her parents what happened at school when Wood came back.

Help!

Who? What?

former big executive: *ex cadre supérieur*
corporation /firm /fɜːm/: *société, compagnie*
philanthropist: someone who freely gives money and help to people in need

committed to V-ING: *engagé*
destitute: *démuni*
deprived of: *privé de*
disadvantaged

quit, (quit, quit) one's job

Goals

inequalities
literacy rate: *taux d'alphabétisation*

be on an equal footing with: *être sur un pied d'égalité avec*
give equal opportunities
bridge the gap: *combler le fossé*
get a fair deal: *être traité de façon équitable*
take measures /ˈmeʒəz/

CD1 PISTE 16

3 Because I'm a girl WB P. 17

Listen to Malala Yousafzai's speech at the United Nations.

video

4 Watch a video

Discover an awareness campaign and turn to your worksheet for help.

PREPARE YOUR TASK

5 My favourite poster

You work for *Room to Read*. They want to launch a new advertising campaign. Select one of these three photos and defend your choice in front of the class.

1

2

3

3 What If...?

1 Get ready

Look at the illustration and read the title. What can you guess about the themes of the song?

IMAGINE

▲ *Bridge the Gap* by Robert Coghill (2003)

Imagine there's no heaven[1]
It's easy if you try
No hell[2] below us
Above us only sky
Imagine all the people
Living for today...

Imagine there's no countries
It isn't hard to do
Nothing to kill or die for
And no religion too
Imagine all the people
Living life in peace...

You may say I'm a dreamer
But I'm not the only one
I hope someday you'll join us
And the world will be as one

Imagine no possessions[3]
I wonder if you can
No need for greed[4] or hunger
A brotherhood of man
Imagine all the people
Sharing all the world...

You may say I'm a dreamer
But I'm not the only one
I hope someday you'll join us
And the world will be as one

John Lennon, *Imagine*, 1971

1. /ˈhevən/ *paradis*
2. /hel/ *enfer*
3. /ˈpəzeʃənz/
4. *appât du gain / cupidité*

2 Find the key information

a. What is the singer's message in stanza 1? (Several answers are possible.)
- He wants us to forget about good and evil (*le bien et le mal*).
- He wants people to be judged on their actions once they are dead.
- He says people should fear (*craindre*) God's judgement.
- He wants people to be free from all judgement.

b. Who does "You" refer to?

c. Group work:

Each group will work either on stanza 2, the chorus (stanza 3) or stanza 4.
In each stanza, pick out all the words referring to:
- the singer's dream.
- the consequences this dream would have, if it came true.

Then, classify them in two columns: Dreams and Consequences.

d. Class work:
- Report to the class.
- What does the singer denounce? Why?

Help!

Stanza 2	Stanza 4	Chorus
border: *frontière*	a utopia	jealousy
soldier	peace activist	rivalry /'raɪvəlri/
cause of war	unity	solidarity = brotherhood
jingoism = strong belief that your country is better than others	hopeful ≠ hopeless	the rich ≠ the poor
extremism /ɪk'striːmɪzəm/	idealistic	powerful
optimism /'ɒptɪmɪzəm/ ≠ pessimism /'pesɪmɪzəm/	committed: *engagé*	strong ≠ weak
denounce	believe in	steal sth from sb
criticise sb for V-ING	come true = become true	help one another
	urge sb to do sth: *inciter fortement qqn à faire qch*	respect one another

3 Action!

You are working on a CD called *"The Songs that Changed History"*. Design a CD cover and write the article to launch it. Explain why *Imagine* is a cult song.

4 Song corner

PREPARE YOUR TASK

a. Outside school, choose one or two songs from the following list. Find the lyrics on the Internet and read them carefully. Sing the song you like best to improve your prononciation.

- *With My Own Two Hands* – Ben Harper
- *Get Up, Stand Up* – Bob Marley
- *If I Can Dream* – Elvis Presley
- *Over the Rainbow* – Ella Fitzgerald
- *Change* – Tracy Chapman
- *Somewhere Over the Rainbow* – Israël Kamakawiwo
- *I Wish I Was a Punk Rocker* – Sandi Thom

b. In class, explain your choice it and find the common points with John Lennon's song.

LANGUAGE AT WORK

+ WORKBOOK
→ Apprendre à apprendre
p. 103 - 104

Le prétérit simple : valeur imaginaire
Les phrases conditionnelles : *If* …

Précis, p.265

Observez

1

*If my dreams **came** true, I **would be** the happiest person on earth.*

*If she **wins** the song contest, she **will become** famous.*

a. De quels éléments sont composés les formes verbales soulignées ?
Quel temps est utilisé après *If* dans chacune des phrases ci-dessus ?

b. Remettez les morceaux dans l'ordre pour former deux schémas qui expliquent comment former des phrases en *If*…

If +	*would* + BV	*will* + BV
présent,	prétérit,	*If* +

c. Traduisez les deux phrases d'exemples en français. Que remarquez-vous concernant les formes verbales employées ?

2 **Lisez les phrases suivantes.**

They wish they had money to do what they want.
She wishes she lived in a more comfortable house.
The poet wishes people were more respectful of the environment.
John Wood wishes more girls were educated in developing countries.
The child wishes his parents allowed him to do what he wants.

a. Quel verbe exprime le regret de la situation présente ?
b. Quelle forme verbale est utilisée dans la subordonnée (verbe en gras) ?
c. Le verbe *wish* signifie « souhaiter », mais dans certains cas il est préférable de le traduire par « regretter ». Traduisez les phrases en entier. Quels changements remarquez-vous lorsque l'on traduit ces phrases en français ?
d. Remplacez *they wish…* par *if only…* dans les phrases ci-dessus et traduisez en français les énoncés obtenus.

3 **Observez les formes soulignées ci-dessous.**

If I were you, I would try again.
"*If I was hungry, you would feed me*" (Katie Melua)
If she were rich enough, she would have a big garden.

a. Que remarquez-vous ?
b. La forme soulignée appartient-elle à la langue courante ou soutenue ?
(cf. Précis grammatical p. 255)

4 **Autre emploi : observez la forme en caractère gras, puis traduisez l'énoncé ci-dessous :**

*It's time we **started** reacting.*

Entraînez-vous

1 *If…*

Associez chaque début de phrase (à gauche) à la fin qui lui convient (droite).

1. *If they accepted my project, I would make a fortune.*	**A.** *I hope I will.*
2. *If I had enough money, I would fly to Dublin.*	**B.** *I'm not sure he will.*
3. *If I have enough money, I will fly to Dublin.*	**C.** *Unfortunately it still exists.*
4. *If he managed to reach his goals, he would be very happy.*	**D.** *But I can't afford the ticket.*
5. *If racism was eradicated, people would live in harmony.*	**E.** *But I don't think they ever will.*

2 **Complétez ces phrases.**

Example: *If I were a genius, I would only get straight As in school without doing my homework!*

- *If I were as small as a mouse, …*
- *If I won a million dollars, …*
- *If I didn't have to work late at night, …*
- *If teachers were replaced by computers, …*
- *If school wasn't compulsory, …*
- *If guns disappeared, ...*
- *If I lost my mobile phone, ...*
- *If ...., I wouldn't have to work.*
- *If ...., people would be on holiday all the time.*

3 **Et si ?**

Example:

• *It will be terrible if I forget my best friend's birthday.*

• *I would be very surprised if he was on time. It would be awesome if my best friend could go on holiday with me.*

A vous de trouver quatre autres exemples de catastrophes, surprises ou joies.

4 **Grammar battle**

Des équipes s'affrontent pour compléter puis fabriquer des phrases contenant *I wish* ou *If…* . L'équipe gagnante sera celle qui aura produit le plus de phrases correctes.

ON YOUR OWN!

a. Lisez cette bande dessinée.

b. Vous aussi vous avez des milliers d'idées. A votre tour de les exprimer. *"I wish…" / "If only…" / "It would be great if…"*

Possible topics: *pupils … / the cafeteria … teachers… / my timetable …*

▲ Bill Watterson, *Calvin and Hobbes, It's a magical world,* 1996

IMPROVE YOUR SPEAKING SKILLS

MP3 PISTE 7 — CD1 PISTE 17

1 Lisez le texte suivant

"I have a dream that my four little
children will one day live in a nation
where they will not be judged by
the color of their skin but by the
content of their character.
I have a dream today!
I have a dream that one day, [...]
right there in Alabama little black
boys and black girls will be able
to join hands with little white boys
and white girls as sisters and brothers.
I have a dream today!"

► Martin Luther King, 1963, Washington D.C.

Recopiez le passage sur papier libre.

a. Quels mots vous attendez-vous à voir particulièrement accentués ? Soulignez-les. Vérifiez à l'écoute.
b. Repérez les formes réduites et barrez-les à l'aide d'un crayon de couleur.
c. Quels mots allez-vous particulièrement mettre en relief ? Vérifiez à l'écoute.
d. Marquez les liaisons consonne-voyelle au fur et à mesure de l'écoute.
e. A quels endroits allez-vous respirer? Indiquez les groupes de souffle à l'aide d'une barre (/)

Lisez le passage à haute voix.

2 Apprenez à prendre des notes en vue d'une prise de parole

a. Observez le passage d'une phrase complète à des notes. Que remarquez-vous ?

Malala was born in 1997. When the Taliban took control of the Swat Valley in Pakistan a few years later, one girl spoke out and fought for her right to an education.

Quand ?	Qui ?	Verbes / Actions
1997 *a few years later*	*Malala* *the Taliban*	*born* *take control Swat Valley Pakistan* *refuse to be silenced* *fight for right to education*

b. Transformez ce paragraphe en notes.

On Tuesday, October 9, 2012, when she was fifteen, she was shot in the head as she was coming back from school.
She was taken to hospital and was operated on in Birmingham. A year later, when she was sixteen, she delivered a speech at the United Nations Headquarters. She now defends the right of girls to go to school. That's why she has become a symbol of peaceful protest and the youngest nominee ever for the Nobel Peace Prize.

YOUR TASK

You are taking part in a poetry contest. Choose a poem or a song you like or write your own. Recite it in front of the audience and explain your choice.

Scénario 1

MP3 PISTE 8 CD1 PISTE 18

1. **Choisissez un poème**, un extrait de discours ou une chanson dans l'unité.
2. **Élargissez votre choix**, lisez les poèmes ci-dessous et utilisez un dictionnaire.

Peace of Patience

I cannot wait to become
A peacemaker.
I cannot wait to help
The world overcome
Anger, and problems of evil.
I cannot wait for the world
To be peaceful,
And for everyone
To live in harmony.
I cannot wait to grow
And be and overcome.
But, I will wait,
With patience,
And hope, and peace.

▲ Mattie J.T. Stepanek, *Journey through Heartsongs*, 2001

Listen to the MUSTN'TS

Listen to the MUSTN'TS, child,
Listen to the DON'TS
Listen to the SHOULDN'TS
The IMPOSSIBLES, the WON'TS
Listen to the NEVER HAVES.
Then listen close to me –
Anything can happen, child,
ANYTHING can be.

▲ Shel Silverstein, *Where the Sidewalk Ends*, 1974

3. **Apprenez-en un par cœur.**
Puis justifiez votre choix. Appuyez-vous sur les notes prises au cours de cette unité.
- Donnez votre opinion : *to me / as far as I'm concerned / in my opinion* … (cf. p. 232)
- Réutilisez les structures vues dans l'unité pour partager vos sentiments : *I wish …/ If only* …
- Réemployez le vocabulaire étudié.
- N'utilisez pas : "*I like it because, it's nice…*", mais dites plutôt :
It makes me feel like / it makes me think of / it symbolises / it stands for / it highlights… .

Scénario 2

1. **Écrivez** une ou plusieurs strophes en vers libre. Commencez le premier vers de chaque strophe en utilisant l'expression "*I imagine*" ou "*I have a dream*".
2. **Suivez** les mêmes étapes qu'au **scénario 1. 3.**

Conseils pour votre prestation!

Parlez lentement, regardez votre auditoire
Vous n'en serez que plus convaincant !
(Le professeur n'est pas votre seul interlocuteur.)

Travaillez votre prononciation
> Lisez le texte choisi à haute voix et vérifiez la prononciation en écoutant **l'enregistrement du texte** (Scénario 1).
Puis récitez-le en imitant le modèle de l'enregistrement.
> **Enregistrez-vous.**
> Mettez-vous **en situation** : restez debout et regardez autour de vous.
Déplacez-vous pour occuper l'espace.

MP3 PISTE 9 — CD1 PISTE 19

Geography Lesson

Our teacher told us one day he would leave
And sail across a warm blue sea
To places he had only known from maps[1],
And all his life had longed to[2] be.

The house he lived in was narrow and grey
But in his mind's eye he could see
Sweet-scented jasmine clinging to[3] the walls,
And green leaves burning on an orange tree.

He spoke of the lands he longed to visit,
Where it was never drab[4] or cold.
I couldn't understand why he never left,
And shook off[5] the school's stranglehold[6].

Then halfway through his final term
He took ill and never returned,
And he never got to that place on the map
Where the green leaves of the orange trees burned.

The maps were redrawn on the classroom wall;
His name was forgotten, it faded away[7].
But a lesson he never knew he taught
Is with me to this day.

I travel to where the green leaves burn
To where the ocean's glass-clear and blue,
To all those places my teacher taught me to love
But which he never knew.

▲ Brian Patten, *Juggling with Gerbils*, 2000

1. *cartes*
2. *désirait ardemment*
3. *(ici) qui grimpe*
4. *(ici) glauque*
5. *(ici) brisa*
6. *(ici) étau*
7. *disparut*

Bums[1] in the Attic[2]

I want a house on a hill[3] like the ones with the gardens where Papa works. We go on Sundays, Papa's day off. I used to go. I don't anymore. You don't like to go out with us, Papa says. Getting too old? Getting too stuck-up, says Nenny. I don't tell them I am ashamed - all of us staring out the window like the hungry. I am tired of looking at what we can't have. When we win the lottery… Mama begins, and then I stop listening.

People who live on hills sleep so close to[4] the stars they forget those of us who live too much on earth. They don't look down at all except to be content to live on hills. They have nothing to do with last week's garbage[5] or fear of rats. Night comes. Nothing wakes them but[6] the wind.

One day I'll own my own house, but I won't forget who I am or where I came from. Passing bums will ask, Can I come in? I'll offer them the attic, ask them to stay, because I know how it is to be without a house.

Some days after dinner, guests and I will sit in front of a fire. Floorboards will squeak upstairs. The attic grumble[7].

Rats? they'll ask.

Bums, I'll say, and I'll be happy.

▲ Sandra Cisneros, *The House on Mango Street*, 1991

1. *clochards*
2. *grenier*
3. *colline*
4. near
5. rubbish
6. except
7. *(ici) grincera*

Évaluation sommative
Spoken Production

J'évalue mes progrès

Je revois les stratégies apprises dans les unités précédentes (*Improve Your Speaking Skills* p.26, p.38 et p.50) afin de faire le bilan de mes compétences.

1. Je me prépare

Entraînez-vous à parler le plus longtemps possible de Michelle Obama (au moins 1 minute). Présentez-la à l'aide des informations contenues dans la fiche.

Birth	Michelle LaVaughn Robinson, January 17, 1964 – Chicago, Illinois
Parents	African-American; middle class, one elder brother
Family	Marriage to Barack Obama: 1992 Two daughters: Malia (1998) and Sasha (2001)
Career	University: Princeton & Harvard First job: lawyer[1] in Chicago Support of her husband's political campaign ⇝ stop working After her husband's elections (2008 & 2012): ⇝ first African-American First Lady
Activities as First Lady	✱ Travels all around the world & holds meetings with foreign leaders ✱ Visits hospitals, homeless shelters[2], schools all over the US ✱ 2010: foundation of Let's Move, an organisation promoting healthy eating, especially in schools ⇝ Goal: to fight childhood obesity in the US ✱ Support of charities for children: PeacePlayers International, Healthy Child Healthy World ⇝ participation in galas and events ✱ Defence of important causes: childhood hunger, cancer research, education, arts.... ⇝ speeches & organisation of receptions at the White House to raise money[3] for these causes

1. *avocate* **2.** *foyers pour sans-abris* **3.** *collecter des fonds*

2. Je me corrige

CD1 PISTE 20 — MP3 PISTE 10

Écoutez l'enregistrement correspondant à cette évaluation et comparez votre production orale à celle enregistrée par un anglophone.

Je fais le bilan

Analysez vos résultats à l'aide de cette grille d'évaluation où sont définis les différents niveaux de compétence en expression orale en continu. Le niveau attendu en classe de seconde est B1.

Je peux…	Niveaux
… présenter ou raconter des faits en points successifs avec des mots de liaison de base (*and, but, because*). … faire des phrases simples en utilisant des expressions toutes faites et courtes, malgré des hésitations et de nombreuses pauses. … utiliser des structures de base, mais je fais encore des erreurs de temps et de grammaire qui ne bloquent pas la compréhension générale de mon message. … me faire comprendre malgré un net accent français.	A2
… raconter une histoire ou la vie de quelqu'un et décrire mes réactions. … me faire comprendre malgré un léger accent français. … utiliser un mot simple de signification semblable, ou une périphrase, si un mot m'échappe. … m'exprimer de manière compréhensible sans trop d'hésitation, mais je fais des pauses pour réfléchir ou corriger ce que je dis.	B1
… communiquer avec aisance et spontanéité.	en route vers B2

Évaluation

Votre professeur va vous distribuer un document portant sur une des unités travaillées en cours.

Unit 1 Me, Myself & I

Unit 2 Choose Your School

Unit 3 Change the World

Vous l'observerez puis vous le présenterez.

Temps de préparation : 5 minutes

Temps de parole : 1 minute minimum

⚠ Ne rédigez pas votre texte, vous n'aurez droit qu'à des notes. (cf. p.50)

⚠ Vous avez le droit d'hésiter et de vous reprendre. (cf. Enrichir sa prise de parole : *Gap Fillers* p.232)

Une fois l'évaluation terminée, votre professeur pourra ainsi déterminer à quel palier vous vous situez par rapport à la grille d'évaluation du Cadre Européen Commun de Référence pour les Langues.

▲ *The Great Gatsby*, Baz Luhrmann, 2013 (starring Leonardo Di Caprio)

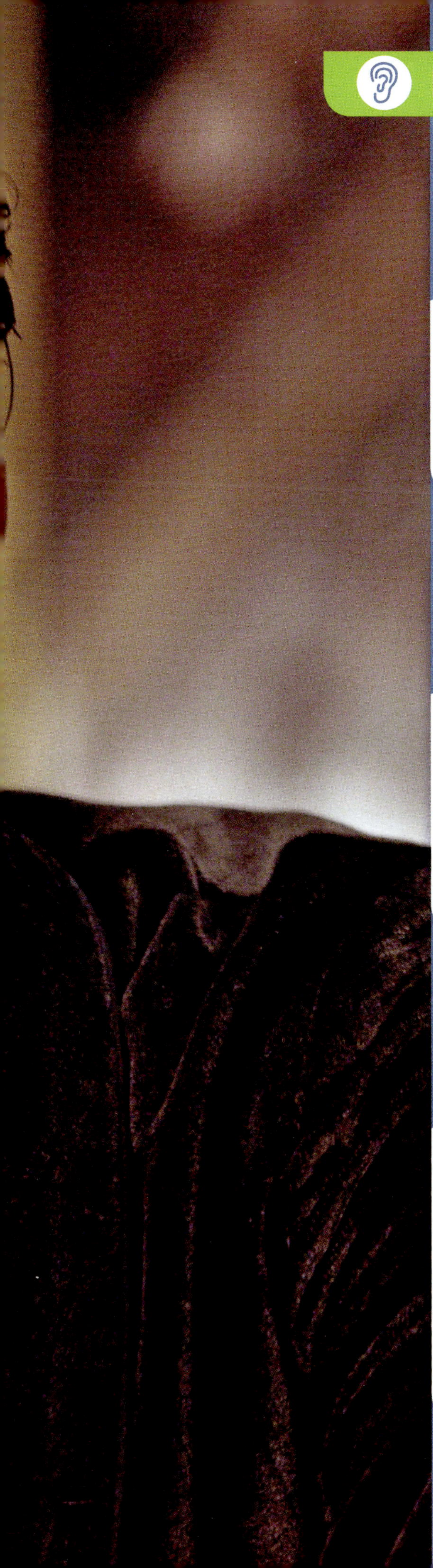

Listening

Unit 4

Destination UK

SENTIMENT D'APPARTENANCE • MÉMOIRE

- Discover the United Kingdom and its different regions.
- How much do you know about British food?
- Learn more about some famous Brits and the country's icons.

YOUR TASK You are going to participate in a quiz show on British culture. Answer the host's questions or, in groups, test the other team. Get the best score to win the contest.

p. 67

Unit 5

Over the Rainbow

MÉMOIRE • VISION D'AVENIR

- Explore South Africa. Learn about its population, troubled past and heroes.
- Discover films and songs about the country.
- Understand the importance of sport and music for South Africans at the end of apartheid.

YOUR TASK You work for the magazine *National Geographic*. Listen to different reports on South Africa and prepare a page entitled "The New South Africa in Focus".

p. 81

Unit 6

Beyond Limits

VISION D'AVENIR • SENTIMENT D'APPARTENANCE

- Learn more about two exceptional people: Felix Baumgartner, and Jessica Cox.
- How did a young man change the life of his village in Malawi?
- Read about Diane Fossey's life and listen to Ishmael Beah speaking about his fight against child soldiers.

YOUR TASK You take part in a quiz show on people who have gone beyond their limits. Listen to the recording and guess their identity. You can also prepare a presentation on a person who has done something extraordinary.

p. 93

Unit 4

SENTIMENT D'APPARTENANCE • MÉMOIRE

Destination UK

YOUR TASK AT THE END OF THIS UNIT

You are going to participate in a quiz show on British culture. Answer the host's questions or, in groups, test the other team. Get the best score to win the contest. *p. 67*

1 Tune In!

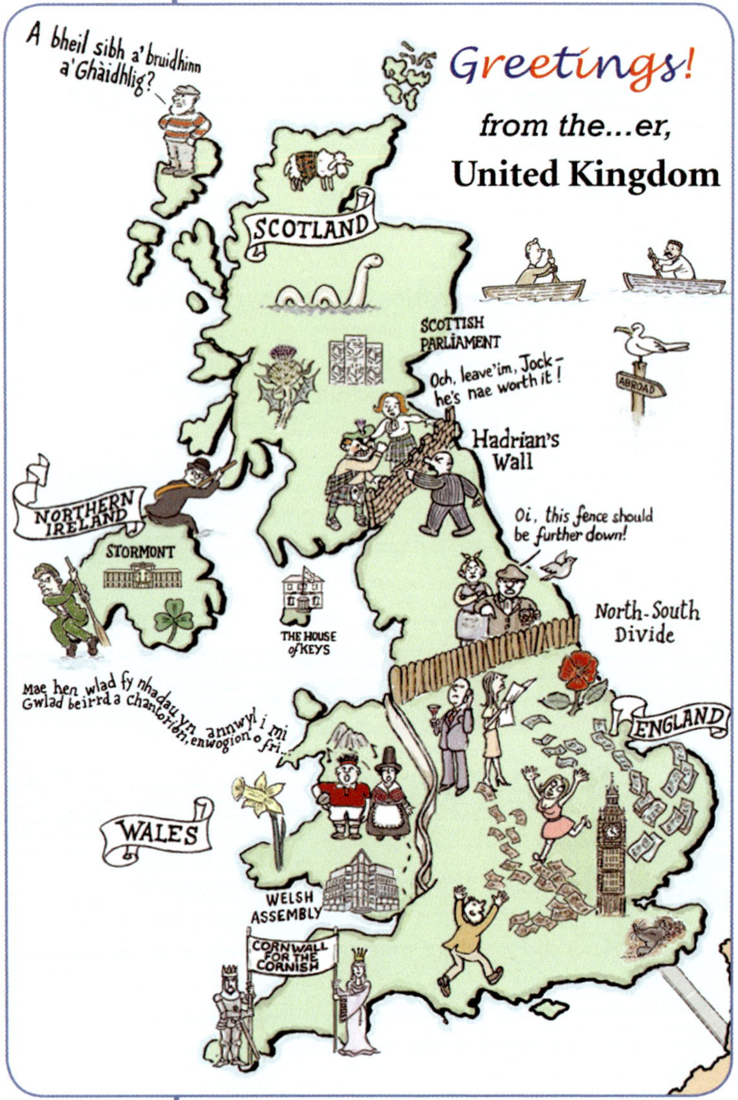

1 A united country?

a. What are the different countries which compose the UK?
b. What are the emblems of each country?
c. Locate and name the different parliaments.
d. What languages are spoken in the UK?
e. Go on the Internet and find information about Hadrian's Wall.
f. Focus on the two men on each side of Hadrian's Wall. What is their attitude? Why?
g. On the map, find an expression corresponding to this definition: "The economic and cultural differences between Southern and Northern England".

Help!

daffodil: *jonquille*
shamrock: *trèfle*
thistle /ˈθɪsəl/: *chardon*
similarities ≠ differences
fence: *barrière*

have an argument = have a row /raʊ/
be prejudiced against

2 Play with words

WB p. 19

Turn to your Workbook to work on the nationalities and geography of the UK.

3 A street survey

WB p. 20

CD1 PISTE 21

PREPARE YOUR TASK

a. Listen to the radio programme. Turn to your Workbook for help.
b. Find the common points and the differences between the three people interviewed.

2 Take a Tour

video

1 Watch a video

a. React to the video: what can you remember (monuments, places, people, music)?
b. What is the goal of the video? Who is targeted?

2 A trip to the countryside!

WB p.21

a. Match each description with the corresponding image of the region. Justify your choice with key words from the texts.
b. Locate these regions on the map. Turn to your Workbook for help.

1

The Highlands is a Scottish region where snow-peaked mountains and breathtaking landscapes can be admired.

2

Devon is a coastal county of southern England well known for its seaside towns surrounded by hillsides.

The Lake District, in North West England, is a mountainous region famous for its 19 lakes.

3

Help!

Activities

go hiking / sailing
go hill-climbing
sunbathe: *bronzer*
take pictures = photos = snapshots

Likes and dislikes

I'd love to… because…
I am fond of V-ING
I have always been keen on V-ING
… is/are definitely worth visiting!
… is/are not really my cup of tea
I don't like… so much…

3 Prepare for your trip

In groups, decide which region above you would like to visit. What activities could you do there? Justify your choice.

3 Food, Glorious Food

1 Guessing game WB p. 22

Describe a dish to your partner, using the vocabulary given. He / She will have to guess which picture you are talking about. Turn to your Workbook for help.
- **Group 1** will concentrate on pictures 1 to 4.
- **Group 2** will work on pictures 5 to 8.

2 Yummy! Yucky!

a. Find information about Marmite.
www.unilever.co.uk/brands-in-action/detail/Marmite/293688/
b. Report to the class:
What is Marmite? When and where was it created?
When was it used and why? What do customers think of this product?

CD1 PISTE 22

PREPARE YOUR TASK

3 A British recipe WB p. 22

a. Listen to a radio programme on cooking. Turn to your Workbook for help.
b. What recipe is given? Match the dish with one of the eight photos above.

4 Act it out!

You participate in a TV show on cooking. Tell the other contestants which dish you would (or would not) like to try. Justify your choice.

Help!

Savoury
bacon and eggs
baked /beɪkt/ beans
chips (GB) = French fries (US): *frites*
meat: beef, chicken, sausages
mushrooms: *champignons*
rice and curry sauce /sɔːs/
roast potatoes: *pommes de terre rôties*
Yorkshire pudding

Sweet
chutney *(condiment)*
custard /ˈkʌstəd/: *crème pâtissière*
pie /paɪ/: *tarte ou tourte*
raspberries: *framboises*
scone /skɒn/
strawberries /ˈstrɔːbriz/: *fraises*
jam: *confiture*

Opinion
yummy ≠ yucky *(familier)*
revolting = disgusting

it looks / tastes good
it's worth trying: *cela vaut la peine d'essayer*
it makes my mouth water
I'd like to have a try: *j'aimerais goûter*

4 The Perfect Brit

1 Observe and react
WB P.23

a. Look at this cartoon carefully for one minute then close your book.

Which characters did you identify?	Which elements did you memorise?	Which adjectives can you remember?

CD1 PISTE 23

b. Match each adjective with the appropriate picture and justify your choice.

arrogant /ˈærəgənt/	tight-fisted /ˌtaɪtˈfɪstɪd/ =	incomprehensible
rude /ruːd/	stingy /ˈstɪndʒi/ *(radin)*	inedible *(inmangeable)*
awful *(affreux)*	stiff *(raide)*	contemptuous *(méprisant)*
tasteless *(insipide)*	rainy	posh *(chic)*
drunk /drʌŋk/	nervous /ˈnɜːvəs/ *(inquiet)*	snobbish

c. Work on your pronunciation. Turn to your Workbook for help. WB P.23

CD1 PISTE 24

PREPARE YOUR TASK

2 A Brit's opinion

We asked Andrew, a British citizen, to react to this cartoon. In his opinion, does it reflect the reality?

3 Be creative!

If the same cartoon were made about the French, what would it be like? Why? You can make a similar cartoon if you like.

Help!

be considered a symbol
be regarded as / seen as / viewed as…
be said / thought to be: *on dit / pense que*
British people are said to be bad cooks.

5 Home, Sweet Home

I like living in England because everywhere else is foreign and strange. The only language I speak is English. [...] But I wouldn't like anyone to think I don't like Abroad. I do. Abroad means adventure and the possibility of danger and delicious food, but Abroad is also tiring and confusing and full of foreigners who tell you that the bank is open when it's not. [...]

I like English weather; like the countryside it's constantly drawing attention to itself. I started this article in a room filled with piercing sunlight, but now a strong wind has materialised and the room is full of gloom[1].

I like the reserve of English people, because I don't particularly want to talk to strangers in trains either, unless of course there is a crisis such as a 'cow on the line'[2] causing an hour's delay[3]. In which case my fellow passengers and I will happily spill out[4] our life stories to anybody we can get to listen.

I like the way in which the English cope with[5] disasters: cut our water off and we will cheerfully queue at a standpipe[6] in the snow. [...] I'm happy to live in a country that produces important things: wonderful plays, books, literature, heart surgeons, gardeners and Private Eye[7].[...] I asked a friend of mine where, given the choice and enough money, he would choose to live. He replied gloomily, 'There isn't anywhere else'.

▲ Sue Townsend, *True Confessions of Adrian Albert Mole, Margaret Hilda Roberts and Susan Lilian Townsend*, 1989

1. *obscurité*
2. a commonly used excuse when British trains are late
3. *retard*
4. *déballer*
5. *font face à*
6. (ici) *point d'eau de secours*
7. a British satirical magazine

1 Understanding the text
WB p.24

Find the different reasons why the narrator likes living in England. Turn to your Workbook for help.

2 Go further!

CD1 PISTE 25

PREPARE YOUR TASK

Listen and learn more about famous British authors. Use your notes to report to the class.

▲ William Shakespeare

▲ Emily Brontë

▲ George Orwell

3 A poem

CD1 PISTE 26

PREPARE YOUR TASK

a. Listen to these lines by D.H. Lawrence.
b. Your teacher will give you a worksheet to improve your pronunciation.
c. Now read this poem aloud.

The English Are So Nice!

The English are so nice
so awfully nice
they are the nicest people in the world.
And what's more, they're very nice about being nice
about your being nice as well!
If you're not nice they soon make you feel it.

▲ D.H. Lawrence

4 Writing workshop

You are hoping to stay with a British family next summer. Send them an email explaining why you would like to visit their country. (100-150 words)

6 Royals in the Limelight

1 Group work

PREPARE YOUR TASK

a. Learn more about Queen Elizabeth I, Queen Victoria or Queen Elizabeth II.
Visit the following website: www.britroyals.com
Decide which of the three queens you want to learn more about.
b. Now watch the trailer of the film corresponding to the queen you have chosen.
- What is the main historical event which is mentioned?
- Describe the queen's personality.

c. Give an oral account of the film to the class.

Help!

The film is about / deals with…
It relates the story of…
The queen is portrayed / described as authoritative / powerful / mysterious / determined because…
She is faced /feɪst/ with = confronted with…
I strongly advise /ədˈvaɪz/ you to + V
≠ I wouldn't recommend it because …

◄ *Elizabeth, the Golden Age*, Shekhar Kapur, 2007

◄ *The Queen*, Stephen Frears, 2006

▲ *The Young Victoria*, Jean-Marc Vallée, 2009

2 Become a historian

Create a timeline about one of the British queens above. You can follow this example:

1533	…
Birth of Elizabeth I	…………………

3 A critic's review

Write a review of one of the films above for a film magazine. Make a short summary and give your opinion: would you encourage people to go and watch it? Why? Why not? (100 words)

LANGUAGE AT WORK

+ WORKBOOK
→ Apprendre à apprendre
p. 105 - 106

A La détermination du nom : *a, an, the,* « l'article zéro » = Ø Précis, p. 250

Observez

1 Lisez les énoncés ci-dessous :

a. *__Tea__ has become __a national drink__.*

b. *__Chips and vinegar__ are very popular.*

c. *To go to Westminster from Waterloo, you have to walk over __a bridge__.*

Chaque groupe souligné renvoie-t-il à :
- un ensemble / une généralité ou un élément parmi d'autres ?
- un indénombrable ou un dénombrable ?

2 ***A / an*** **: observez et comparez.**

*Oxford has **a** famous university.*
*Stonehenge is **an** interesting site.*
*Stonehenge is **a** unique site.*
*It will take us **an** hour to go to the Globe Theatre.*

Quel article indéfini est utilisé devant *unique* et pourquoi ?

Déduisez

On emploie ***a / an*** pour désigner un ... .
Pour parler de quelque chose « en général », on emploie l'article zéro (ø) si le nom est un ... au ..., ou si le nom est un ... au ... .

On emploie ***a*** devant les ... , sauf « ... » non-prononcé comme dans ... .
On emploie ***an*** devant les ... , sauf devant « ... » prononcé comme dans ... .

Observez

3 Observez.

Sherlock Holmes is a detective.
Who was Sir Christopher Wren? He was an English architect.

Traduisez ces énoncés en français.

Déduisez

A la différence du français, on emploie l'article indéfini (*a / an*) lorsqu'on indique la catégorie à laquelle appartient quelque chose ou quelqu'un, donc devant les noms de ... .

4 Lisez les énoncés suivants.

a. *Big Ben is __the name__ of __the bell__ inside St Stephen's clock tower attached to __the Houses of Parliament__.*

b. *__The chime__ of Big Ben is __the sound__ that announces __the New Year__.*

c. *__The clock__ tells __the time__ with great accuracy (*précision*).*

d. *__The Millennium Bridge__ was closed four days after being opened because of technical problems.*

Pourquoi emploie-t-on *the* dans chacun des éléments soulignés ? Parce que :
- le mot est défini par ce qui suit.
- le mot fait référence à un élément connu de tous.
- le mot fait référence à un élément particulier et bien défini.
- le mot est défini par le contexte, on vient d'en parler.

Observez

5 Lisez ces énoncés.

The symbol of England is a rose.
The symbol of Scotland is a thistle.
Uncle Sam often symbolises the United States.
The United Kingdom is worth visiting.

Déduisez

Les noms de pays au singulier s'emploient sans ... .
La plupart des noms de pays formés à partir de noms communs sont précédés de ... .

Entraînez-vous

1 Complétez avec *the* ou *a/an* lorsque c'est nécessaire. Si aucun article n'est nécessaire (ø), rétablissez la majuscule en tête de phrase.

a. ... pubs are an important part of life in Britain. ... people go there to relax, meet ... friends and sometimes to do business. ... pub food (called "pub grub") is often good and cheaper than ... restaurant food. In a pub you often have to go to ... bar to get your food and drink. ... beer is ... popular drink.

b. ... people of Wales are very musical. Every year almost every town or region organises ... festival of poetry and music called "*eisteddfod*".

c. Britain is ... island and you are never very far from ... sea.

d. The West of England produces ... milk, ... cream, ... butter, ... cheese (especially Cheddar cheese) and ... apples, which go to make ... cider, ... very popular drink.

2 Complétez les espaces blancs avec *the* ou *a/an* lorsque c'est nécessaire. Attention aux majuscules.

... miniskirts were designed by ... British designer Mary Quant in 1966. ... miniskirts caused ... controversy and ... car crashes when women first started wearing them. They are ... symbol of ... London as ... pop culture capital of ... world.

... woman wearing ... miniskirt in .... 1960s.

3 Lisez le paragraphe suivant, puis complétez les espaces blancs avec *the* ou *a/an* lorsque c'est nécessaire. Attention aux majuscules.

Edinburgh is ... Scotland's capital. ... heart of Edinburgh is ... castle where ... kings of ... Scotland lived for ... centuries. Edinburgh has ... busy cultural life. Every year, in September, ... International Festival takes place. ... musicians, ... actors and ... singers from all over ... world and thousands of visitors from ... Australia, ... Canada, ... Japan, ... United States and ... Netherlands fill ... city. In ... evening, ... opera house, ... theatres and ... concert halls of the city are full. In ... cafés and ... pubs of ... capital of Scotland, ... small groups sing, act, and read ... poetry.

4 Pour traduire ces phrases en anglais, demandez-vous quel déterminant (*a / an / the* / ø) utiliser devant les mots soulignés.

a. Brick Lane est une rue célèbre en Grande Bretagne. Des immigrants originaires du Bengladesh et d'Inde se sont installés là.

b. Monica Ali est romancière *(novelist)*, elle a écrit un roman sur ce quartier *(this area)*.

c. Les Londoniens *(Londoners)* vont à Brick Lane pour manger un curry.

1 Who's who?

1. Anticipez

Avant d'écouter plusieurs messages oraux, regardez les images ci-contre. Pouvez-vous identifier certaines personnes ? (*Cf. Fast Facts p. 245*)

2. Associez son et écriture

MP3 PISTE 11 — CD1 PISTE 27

a. Écoutez une liste de mots. Écrivez sur papier libre chaque mot entendu.
b. Repérez à chaque fois la syllabe accentuée.
c. Entraînez-vous ensuite à prononcer chaque mot.

3. Écoutez

MP3 PISTE 12 — CD1 PISTE 28

a. Repérez tous les mots connus ainsi que les mots accentués (ce sont les mots importants qui se détachent dans le discours car ils portent le message).
b. A l'aide de ces indices, associez chaque portrait à la photo qui lui correspond.

4. Entraînez-vous

MP3 PISTE 13 — CD1 PISTE 29

Découvrez d'autres personnages célèbres. N'oubliez pas de repérer les mots accentués qui vous permettront de trouver de qui il s'agit.

2 Écoutez un audioguide de la National Portrait Gallery

MP3 PISTE 14 — CD1 PISTE 30

Que représente ce portrait d'Henry VIII ?
a. Prenez en notes les mots-clés (ceux qui sont accentués). Mettez en œuvre les stratégies étudiées précédemment pour relever les informations principales.
b. Restituez le message en une minute : quels sont les éléments frappants de ce tableau ? Que symbolisent-ils ? Comment le roi est-il présenté ?

◄ *Henry VIII*, Hans Holbein, 1537

YOUR TASK

You are going to participate in a quiz show on British culture. Answer the host's questions or, in groups, test the other team. Get the best score to win the contest.

Préparez-vous

1. Réactivez vos connaissances.
Revoyez ce que vous avez appris. Pour vous aider à réviser, vous pouvez aller sur le site internet du *British Postal Museum & Archives*
www.postalheritage.org.uk/page/icons

2. Prononcez à haute voix les mots des rubriques *Help* p. 58-60. Vérifiez à l'écoute.
MP3 PISTE 15 CD1 PISTE 31

3. Ecrivez les mots que vous allez entendre sur papier libre, vérifiez leur orthographe, lisez-les à haute voix.
MP3 PISTE 16 CD1 PISTE 32

4. Entraînez-vous
Préparez quelques questions afin de tester votre voisin / un autre groupe sur leurs connaissances.

Scénario 1

CD1 PISTE 33

Comment se déroulera le jeu ?

a. Une fiche réponse va vous être distribuée. Vérifiez si vous faites partie du groupe A ou B.
b. Le jeu est composé de questions qui portent sur tous les aspects du Royaume-Uni : géographie, monarchie, nourriture, culture populaire, etc.
c. Chaque question sera répétée deux fois, et vous aurez quelques secondes pour écrire votre réponse.
d. Avant de ramasser les fiches, le professeur vous laissera une minute pour vous relire.

Scénario 2

A l'aide de vos notes sur l'unité, préparez les questions que vous poserez à un autre groupe. (Revoyez comment poser les questions p.218)

Reading Corner

I don't understand!

Paul West, a young London marketing agent, is starting a new job in Paris. This is his first meeting with his French colleagues.

"My name is Paul West," I told them. I saw them all practise saying my name...
"You rilly yong," said the skinny[1] bloke[2]. Not accusingly, but annoyingly[3].
"Not really, I'm 27. If I was a rock star I'd be dead." The bloke made apologetic[4] gestures. "No, no. Ah'm not criti-sahsing. Ah'm just... admirative." He had a weird[5] accent. Not quite French. I couldn't place it [...].
"Why don't everyone present himself? "[...]Bernard, start please" [...] Bernard smiled nervously and began.
"Yam bare narr, yam responsa bull ov commu-nikasyon, er...."
Shit I thought, didn't Jean-Marie[6] say the meeting was going to be in English? How come some people were allowed to speak Hungarian? Bernard of Budapest carried on in the same incomprehensible vein for a couple of minutes and then started to enunciate something which, to judge by the look of acute constipation on his face, was of great importance.
"Alok for wah toowa king wizioo."
Hang on, I thought. I don't speak any Central European languages, but I got that. He's looking forward to working with me. Holy Babel fish[7]. It's English, Jim, but not as we know it.

▲ By Stephen Clarke, *A Year in the Merde*, 2004

1. /'skɪni/: very slim **2.** /bləʊk/ (GB): guy **3.** in an irritated way **4.** expressing regret **5.** /wɪəd/ strange **6.** Jean-Marie is the boss of the French company **7.** *site de traduction très connu des Britanniques*

CD1 PISTE 34

"I wandered[1] lonely as a cloud
That floats on high o'er vales and hills[2],
When all at once I saw a crowd,
A host, of golden daffodils;
Beside the lake, beneath the trees,
Fluttering[3] and dancing in the breeze."

▲ William Wordsworth, 1807

1. /wɒndəd/ walked without going in a particular direction **2.** *vallées et collines* **3.** *frémissant*

What aspects of British culture do these two documents focus on?

▲ *The Royal Family, A Centenary Portrait*, John Wonnacott, 2000

Tongue twisters

CD1 PISTE 35

Ruth threw this thick thing through the bathroom. I thought this thick thing she threw was a tooth from her mouth.

Mother and father left Southampton last Thursday for their brother's birthday.

The Smiths wear thin clothes throughout the winter months.

Unit 5

Over the Rainbow

YOUR TASK AT THE END OF THIS UNIT

You work for the magazine *National Geographic*. Listen to different reports on South Africa and prepare a page entitled "The New South Africa in Focus."

p. 81

1 Tune In!

1 2 3

1 Observe and react

React to the pictures above. Choose from these words to describe them:

flag · tribe · multicultural · uniformity · diverse · colourful · traditional · origins

2 Main facts

WB p.26

PREPARE YOUR TASK

CD2 PISTE 1

Listen and learn more about South Africa. Turn to your Workbook for help.

video

3 Watch a video: Discover South Africa

Turn to your worksheet for help.

a. What aspects of the country are presented?

b. Who is the target?

c. Do you feel like visiting this country? Why? Why not?

4 Play with words

WB P.26

Turn to your Workbook to improve your vocabulary.

5 The Rainbow Nation

WB P.27

a. Group A: Understand the text with the help of your Workbook.

www.southafrica-travel.net

Numerous population groups with different languages, cultural backgrounds and origins all coexist in South Africa. The bigger groups are Zulus (21%), Xhosas (17%) and the Sotho (15%). The province of Natal is home to about one million Indians, whose forefathers[1] came to South Africa to work on the sugarcane plantations. And there are three million people of mixed race, the so-called "coloureds" [...]. They are descendants of the first Dutch settlers[2] and the native population of the Cape (Khoikhoi) or the Malays, who were taken to South Africa as slaves from East India in the 18th century.

The portion of the relatively prosperous white part of the South African population amounts to[3] 8% (4 million) of the national population. Most of them derive from Dutch, German or French immigrants. They are called Afrikaners and speak Afrikaans, which is closely related to the Dutch language. The English speaking part of the white population is concentrated in the Western and Eastern Cape province and in Natal.

1. *ancêtres* **2.** *colons Hollandais* **3.** *s'élève à*

PREPARE YOUR TASK

CD2 PISTE 3

Group B: Listen to Merylin, a South African woman, talking about her country. Turn to your Workbook for help.

b. Report to the class.

c. Learn more about South Africa.

- Understand the South African flag. On the Internet, search for the following key words: South Africa, flag, symbolism.
- What are South Africa's capital cities?

d. Locate on the map:

- city names of Dutch, African or British origin
- the name of a desert
- the name of a national park

e. Use the information collected on this double page to explain why South Africa is nicknamed "the Rainbow (*arc en ciel*) Nation."

Help!

diversity /daɪˈvɜːsəti/

landscape / scenery: *paysage*

tribe: *tribu*

breathtaking: *à couper le souffle*

magnificent /mæɡˈnɪfɪsənt/: *magnifique*

6 Writing Workshop

Write a short article about South Africa for a holiday brochure. (100 words)

2 The Fight

► Signboard on a Durban beach during apartheid

1 Separated and unequal

a. Locate Durban on the map p. 71 and react to the photograph.
b. What does it reveal about the situation of black and coloured people under apartheid?

2 A time of fire

WB p. 29

a. Read the text and turn to your Workbook for help.

It was a "time of fire" as Grace called it, when she and Dumi[1] had marched in the streets with thousands of other schoolchildren. They were protesting that their schools taught them only what the white government wanted them to know.

On the banner that Dumi and his friends carried, they had written: "BLACKS ARE NOT DUSTBINS[2]."

Everything went all right until the police saw the schoolchildren marching, and then the trouble started. The police aimed their guns and began to shoot with real bullets, killing whoever was in the way.

It was terrible. The police shot tear gas too, making everyone's eyes burn.

People were screaming, bleeding[3], falling. More police came in great steel[4] tanks, and more in helicopters, firing from above. A little girl standing near Grace, about eight years old, raised her fist[5], and next thing she was lying dead.

People became fighting mad, throwing stones at the police, burning down schools and government offices. Smoke and flames were everywhere.

But the police kept shooting, until hundreds were dead. Hundreds were hurt and hundreds were arrested. Dumi was one of those arrested.

When he came out of prison, he said that the police had beaten him up badly, but he would go on fighting even if they killed him.

▲ Beverley Naidoo, *Journey to Jo'burg*, 1985

1. Grace's brother **2.** *poubelles* **3.** *saignaient* **4.** *acier* **5.** *poing*

3 Rebels with a cause

CD2 PISTE 4-5

PREPARE YOUR TASK

WB p. 30

a. - **Group 1** will learn more about apartheid.
- **Group 2** will focus on the Soweto riots.

Turn to your Workbook for help.
b. Report to the class what you have understood.

4 Newsflash

You are a journalist and you witnessed the scene. Prepare a one-minute news report including the following points:

- Who are Grace and Dumi?
- Why were they there?
- How did the police react?
- What happened to the people present?
- What happened to Dumi in particular?

Help!

civilians / rebels
protest
apartheid /ə'pɑːtaɪt/ /ə'pɑːteɪt/

aggressive
brave = courageous
injured = wounded: *blessé*
humane ≠ inhumane
pitiless / merciless

be discriminated against
demonstrate against: *manifester contre*
complain about
crush a riot /'raɪət/: *écraser une émeute*
rebel against

3 Apartheid in Films

video

1 Watch a video

Watch an extract from *Goodbye Bafana* by Bille August (2007). Turn to your worksheet for help.

a. Whose point of view on apartheid is given here?

b. The little girl in the movie relates the scene in her diary. Imagine her narrative. (150 words)

2 Compare

Look at the DVD covers of two films about apartheid. What strikes you? What are the common points and differences?

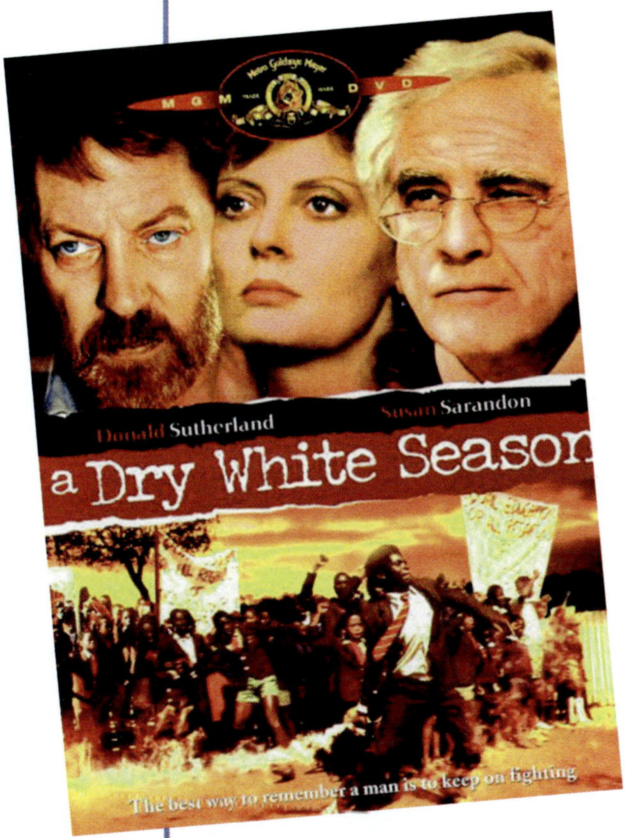

PREPARE YOUR TASK

CD2 PISTE 6

3 A film review

a. Listen to a journalist reviewing one of these films. Which one does he present?

b. Go on the Internet and watch the trailer of the other film. Write a summary.

Help!

Characters	Plot	Reactions
lawyer gardener witness: *témoin* opponent: *opposant* activist: *militant* determined / strong-minded bitter / resentful : *amer* side with: *prendre parti pour* realise: *se rendre compte*	cruelty involved in: *impliqué* on an equal footing: *sur un pied d'égalité* investigate: *mener l'enquête* struggle: *lutter* expose = denounce uncover the truth threaten: *menacer*	condemnation happy ending brilliant ≠ disappointing effective ≠ ineffective impressive moving: *émouvant* powerful shocking unfair = unjust

4 A Long Walk to Freedom

1 Get ready

With the help of the cartoon below, share with the class what you know about Nelson Mandela.

2 When Buti became Nelson

Buti grew strong and smart, and when he was seven years old, two old friends of his father recognized how smart he was and told his mother he should go to school. Even Buti's father, who had never gone to school himself, thought this was an excellent idea.

On the first day of school, the English teacher gave all the African children English names. Buti's new name was Nelson.

He wasn't certain if he liked his new English name, but Nelson knew he liked school. He liked [...] the way his father prepared him for school by telling him always to stand firm[1] for what he believed was fair and right[2]. [...]

Next Nelson advanced to Fort Hare, a missionary college for African scholars[3] from all over Africa. [...] He became a school leader and in his final year was elected to serve on the student council. When, in a protest for better food, he quit the council, the principal threatened him: come back, or be expelled! Nelson refused. He stood firm for what he believed was fair and right, and was expelled. Nelson never imagined the unfairness and inequality that he would find in Johannesburg. He'd known the attitude most English men had toward anything African. [...] But he could hardly believe what he saw.

▲ Floyd Cooper, *Mandela: From the Life of the South African Statesman*, 1996

1. *(ici) défendre*
2. *juste et bon*
3. *intellectuels / érudits*

3 Understand the text WB P.32

a. Read the text and turn to your Workbook for help.
b. In your own words, write a portrait of Nelson Mandela when he was a student. Use the adjectives opposite.
c. Focus on the following sentences and explain the Whites' attitude to Africans at that time.

"Buti's new name was Nelson. He wasn't certain if he liked his new English name ..." – "He'd known the attitude most English men had toward anything African." – "Nelson never imagined the unfairness and inequality that he would find in Johannesburg."

Help!

obedient ≠ rebellious
determined /dɪˈtɜːmɪnd/
committed: *engagé*
responsible
popular
courageous = brave
bold: *audacieux*
wilful: *volontaire*
resolute
provocative

CD2 PISTE 7-8

PREPARE YOUR TASK

4 A timeline WB P.33

In groups, listen to different parts of Mandela's biography. Turn to your Workbook to complete a timeline, then share what you have learnt with the class.

5 Mandela Days

1 Groupwork

a. Choose one of the following songs and go on the Internet to discover the lyrics.

Mandela Day, Simple Minds

Free Nelson Mandela, The Special A.K.A

Freedom Now, Tracy Chapman

b. Answer the questions corresponding to the lyrics you have read.

Mandela Day

a. Which words are repeated? What is their impact?
b. Focus on line 1. What does it refer to?
c. Find references to: - prison - apartheid - change
Justify with words and phrases from the song.
d. Which emotions does this song convey?

happiness • injustice • hope • revolt

Freedom Now

a. One verb in the preterit tense is incorrect. Rewrite the correct form.
b. List all the words and phrases referring to freedom.
c. Find the reasons why 'they' put Mandela in jail.
d. What is the tone of the song? Justify.

angry • desperate • uncertain • joyful • bitter

Free Nelson Mandela

a. What does '*twenty-one years*' refer to?
b. In this song, does the singer ask for / celebrate / condemn the release of Mandela? Justify.
c. Which party did Nelson Mandela belong to? Quote the song to justify.
d. Do you think this song is optimistic or pessimistic? Justify your choice.

Fast Fact

The ANC (African National Congress) is a political party that fought to put an end to apartheid.

c. Sum up the message of the song you have chosen and report to the class.

2 Mandela Day

Choose a song to celebrate Mandela Day (on 18th July). In groups, decide which one you consider the best and justify your choice to the class.

Help!

Song	Message	Feelings / Reactions
chorus: *refrain*	hope ≠ despair	revolted
line = verse	demand the release /rɪˈliːs/: *exiger la libération*	hopeful ≠ hopeless
lyrics	fight for justice	inform sb of sth
rhyming verses /ˈvɜːsɪz/	promote freedom	make sb aware of sth
stanza: *strophe*		alert sb to sth

6 Crossover

The Soweto Strings

▲ Frank Ross, *Cape Township*

The Soweto[1] suburbs[2] are an unlikely[3] location for a globally-renowned classical music school. But that is where the British viola player Rosemary Nalden has spent the last 20 years, sharing her passion for stringed instruments[4] with hundreds of township children and transforming their lives. [...]

Although Nalden says the school does not select by talent, preferring instead to help some of the many Diepkloof[5] children for whom life remains tough[6] some two decades after apartheid ended, she has unearthed some gems[7] "out of nowhere".[...]

"What's extraordinary is how many children are extremely talented," Nalden added, "especially when you consider there's no family background [of classical music], no parents saying 'you should practice'. The child is always almost totally responsible."

She remembers arriving in Soweto. "It was very, very unusual for a white woman to suddenly appear in a South African township. It was unheard of." She describes "a mutual fascination" that snowballed as her relationship with the children deepened. "I was fascinated by the whole phenomenon of these incredibly talented children who were so thirsty for violin lessons. I couldn't turn back although I don't remember making a conscious decision. I was just captivated and had this feeling that after having shown them what was possible I couldn't walk away."

Hundreds of children and their extended families will be forever thankful that she didn't.

▲ *The Independent*, 12 May, 2013

1. **S**outh **W**est **T**ownship of Johannesburg **2.** *banlieues* **3.** *(ici) inattendue* **4.** *instruments à cordes* **5.** district of Soweto **6.** *dure* **7.** *(ici) a découvert des perles rares*

1 Understand the article

a. Turn to your Workbook for help. WB p.34

b. Who is Rosemary Nalden (country of origin, skin colour, job and place where she works)?

c. What did she go to South Africa for? How did the children react to her project?

d. What positive role have Rosemary Nalden and the children had on each other?

2 A thank you letter

You are one of the children who went to the music school. Write a letter to Rosemary Nalden explaining why this experience has changed your life. (*Improve Your Writing Skills* p.208)

Help!

determination
prejudice: *préjugé*

eager to + BV: *impatient de*
enthusiastic

act for peace
bridge the gap: *combler le fossé*
overcome the barriers
respect one another
succeed in V-ING: *réussir à*
urge sb to do sth: *inciter fortement qqn à faire qqch*

PREPARE YOUR TASK

CD2 PISTE 9

3 The white Zulu

a. Observe the photo below and try to explain who Johnny Clegg is and why he has been nicknamed 'the White Zulu.'

b. Listen to a report about Johnny Clegg. Go to your Workbook for help. WB P.35

▲ Johnny Clegg in concert

c. Recap

- Who taught Johnny Clegg music and dancing?
- What was special about his band when he first started it and what consequences did it have?
- What has always been important in Johnny Clegg's music?

d. Go on the Internet and find out more about Johnny Clegg.
www.gatewayofafrica.com/artists/biography/208.html

e. Use what you have learnt to write a short article for a music magazine about Johnny Clegg and how music can help unite people. (80 words)

Useful words

"*Asimbonanga*": title of a song
banned = forbidden
crossover: *croisement / mélange*
issue = problem
rub shoulders with: *côtoyer*

PREPARE YOUR TASK

CD2 PISTE 10

4 Bridging the gap

a. At home, go on the Internet and watch the trailer of *Invictus*.

b. Prepare a short report for the class:
- When does the film take place? What has just happened?
- Who are the main characters? Why do they meet?

c. Now listen to a radio report about the role of sports after apartheid. Turn to your Workbook for help. WB P.36

d. Use the information from the report to write a short introduction to *Invictus* in a film magazine.

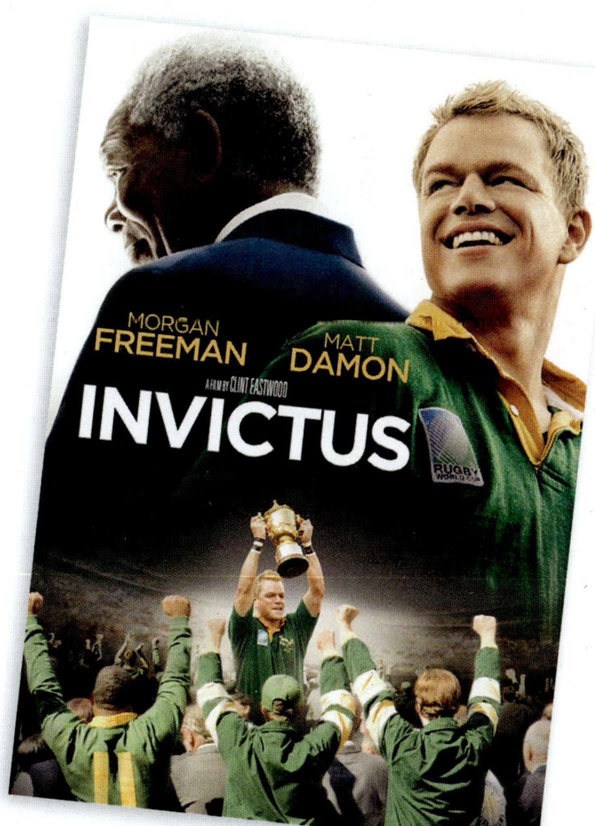

LANGUAGE AT WORK

+ WORKBOOK
→ Apprendre à apprendre
p. 107 - 108

A Le *present perfect*

Précis, p.262-263

Observez

1 Quels énoncés nous renseignent sur le présent ? Lesquels renvoient à un moment coupé du présent?

a. *Mandela has now become a legend.*
b. *Nelson Mandela was born in Transkei in 1918.*
c. *He stayed in prison for 27 years and was finally released in 1990.*
d. *Things have changed a lot since 1994.*
e. *The situation in South Africa has improved over the last few years.*
f. *I've just heard a song by Johnny Clegg.*

2 Sur papier libre, classez les formes verbales ci-dessus dans les colonnes *present perfect* ou prétérit. Notez le marqueur de temps auquel chacune de ces formes est associée.

	Present perfect	Prétérit
Formes verbales		
Marqueurs de temps		

3 Traduisez les énoncés de l'exercice 1. Quelles sont les deux formes verbales en anglais qui peuvent correspondre au passé composé français?

Déduisez

Selon le contexte, le passé composé français peut se traduire en anglais par un … ou un … .

4 Récapitulez :

Le prétérit sert à parler d'un fait, d'une période … . Les marqueurs de temps associés sont … .

Le *present perfect* (*Have* au présent + participe passé) sert à faire un lien entre … et … .

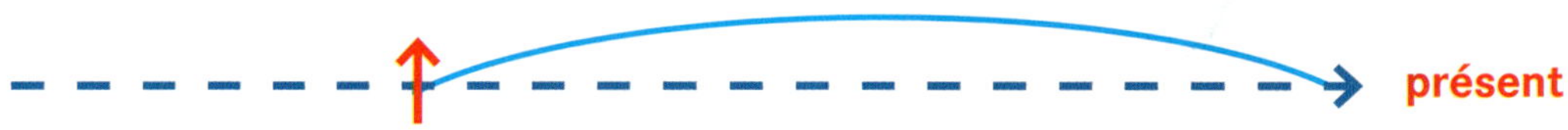

Observez

5 Observez les questions et les réponses données.

A: *Have you ever heard of Frederik De Klerk?*
B: *No, I've never heard of him.*

A: *Have you ever heard of Steve Biko?*
B: *Yes, I've already heard a song about him.*

A: *Have you seen* Cry Freedom*?*
B: *No, I haven't seen it yet.*

Traduisez les marqueurs de temps soulignés en rouge.

Déduisez

Le … s'emploie avec *never*, *already* et *not...yet*, etc. La date n'est pas mentionnée. L'énonciateur s'intéresse uniquement au … au moment présent.

6 Traduisez les énoncés suivants.

How long has South Africa been a democracy?
It has been a democracy ***since 1994 / since Mandela was elected / since the 1994 elections****.*

How long have Johnny Clegg and Sipho Mchunu been playing together?
They have been playing together ***for more than 40 years, since 1969*** *in fact.*

Déduisez

« Depuis combien de temps » se traduit en anglais par … .
« Depuis » se traduit par …, lorsque l'on parle d'une durée dans la globalité.
« Depuis » se traduit par …, lorsque l'on veut préciser le point de départ de la durée.

Entraînez-vous

1 **Complétez la carte postale en mettant les verbes au *present perfect*.**

Dear Liz and Chris,
We (be)... in South Africa for a week and we cannot believe our eyes. What we (see) ... so far (be)... astonishing, but Kruger Park is probably the most beautiful park we (ever – visit)...! The scenery here is breathtaking.
We (see)... giraffes, elephants, rhinos, lions ...
So far we (not – be attacked) ... but we (never – drive) ... through the park without our guide!
... (you – ever – fly) in a helicopter? I'm really excited because next week we're flying above Kruger Park.
See you in two weeks.
Kate and Pete

Mr and Mrs Smith
28 Belmont Road
Watford
Herts, WD1 1JS
United Kingdom

2 **Mettez les verbes entre parenthèses au prétérit ou au *present perfect*.**

a. *Spending on education (increase / greatly) over the last ten years.*

b. *Mahatma Gandhi (live) in South Africa from 1893 to 1914.*

c. *Alan Paton's book,* Cry, the Beloved Country, *(be) published in 1948. It (become) a massive success and (make) people aware of apartheid abroad.*

d. *I (never / read) a novel by a South African author.*

3 **Classez les énoncés selon qu'ils donnent un renseignement sur le présent ou renvoient à un événement coupé du présent. Repérez le marqueur de temps et / ou la forme verbale utilisée. Traduisez.**

a. Avant 1994, les deux communautés étaient séparées.

b. La situation s'est améliorée ces dernières années.

c. Certains Sud-Africains ne se sont pas encore débarrassés de tous leurs préjugés.

d. Steve Biko mourut dans sa cellule de prison (*prison cell*) en 1977.

e. Johannesburg est la capitale économique de l'Afrique du Sud depuis plus d'un siècle.

B Improve your vocabulary

Complétez les énoncés ci-dessous à l'aide de noms ou d'adjectifs de nationalité correspondant aux pays entre parenthèses.

South Africa's largest ethnic group is black. The white population consists of Afrikaners – descendants of (the Netherlands)..., (France) ... and (Germany)... settlers (colons) *who speak their own language – Afrikaans, and people of (Britain)... descent who speak English.*

There are also coloureds, as people of mixed race are called in South Africa, and descendants of (South Asia) ... immigrants.

The colonisation by the (the Netherlands) ... and the (Britain) ... has left two official languages - Afrikaans and English.

The (France) ... came to South Africa after 1685 (after the revocation of the Edict of Nantes) but they were soon assimilated in the (the Netherlands) ... culture.

Pour saisir l'essentiel d'un document oral, il n'est pas nécessaire de tout comprendre. Repérez les mots accentués pour reconstruire le sens du message. Entraînez-vous en écoutant une interview de Johnny Clegg.

1 Anticipez

Utilisez l'affiche ci-contre pour émettre des hypothèses sur le document que vous allez entendre. Quels sont les mots qui vous viennent à l'esprit en lisant le titre ?

2 Première écoute MP3 PISTE 18 CD2 PISTE 11

Le contenu correspond-il à ce que vous aviez anticipé ? Quels éléments supplémentaires avez-vous repérés ?

3 Deuxième écoute et prise de notes

- Relevez les mots porteurs de sens (ils sont plus accentués et se détachent).
- Laissez de l'espace pour pouvoir compléter vos notes lors de l'écoute suivante.

4 Dernière écoute

Complétez vos notes et classez les informations relevées en deux colonnes :
- Johnny Clegg
- The show

Présentez à la classe le compte-rendu de ce que vous avez compris.

5 Un journaliste parle de Johannesburg MP3 PISTE 19 CD2 PISTE 12

La ponctuation a été enlevée.
Mettez une barre verticale (|) lors des pauses brèves et deux barres (||) lors des pauses plus longues. Rétablissez la ponctuation et les majuscules sur la fiche distribuée par votre professeur.

"When I go for a walk at Zoo Lake Park or visit my local shopping centre in Johannesburg's northern suburbs the crowds around me are multiracial and getting along just fine when I attend a concert I'm surrounded by youth from all races and religions listening to their favourite band when I watch South African television I can see that rugby and cricket are no longer just for white athletes but under all the superficial harmony racial tensions still exist regularly those tensions explode into accusations of racism coming both from black groups and white groups."

YOUR TASK

You work for the magazine *National Geographic*. Listen to different reports on South Africa and prepare a page entitled "The New South Africa in Focus."

Les étapes à suivre

1. Réactivez vos connaissances.

• Relisez vos notes sur l'unité et révisez le vocabulaire appris.
• Revoyez les stratégies de compréhension (*Improve Your Listening Skills* p.80).

2. Avant l'écoute

a. Vous allez écouter un enregistrement et une fiche va vous être distribuée.
b. Lisez attentivement les consignes afin de savoir quelles informations il faudra repérer.
c. À partir du titre et des illustrations de cette double page, anticipez rapidement les mots que vous pourrez entendre et le contenu de l'enregistrement.

3. Première écoute CD2 PISTES 13 +14 +15

a. Combien de voix avez-vous entendues?
b. Repérez et mémorisez les mots porteurs de sens.
c. À la fin de l'écoute, reportez sur papier libre les mots que vous avez retenus.
Déduisez le thème de l'enregistrement.

4. Deuxième écoute

a. Complétez vos notes.
b. Après l'écoute, commencez à remplir la fiche distribuée.
N'oubliez pas de laisser de l'espace pour compléter vos notes lors des écoutes suivantes.

5. Dernière écoute

Complétez vos réponses.

Scénario

À l'aide de vos notes, en groupes, utilisez ce que vous avez compris.
Dégagez les thèmes principaux et rédigez votre page du *National Geographic*.
L'article développera les principaux points de l'enregistrement.
Vous pourrez utiliser le site :
madmagz.com/fr

Vous devez inclure

- un titre qui annonce le sujet de votre article et qui donne envie aux lecteurs de poursuivre leur lecture.
- une ou deux illustrations en rapport avec le sujet.

Reading Corner

Ben Du Toit, a white teacher in a South African school, is investigating the murder of his black gardener, Gordon Ngubene. He meets the police officer in charge of the case…

"What can I do for you, Mr Du Toit? I do feel honoured."

"Colonel[1], I thought it was high time we had a frank discussion."

"I'm very glad to hear that. What is it you would like to discuss?"

"I think you know very well."

"Please be more specific." […]

"I'm not sure how you people operate. But you must be aware of the fact that your men have been waging[2] a campaign of intimidation against me for months on end."

"You must be exaggerating, Mr Du Toit."

"You know that they searched my house, don't you?"

"Simple routine, I trust they were polite?"

"Of course they were. That's not the point. What about all the other things? Questioning my colleagues about me."

"Why should that upset you? I'm sure you don't have anything to hide."

"It's not that, Colonel. It's – well, you know what people are like. They start talking. All sorts of rumours are being spread. One's family has to bear the brunt[3]."

A quiet chuckle. "Mr Du Toit, I'm no doctor but it seems to me what you need is a good holiday." Adding, with the smallest hint of an undertone[4]: "Just to get away from it all for a while."

"There are other things too," Ben persisted, refusing to be put off. "My telephone. My mail."

"What about your telephone and your mail?"

"Don't tell me you're not aware of it, Colonel."

"Of what?"

Ben could feel a throbbing in his temple. "When I come into my classroom, I find insults scrawled[5] all over the board. There was a hammer-and-sickle[6] painted on my front door. I've had my car tyres[7] cut to bits. Night after night we're pestered by anonymous phone calls."

The Colonel allowed his chair to tilt forward, back on the floor. He leaned over. "Have you reported all this to the police?"

"What's the use?"

"That is what they're there for, isn't it?"

"All I want to know, Colonel, is why don't you leave me in peace?"

"Now wait, wait a minute, Mr Du Toit. You're not trying to blame me for it, are you?"

He had no choice but to persist: "Colonel, why is it so important to you people to stop my inquiries about Gordon Ngubene?"

"Is that what you're doing?"

It seemed as if he would never be allowed an opening. And yet he had persuaded himself that with this man, unlike all the others, he could be frank; and that he would get an equally frank reply. He'd thought that they would speak the same language. For a while he sat staring at the framed photograph of the two blond boys, standing at an angle on the desk between them.

"Colonel," he said, suddenly impetuous, "doesn't it haunt you sometimes? Don't you wake up at night about what happened to Gordon?"

"All the available evidence was placed before a competent magistrate who examined everything in depth and gave his finding."

"What about the evidence that was deliberately kept from the court?"

"Well, now! Mr Du Toit, if you possess any information that may be of use to us I trust you won't hesitate to discuss it with me."

Ben looked at him, rigid on his straight-backed chair.

The Colonel leaned over[8] more closely towards him, his tone darkening: "Because if there are facts you are deliberately hiding from us, Mr Du Toit – if you give us reason to believe that you may be involved in activities that may be dangerous both to yourself and to us – then I can foresee some problems."

"Is that a threat, Colonel?" he asked, his jaws[9] very tight.

▲ André Brink, *A Dry White Season*, 1979

1. /kɜːnəl/ **2.** *(ici) mener* **3.** *en faire les frais* **4.** *(ici) avec un léger sous-entendu* **5.** *griffonées* **6.** *marteau et enclume* (emblem of the Communist Party) **7.** *pneus* **8.** *se pencha* **9.** *les mâchoires*

CD2 PISTE 16

Freedom

The shackles[1] have been cast off.
Chains broken.

People once squashed[2],
under the jackboot of Apartheid,
are free.

Free at last!

Freedom came on the 27th day in that April, 1994.

Freedom from prejudice.
From institutionalised racism.
From being relegated to second-class citizenship[3].

Freedom came and we danced.
We cried.
We ululated[4] as we elected
our revered Mandela.

President Nelson Mandela.
Our very own beloved 'Madiba'.

Black and white and brown and those in-between,
All hues[5] of this rainbow nation,
rejoiced as we breathed in the air of freedom and democracy. [...]

▲ Afzal Moolla, 2012

1. *les fers*
2. *écrasés*
3. *citoyenneté de second rang*
4. shouted our joy
5. *nuances*

Beyond Limits

YOUR TASK AT THE END OF THIS UNIT

You take part in a quiz show on people who have gone beyond their limits. Listen to a recording of the show and guess their identity. You can also prepare a presentation on a person who has done something extraordinary. p. 93

1 Tune In!

1 Fearless Felix

a. Read this page from a newspaper website (*Mail Online*, 13 October 2012) and react.
b. What makes this man exceptional? Justify your answer by listing his qualities. Use the vocabulary given on the opposite page.

Mail Online

Faster than the speed of sound: Supersonic skydiver Fearless Felix hits mach 1.24 in terrifying plummet to Earth from 128,000ft.

- 'Fearless Felix' Baumgartner completes astonishing drop from the top of the stratosphere
- Breaks the speed of sound after travelling at mach 1.24
- Austrian daredevil had been planning the feat for five years

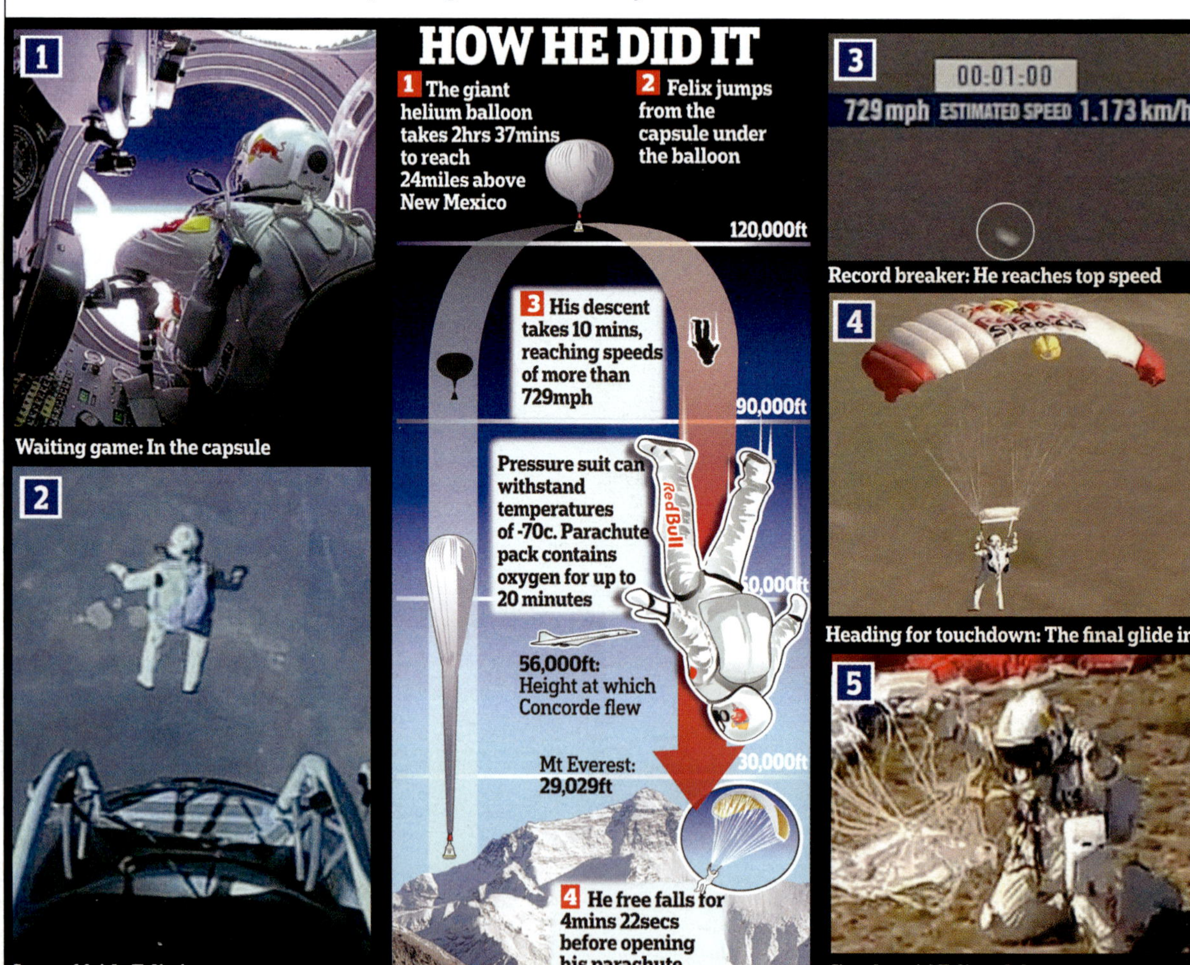

1 Waiting game: In the capsule

2 Leap of faith: Felix jumps

3 Record breaker: He reaches top speed

4 Heading for touchdown: The final glide in

5 I've done it! Felix celebrates

2 Play with words

WB p.37

Turn to your Workbook to improve your vocabulary.

3 Pilot without arms

a. Read the text below, then close your book and say what you can remember.
b. List the elements showing that Jessica is remarkable.

Born in 1983 in Sierra Vista, Arizona, Jessica has learned to live her life with her feet. With the support of her parents and family, Jessica became confident in herself as an adult and continued to explore the world with her feet.

At the age of 14, Jessica earned her first Black Belt in the International Taekwondo Federation. After graduating from high school, Jessica attended the University of Arizona where she earned a bachelor's degree[1] in Psychology. [...] Jessica's most famous accomplishment was learning how to fly. She received the Guinness World Record for being the first person certified to fly an airplane with only their feet.

Jessica now works as a motivational speaker. She travels the world sharing her story and encouraging people to be creative and innovative with the slogan "Think outside the shoe"™.

▲ www.rightfooted.com/about-jessica

1. *licence*

4 Watch a video: An amazing woman

video

a. Learn how Jessica became a pilot. Turn to your worksheet for help.
b. Sum up what you have understood in your own words.

5 Your reaction

Post a comment on the website to react and give your opinion about this woman's achievements.

Help!

Achievements	Qualities
be born /bɔːn/ ≠ die /daɪ/	adventurous /ədˈventʃərəs/
overcome a physical disability	bold: *audacieux*
discover	clever = intelligent
be awarded /əˈwɔːdɪd/	courageous = brave
fight /faɪt/ for ≠ against	determined /dɪˈtɜːmɪnd/
spend one's life V-ing	energetic
reach one's goal: *atteindre son but*	persevering
give up: *abandonner*	reckless /ˈrekləs/: *téméraire*
	selfless /ˈselfləs/: *altruiste*

2 Wind of Change

1 Discover Malawi

List the problems this country is confronted with.

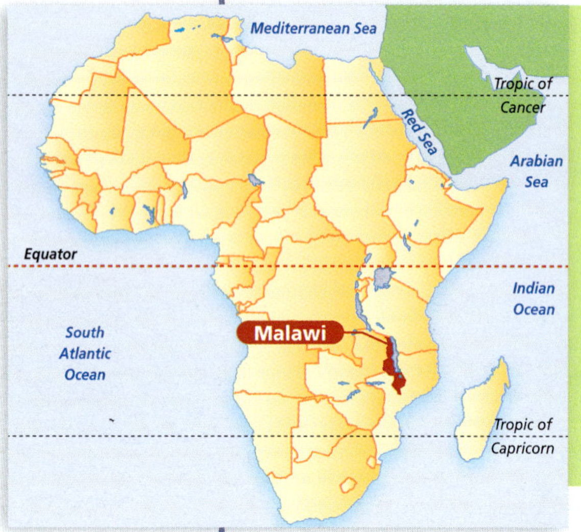

The Republic of Malawi is in Southeast Africa.
Malawi is one the world's least-developed countries. The economy is based on agriculture, the population is largely rural. The Malawian government faces challenges in building and expanding the economy, improving education, health care[1] and environmental protection.
Malawi has about 15 million inhabitants. Life expectancy is low and infant mortality high. The country is plagued with[2] HIV/AIDS, which claims the lives of many people every year; 14% of the population is affected. One million children have been left orphans.
The main agricultural products of Malawi include tobacco, sugarcane, cotton, tea, corn, potatoes, sorghum[3] and cattle.

1. *service de santé* **2.** *confronté au fléau* **3.** tropical grass grown for food

2 The whole story

a. Look at the photo. What do you think this young man did to help his country?
b. Listen to William Kamkwamba's story. WB p. 38

CD2 PISTE 17

PREPARE YOUR TASK

3 Creative writing

You are a journalist and have heard of William Kamkwamba's invention.
Write an article after meeting the young boy (100-150 words).

Help!

Family background
- standard of living
- destitute: *misérable*
- (below) the poverty line: *(sous) le seuil de pauvreté*
- basic commodities: *produits de base*
- have access to
- starve = suffer from hunger
- be confronted / faced with

William
- daring: *audacieux*
- smart = clever
- skilful: *habile*
- determined /dɪˈtɜːmɪnd/
- inventive
- design: *concevoir*
- construct
- overcome (obstacles): *surmonter*
- dream of V-ING

Results
- pioneer /paɪəˈnɪə/
- living conditions
- succeed
- improve: *améliorer*
- manage to: *réussir à*
- provide sb with sth: *fournir qch à qqn*
- rescue from: *sauver de*

3 Gorillas in the Mist

1 Get ready

a. Read the information given on the post-it, then close your book. What can you remember?

b. Look at the photo. What can you guess about Dian Fossey (job, relationship with the gorillas)?

Gorillas are mammals
- diet: *omnivore*
- average lifespan: *35 years*
- size (standing): *1. 2 – 1. 8 m*
- weight: *135 – 220 kg*
- protection status: *endangered*

2 More about Dian Fossey

Read these paragraphs on Dian Fossey's life. Put them in chronological order.

A. The Canadian orangutan expert, Dr. B. Galdikas, has written of her colleague, Dian Fossey: "In her devotion to these animals, Dian will be remembered for generations as one of the heroes of the twentieth century. Without her work, it is doubtful that mountain gorillas would have survived to the twenty-first."

B. In 1980 she went to England to attend Cambridge University, where she obtained a PhD[1] in zoology.

C. In 1985, she was found murdered in her cabin. No one has ever found her killer, although it is suspected that the person was a gorilla poacher[2].

D. Her work took her to Zaire and then to Rwanda, where she opened the Karisoke Research Center. After years of patient observation, the gorillas came to know and trust her, and she found that she could sit in the midst[3] of a group and even play with their young. She came to know the animals as individuals, and even gave them names.

E. Thanks to her work, the world's awareness of the endangered status of the mountain gorilla has increased, and the animals are now protected by the government of Rwanda and various international conservation organisations, including the Dian Fossey Gorilla Fund.

F. She wrote an account of her experiences in Rwanda. In 1983, it was published as *Gorillas in the Mist*[4]. The next year she returned to the Karisoke Research Center to continue her fieldwork.

G. Dian Fossey decided to study the endangered mountain gorilla in Africa.

H. When her favorite gorilla, Digit, was killed (in 1977) by poachers for his hands, Fossey began a campaign against poaching. Her outspokenness, unfortunately, made her a target for violence.

1. *doctorat*
2. *braconnier*
3. in the middle
4. *brume*

3 Role play

You have just read the text. You decide to raise funds for the Dian Fossey Gorilla Fund. Try to convince your friends to donate money. Include the following points:
- Who was Dian Fossey? What is she famous for? Where did she work?
- Who opposed her work? Why? What happened to her?
- Why should gorillas be saved? Why is Dian Fossey considered a key figure of the twentieth century?

4 War and Peace

1 Rebel without a cause WB p.40

a. Look at the front cover of the book below, then read the back cover. Find as much information as you can about Ishmael Beah. Turn to your Workbook for help.

b. Read the following extract from Ishmael Beah's book and list the reasons why he became a soldier.

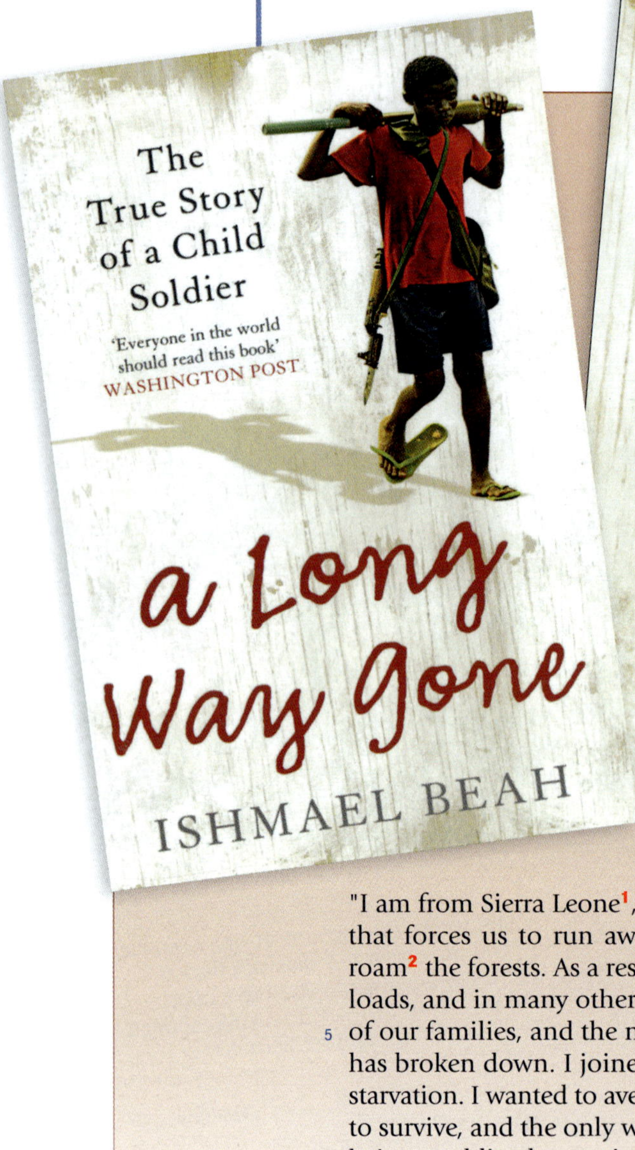

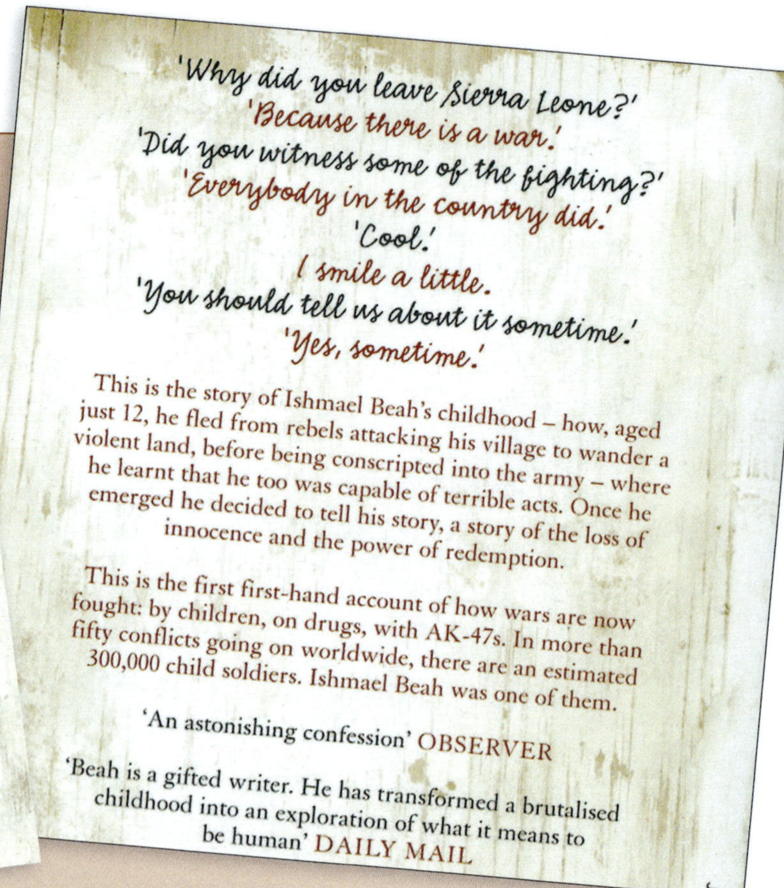

'Why did you leave Sierra Leone?'
'Because there is a war.'
'Did you witness some of the fighting?'
'Everybody in the country did.'
'Cool.'
I smile a little.
'You should tell us about it sometime.'
'Yes, sometime.'

This is the story of Ishmael Beah's childhood – how, aged just 12, he fled from rebels attacking his village to wander a violent land, before being conscripted into the army – where he learnt that he too was capable of terrible acts. Once he emerged he decided to tell his story, a story of the loss of innocence and the power of redemption.

This is the first first-hand account of how wars are now fought: by children, on drugs, with AK-47s. In more than fifty conflicts going on worldwide, there are an estimated 300,000 child soldiers. Ishmael Beah was one of them.

'An astonishing confession' OBSERVER

'Beah is a gifted writer. He has transformed a brutalised childhood into an exploration of what it means to be human' DAILY MAIL

"I am from Sierra Leone[1], and the problem that is affecting us children is the war that forces us to run away from our homes, lose our families, and aimlessly roam[2] the forests. As a result, we get involved in the conflict as soldiers, carriers of loads, and in many other difficult tasks. All this is because of starvation, the loss of our families, and the need to feel safe and be part of something when all else has broken down. I joined the army really because of the loss of my family and starvation. I wanted to avenge the deaths of my family. I also had to get some food to survive, and the only way to do that was to be part of the army. It was not easy being a soldier, but we just had to do it. I have been rehabilitated[3] now, so don't be afraid of me. I am not a soldier anymore; I am a child.
The issue[4] of children in war is not only an African issue, it's a global issue and my trauma is a small price to pay to expose[5] what continues to happen to children all over the world."

▲ Ishmael Beah, *A Long Way Gone*, 2007

1. /sierəli'əʊn/ a country in West Africa **2.** *errer dans* **3.** *(ici) rééduqué* **4.** problem **5.** denounce

PREPARE YOUR TASK
CD2 PISTE 18

c. Now listen to Ishmael Beah explaining why he is now a member of Human Rights Watch. Turn to your Workbook for help. WB p.41

2 Act it out

You are a journalist and you introduce Ishmael Beah before his speech at the United Nations. Prepare what you will say to the audience.

Prompts for the introduction

Ladies and gentlemen... Today Ishmael Beah is with us and it is a great honour to... . Please welcome ..."

- **Include the following points:**
  - Major disaster in Sierra Leone
  - Consequences for children
  - Age when it happened
  - Role in the conflict
  - Reasons for joining the army
  - Major change in his life
  - New cause
- **Use gap fillers:** *'Well, let me see, um, what else?...'*
- **Use link words:** *'First, then, later on ...'*

Help!

widespread phenomenon: *phénomène répandu*
ammunition
cartridges
combat dress
machine gun
ill-treated
defenceless
weak /wiːk/: *faible*
committed: *engagé*
positive / optimistic
outraged / indignant

speak out for sb: *parler au nom de qqn*
stand by sb: *être solidaire de qqn*
ban: *interdire*
improve: *améliorer*
be drafted: *être enrôlé*

3 War times

What do the mural below and Ishmael Beah's story have in common?

▲ *Child Soldiering* by Banksy, mural Los Angeles 2011

LANGUAGE AT WORK

+ WORKBOOK
→ Apprendre à apprendre
p. 109 - 110

A Le superlatif

Précis, p. 252

Observez

- Sir Edmund Hillary is the most famous New Zealander of all time. His biggest achievement was when he reached the top of Mount Everest in 1953. He was also one of the most generous men people in Nepal knew.
- Amelia Earhart was the first woman to fly across the Atlantic Ocean. She is one of the best and bravest women pilots I've read about. She is one of the most famous women in the USA.

a. Identifiez les adjectifs à partir desquels ces superlatifs sont formés. Classez-les en trois colonnes : adjectifs courts, adjectifs longs, adjectifs ayant un superlatif irrégulier.
b. Que remarquez-vous dans l'orthographe des superlatifs suivants :
the luckiest - the prettiest - the happiest - the biggest
c. Observez les compléments des superlatifs dans les phrases ci-dessus. Par quelles prépositions sont-ils introduits ?

Déduisez

Pour exprimer **le superlatif de supériorité** (« le plus … »), on emploie :
- … + **terminaison** … pour les adjectifs d' … syllabe et les adjectifs de … syllabes se terminant par … .
- … + … pour les autres adjectifs.

… devient … s'il est précédé d'une consonne.
Une consonne finale qui suit une voyelle est … .

B Être ou avoir ?

Précis, p. 251

1 Lisez ce paragraphe.

Squanto was the first Native American who bridged the gap between his tribe and the first settlers. He was born in 1585 in Plymouth Bay, Massachussetts, USA. In 1565 he was kidnapped by Captain Hunt, an English trader. Squanto was dark-haired and strong. The trader took him to Spain and sold him as a slave. Then the trader sailed on a ship to England. In 1619 he was lucky to cross the Atlantic again.
In 1621 he met the Pilgrims landing at Plymouth Rock in December. He decided to help them. He was not afraid of the colonists because he could speak English. The first winter the settlers were sick, cold and hungry. Half of them died. The first spring Squanto showed the colonists how to plant corn, pumpkin and beans, and where to hunt and fish. During the fall there was enough food for the colony. The Pilgrims invited the Native Americans to a three-day feast to thank them. When he died in 1622 he was 37.

Traduisez en français les expressions soulignées. Que constatez-vous ?

2 À quoi correspond *'s* dans les phrases suivantes?

- *Ishmael's a peace-maker.*
- *Ishmael's book is entitled* A Long Way Gone.
- *He's just read a book on Dian Fossey's life.*

3 Écoutez les phrases suivantes. Classez-les sur papier libre dans un tableau de ce type. Trouvez un titre à chaque colonne.

CD2 PISTE 19

Ex: *Ishmael's a peace-maker.*	**Ex:** *Ishmael's book*	**Ex:** *He's just read …*

Entraînez-vous

1 Mettez les adjectifs entre parenthèses au superlatif.

a. T. Edison was (young) American inventor: he started when he was 16. He became (good) scientist of modern times when he invented the light bulb, (important) discoveries of all time.
b. Ellen MacArthur broke the world record for (fast) solo voyage around the globe on 7th February 2005. She is (brave) sailor I've heard about. She is also (young) person to be awarded the title of Dame Commander of the Order of the British Empire.

2 Lisez le paragraphe suivant et traduisez les formes verbales en gras.

Margaret Brown **became** famous as one of the lucky survivors of the Titanic tragedy and **was** then nicknamed "The Unsinkable Molly". She **was born** in Missouri in 1867. Later she **moved** to Colorado where she **met** her husband James who **worked** for the silver mines. He **struck** it rich. Molly **travelled** around the world. She **was** on her way home on the transatlantic liner Titanic when the ship **hit** an iceberg and **sank**. During the disaster she **helped** victims and everybody **acclaimed** her heroism. Back home she **gave** money to poor immigrants who **were** on board. She **was** an incredible woman who **spoke** her mind and **joined** many causes such as the rights of women and the education of all children.

3 Traduisez les phrases suivantes :

a. Bethany Hamilton avait 14 ans quand elle fut attaquée par un requin (*shark*).
b. Il y avait beaucoup de requins à ce moment-là.
c. Elle ne savait pas qu'il y avait beaucoup de dangers.
d. Elle eut la chance de survivre.
e. Un mois plus tard, elle n'eut pas peur et elle recommença à faire du surf sans son bras gauche.

4 Rédigez une biographie de Terry Fox avec les éléments ci-contre. N'oubliez pas de mettre les verbes au prétérit.

5 Jeopardy

Le jeu consiste à retrouver la question à partir de la réponse. Votre professeur va vous donner des réponses, soyez le premier à reconstituer la question en incluant un superlatif.
Example: *Usain Bolt → Who is the fastest sprinter of all time?*

Terry Fox
Canadian humanitarian, athlete and cancer activist, one of Canada's greatest heroes

July 28, 1958: birth in Winnipeg, Manitoba, childhood near Vancouver
1977: • bone cancer and right leg amputation above the knee
• In hospital decides to run across Canada and raise money for cancer research
• Name of his journey: The Marathon of Hope
Goal: get attention, collect money, raise $1 from each Canadian citizen
Preparation: 18 months, 5,000 kilometers (3,107 miles)
Starting point: St John's, Newfoundland
Departure: April 12, 1980
Distance every day: 42 kilometers (26 miles) through Quebec and Ontario
September 1, 1980: end of the run after 143 days and 5,373 kilometers (3,339 miles)
June 28, 1981: death
Today: • Organisation of The Terry Fox Run around the world every year
• Goal: raise money for cancer research
2005: issue of the Terry Fox dollar
Fox first Canadian on coins

IMPROVE YOUR LISTENING SKILLS

1 Comment prendre des notes ?

a. Let me tell you about Sebastian Clover
Un élève américain a pris ces notes.

- *Unknown teenager: Sebastian Clover*
- *sailed Atlantic solo - Age: 15*
  2003 youngest person to cross ocean alone
  left Tenerife and reached Antigua 24 days later
- *Most fantastic moments = when saw dolphins*
  + whales swimming near boat
- *Worst day = bad weather*
  → mast nearly broken → spent twenty hrs repairing
- *Dream = sleep real bed + eat lots of chocolate*
  admire him → ♥ sailing + know difficult and dangerous
- *Opinion: both courageous + strong = awesome experience!*

MP3 PISTE 20 — CD2 PISTE 20

b. Que remarquez-vous ? Quels mots les signes utilisés remplacent-ils ? Rétablissez à l'oral les éléments manquants.

2 Stratégies d'écoute

a. Anticipez
Regardez la photo et imaginez le contenu de l'enregistrement.
Quels mots vous attendez-vous à entendre ? Choisissez dans cette liste :
peak - summit - climb - reach - rubbish - effort - camping site - crowded - tired - sunbathing - go on holiday - hiking

MP3 PISTE 21 — CD2 PISTE 21

b. Première écoute
- Combien de voix avez-vous entendues ?
- Avez-vous entendu une interview, une dispute, un débat ?
- Pour reconstruire le message, identifiez autant de mots que possible. Repérez :
  - les mots connus.
  - les nombres.
  - les mots accentués, ils sont porteurs d'informations importantes.

c. Deuxième écoute
- Complétez vos notes. Notez quelques expressions utilisées pour exprimer son admiration et donner son opinion.
- Utilisez-les pour dire ce que vous avez compris.

3 Mémorisez

MP3 PISTE 22 — CD2 PISTE 22

Écoutez ce reportage et retenez un maximum d'informations (dates, noms propres, chiffres et mots-clés).

YOUR TASK

You take part in a quiz show on people who have gone beyond their limits. Listen to a recording of the show and guess their identity. You can also prepare a presentation on a person who has done something extraordinary.

Scénario 1

CD2
PISTE 23

1. Réactivez vos connaissances

Revoyez le vocabulaire et les structures ainsi que les documents étudiés dans cette unité.

2. Entraînez-vous

Relisez les conseils donnés p. 92.

3. Déroulement de l'écoute

Une fiche pourra vous être distribuée. Vous allez entendre différentes personnes vous parler de leur héros. Les noms ne seront pas révélés. A l'aide des différents indices recueillis, vous devinerez de qui il s'agit.

- La première écoute se fera en continu pour que vous puissiez prendre connaissance des différents extraits.
- Puis chaque extrait sera passé trois fois. Vous disposerez de quelques minutes pour prendre des notes.
- Avant de ramasser les fiches, votre professeur vous laissera quelques minutes pour relire votre fiche.
- Les élèves qui auront le plus de bonnes réponses gagneront le quiz.

Scénario 2

- **Choisissez** un autre personnage qui a su se dépasser et faites une recherche sur lui/elle.
- **Préparez** son portrait. Donnez des indices précis pour permettre au reste de la classe de deviner de qui il s'agit, mais ne révélez pas son nom.
- **Présentez-le** brièvement, les indices doivent être clairement donnés.

The Times are Changing

Kitty Kitty, the narrator's mother, has been arrested for public disorder after demonstrating for the vote for women. She is in prison with Caroline Black. Her husband, Richard, and her daughter, Maude, visit her.

'Kitty,' Daddy said quietly.[...]

'Have you learned your lesson in here?' Daddy asked.

Mummy frowned. 'What do you mean by "lesson"?'

'Enough is enough, now. When you get out we can get back to normal.'

'That rather depends on what you mean by "normal." Daddy did not reply.

'Are you suggesting that I give up the fight when I've got out?'

'Surely you're not going to continue?'

'On the contrary, Richard, I think prison has been the making of me. Oddly enough, dullness has made me into a rod of iron. "That which does not defeat me makes me stronger." That's Nietzsche, you know.'

'You read entirely too much,' Daddy said.

Mummy smiled. 'You didn't think that when you first met me. Anyway, when I get out I will have far too much to do to read.'

'We'll discuss this when you are back home,' Daddy said, glancing at Caroline Black. 'You can't be expected to think properly[1] in here.'

'There's nothing to discuss. It's a decision I have made. It has nothing to do with you.'

'It has everything to do with me — I'm your husband!'

'Pardon me, Richard, but nothing I've done in my little life has had any significance whatsoever until I joined the WSPU[2].'

'How can you say that in front of Maude?'

Mummy looked at me. She seemed genuinely puzzled.

'What about Maude?'

'Are you saying having a child has not been significant?'

'Of course it has. Maude is the reason I'm sitting in this prison cell. I'm doing this so that she will be able to vote.'

'No, you're doing it so that you can swan[3] about town, feeling self-important, making silly speeches and neglecting your home and family.'

'I do feel important,' Mummy replied. 'For perhaps the first time in my life I have something to do, Richard. I'm working!

1. *correctement* **2.** The Women's Social and Political Union **3.** *(ici) vous pavaner / frimer*

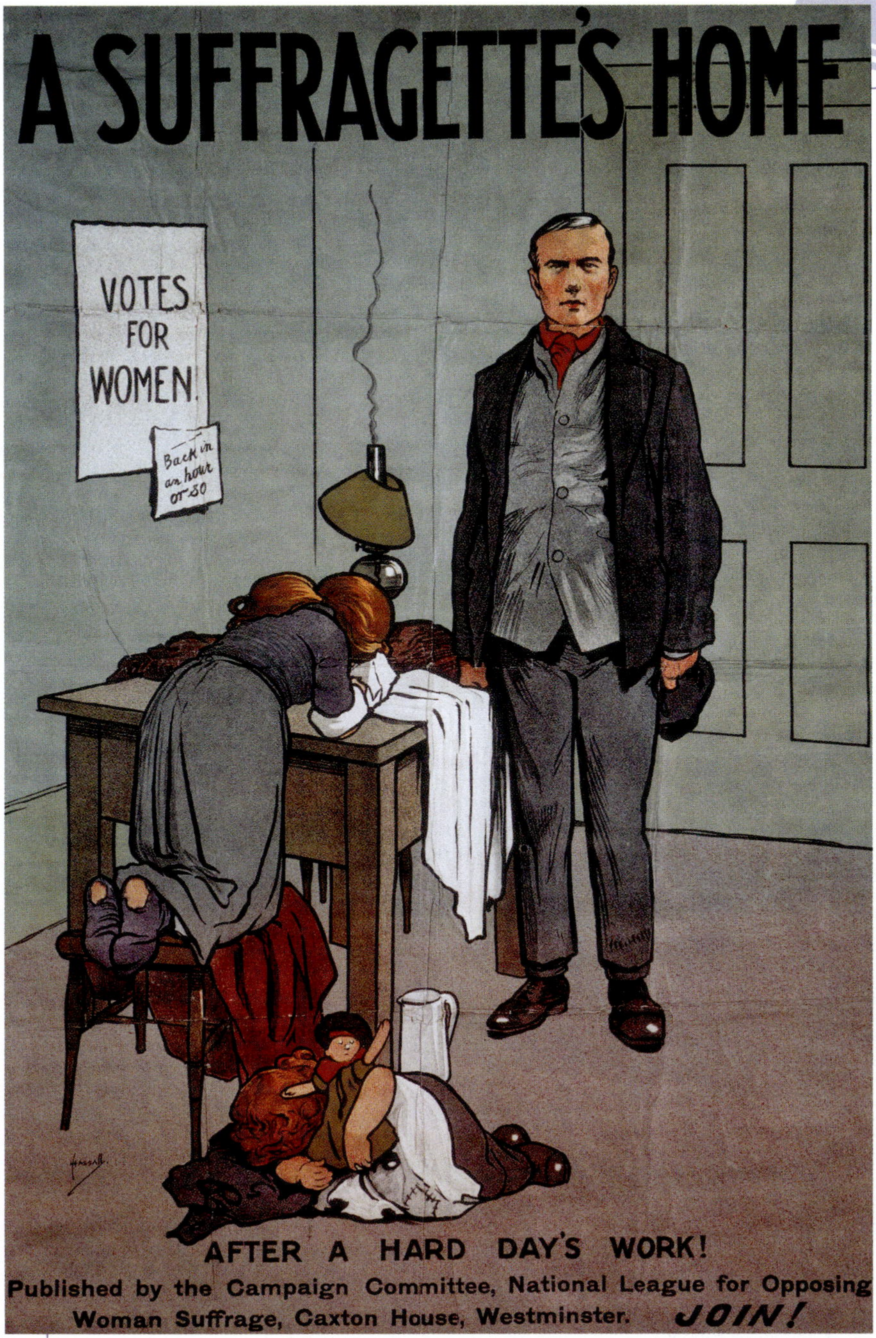

I may not be optimistic like Caroline and the Pankhursts[4] that we'll see suffrage voted in my lifetime. But our work will one day lead to it. Maude will see those results, even if I don't.'

'Oh, climb down from your soapbox[5]!' Daddy cried. 'You claim to be doing this for your daughter. Have you ever asked Maude what she thinks of you leaving her all alone like this? Have you?'

Five sets of eyes turned on me. Daddy's were furious, Mummy's curious. The two wardresses[6] inspected me without interest. Only Caroline Black's dog-like brown eyes showed any sympathy. I turned red. My stomach was aching.

I took a step backwards and then another, and before I knew it I had turned and started to run.

▲ Tracy Chevalier, *Falling Angels*, 2001

4. Emmeline Pankhurst was a British political activist and leader of the British suffragette movement that helped women win the right to vote. **5.** *(ici) descend de ta tribune:* In the 19th century, politicians used to literally stand on soap boxes to give their speeches. **6.** *gardiennes de prison*

Évaluation sommative
Listening

J'évalue mes progrès

Je revois les stratégies apprises dans les unités précédentes (*Improve Your Listening Skills* p.66, p.80 et p.92) afin de faire le bilan de mes compétences.

1. J'anticipe

Observez ces deux photographies de Johannesburg.

a. Quels éléments justifient le titre du reportage *'A city of contrasts'* ?

b. Faites la liste des mots et expressions qui vous viennent à l'esprit.

c. Complétez votre liste : prenez en note les mots que vous allez entendre. CD2 PISTE 24 MP3 PISTE 23

d. Entraînez-vous à les prononcer.

2. Je m'organise CD2 PISTE 24 MP3 PISTE 23

a. **Première écoute**
Une fois l'écoute terminée, notez au moins cinq mots que vous avez entendus.

b. **Deuxième écoute**
Relevez au moins dix mots supplémentaires.

c. **Classez les mots que vous avez relevés en deux colonnes : *positive aspects, negative aspects*.**

d. **Troisième écoute**
Complétez vos notes.

3. Je reconstitue le message

A l'aide des informations relevées, préparez un compte-rendu de ce que vous avez compris.

Tips!
Le titre du document me donne des indices sur le thème principal.
A la première écoute, je collecte des indices. Je repère : - le nombre de voix, les indices sonores, - le thème principal de l'enregistrement, - quelques mots accentués.
A la deuxième écoute, j'affine ma compréhension. - J'identifie les noms de lieux et les noms propres, les dates, les nombres... - Je m'appuie sur les mots accentués et j'essaie de classer les informations pour reconstituer le message.
A la troisième écoute, je complète mes notes.
ATTENTION ! J'espace mes notes pour compléter au fur et à mesure des écoutes.

Je fais le bilan

Analysez vos résultats à l'aide de cette grille d'évaluation où sont définis les différents niveaux de compétence en compréhension de l'oral. Le niveau attendu en classe de seconde est B1.

Hors cadre	A1	A2	B1
Je n'ai réussi à repérer que des mots isolés sans établir de lien entre eux. Je n'ai pas identifié le sujet ou le thème du document. Dans un dialogue, je n'ai pas identifié les interlocuteurs.	J'ai relevé des mots isolés, des expressions courantes que j'ai mis en relation. J'ai une vague idée du sens du document. Je n'ai compris que les phrases et idées les plus simples.	Dans un dialogue, j'ai identifié le thème de la discussion et la fonction ou le rôle des interlocuteurs. J'ai compris certaines informations mais le relevé est incomplet. La compréhension est seulement partielle.	J'ai compris les informations principales (contexte, objet, interlocuteurs, conclusion de l'échange ou de la narration). J'ai correctement compris l'essentiel.

Évaluation

Votre professeur va vous faire écouter un enregistrement portant sur une des unités travaillées en cours. Vous l'entendrez trois fois et vous remplirez la fiche distribuée.
Une fois l'évaluation terminée, votre professeur pourra déterminer à quel niveau vous vous situez par rapport à la grille du Cadre Européen Commun de Référence pour les Langues.

Unit 4 **Destination UK** CD2 PISTE 25 — MP3 PISTE 24

Unit 5 **Over the Rainbow** CD2 PISTE 26 — MP3 PISTE 25

Unit 6 **Beyond Limits** CD2 PISTE 27 — MP3 PISTE 26

▲ *Dear John*, Lasse Hallström, 2010 (starring Amanda Seyfried)

Reading

Unit 7 Geeks

VISION D'AVENIR • SENTIMENT D'APPARTENANCE

- Learn about the history of computer science. When and where did it start?
- Who are the people who have changed our world?
- What impact do new technologies have on our lives?

YOUR TASK You are surfing the Internet when an article catches your attention. After reading it, choose the best illustration or write a letter to the editor.

p. 111

Unit 8 Go West!

SENTIMENT D'APPARTENANCE • MÉMOIRE

- Discover the most famous tourist sites in the western United States.
- Who were Lewis and Clark? How did their adventure change American history forever?
- What does it mean to be a Native American today?

YOUR TASK You are working on a children's book. Read the short story (from p.124 to p.127), then adapt it for young readers.

p. 123

Unit 9 Free at Last

MÉMOIRE

- Learn more about the slave trade. How did slaves cross the Atlantic?
- Find out about the difficulties of their daily lives.
- Learn about the Underground Railroad. Which key figures led the way to abolition?

YOUR TASK You are an artist and you have been asked to illustrate a story. Read it carefully and create a "Wanted" poster or write speech bubbles for a storyboard.

p. 139

Geeks

YOUR TASK AT THE END OF THIS UNIT

You are surfing the Internet when an article catches your attention. After reading it, choose the best illustration or write a letter to the editor. *p. 111*

1 Tune In!

1 SOS

a. Look at the cartoon and explain the situation (Who? Where? When? What?).
b. What are the cartoonist's goals?
c. Do you find it funny? Why? Why not?

Help!

nightmare
mobile (phone) (GB)
cell (phone) (US)
scared: *effrayé*
stunned = very surprised shout

wake sb up
call for help
be addicted to
do without sth: *se passer de qch*
instead of V-ING: *au lieu de*

2 Act it out!

Imagine the dialogue between the parents and the children, then the conversation between the parents.

3 Play with words WB p. 43

Turn to your Workbook to improve your vocabulary on new technologies.

2 The New Tech Generation

Getting rid of bad tech habits

Two years ago, on an unusually warm winter afternoon, Nina Auslander-Padgham and her younger brother were battling over the family laptop. They were irritable and moody. The sun was shining, and neither had stepped foot outside into their back yard, despite the trampoline and large wooden play set. It was an epiphany[1] for her parents, Bonnie and Jon. All technology had to go.

Their decision has put them in the minority. Six in 10 US children older than nine own a mobile phone, according to the Pew Internet & American Life Project. Teens text 60 times a day and four in 10 use video chats, according to Pew. Kids 8 to 18 years old spend about 10.5 hours a day in front of a computer, television or mobile device, up from 7.5 hours a decade ago, according to the Kaiser Family Foundation.

The Auslander-Padghams sometimes struggle to keep technology out of their kids' lives. When Nina turned 12 in March, she begged for an iPhone, something many of her friends had already. Her parents compromised with a purple digital music player that doesn't connect to the internet. "There is definitely leakage[2]," her father said. "We know we can't resist forever."

▲ *The Washington Post*, "High-tech vs. no-tech", May 12, 2012

1. sudden revelation 2. *(ici) brèche*

1 Main Facts
WB P.44

a. Find the following information:

Who? Family members (names, age if possible)	Where? When (year and time of year)?	What (problem, decision taken, consequences)?

b. What problems are the parents confronted with?

PREPARE YOUR TASK

c. Post a comment on the newspaper's website.
Do you feel concerned by the problems raised, if so why? What advice would you give to the parents? (100-120 words)

2 Debate

a. In groups, discuss your tech habits and your use of:

computers / the Internet	social networks (Facebook, Instagram ...)	video /online games

b. Organise a poll:
- Each of you will prepare four questions about each topic above (with three possible answers to each question). Decide on the 10 best questions and put your poll online.
- Each student will answer the class survey.
- Prepare a written account of your results.

Help!

harmful: *nocif*
time-consuming
dependent on
addictive

be hooked on = be addicted to
be used to V-ING: *être accoutumé à*
prevent / stop sb from V-ING
give up / quit V-ING: *arrêter de*
make sb realise
get out of the habit of V-ING: *perdre l' habitude de*
usually: *habituellement*

3 Too Many Friends?

My computer thinks I'm gay
I threw that piece of junk[1] away
on the Champs-Elysées
as I was walking home.

This is my last communiqué
down the super highway
all that I have left to say
in a single tome.

I got too many friends
too many people that I'll never meet
and I'll never be there for (x2)
'cause I'll never be there.

If I could give it all away
will it come back to me someday
like a needle in the hay[2]
or an expensive stone.

But I got a reason to declaim[3]
the applications are to blame
for all my sorrow and my pain[4]
a feeling so alone.

Chorus

My computer thinks I'm gay
What's the difference anyway
when all that people do all day
is staring to[5] a phone.

1. rubbish, trash
2. *une aiguille dans une botte de foin*
3. declare
4. *mon chagrin et ma douleur*
5. look fixedly at

◄ Placebo, "*Too Many Friends*", from *Loud Like Love* 2013

PREPARE YOUR TASK

1 Understand the lyrics

a. What has the narrator decided to do?
b. List the arguments given to explain his decision.
c. Do you share the narrator's point of view in the chorus? Why? Why not?

2 Writing workshop

You are launching an awareness campaign highlighting the dangers of the Internet. You want to use the song by Placebo, *Too Many Friends*, in your video clip. You write a letter to ask for the band's permission and explain your reasons (150-180 words).

Help!

Incident	Reactions	Reasons
gossip = rumours	lack of: *manque de*	virtual ≠ real
lie	lonely	harmful: *nocif, nuisible*
be fed up with	hypocritical	cyberbullying
be aware of = realise	be tired of	invade sb's private life
spread rumours / gossip	get rid of: *se débarrasser de*	criticise sb for V-ING
	frighten of: *effrayer*	warn about: *prévenir de*
	rely on = count on	

4 Back to Basics

1 A brief history of computers

PREPARE YOUR TASK

a. Read the information on the timeline. What surprises you? Why?
b. In your opinion, who are the three most important names in the history of computer science? What did they invent?

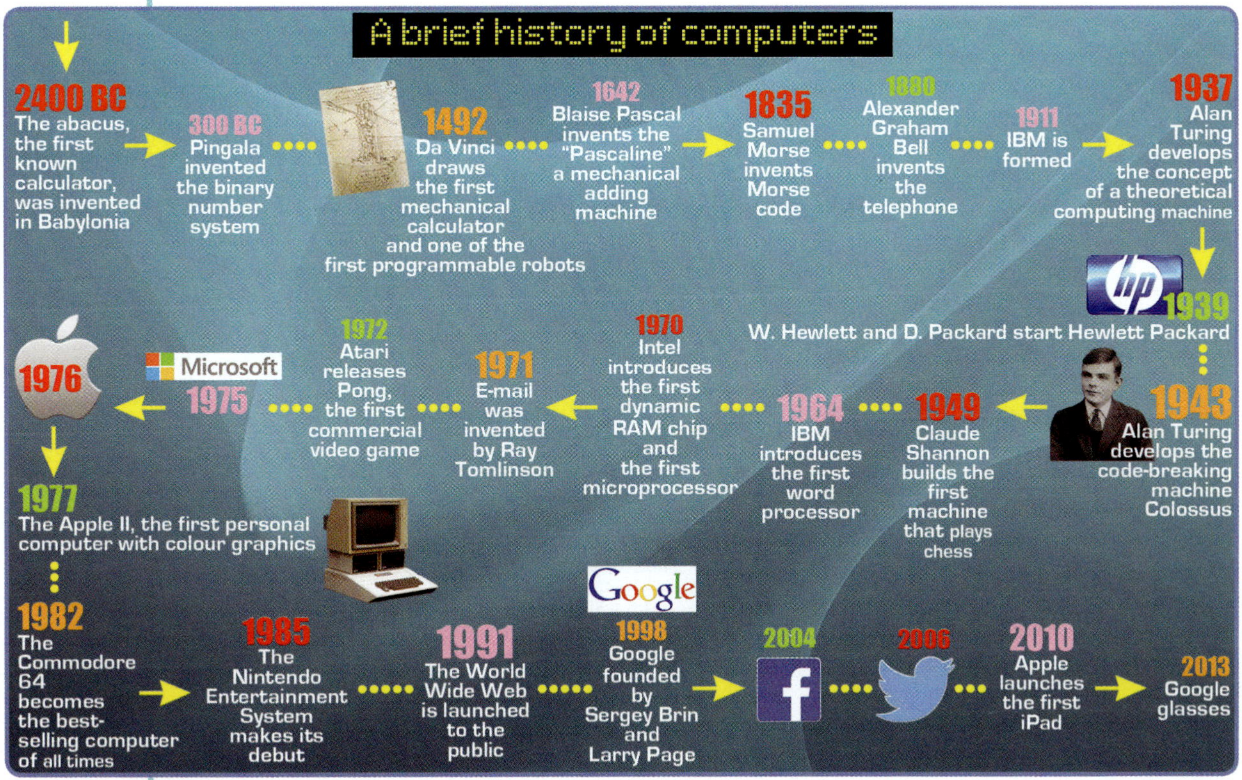

2 Watch a video

video

BRITAIN'S GREATEST CODE BREAKER

a. Learn more about the inventor of computers. Which name appears twice in the timeline above? Turn to your worksheet for help.
b. You have decided to name the computer centre of your school after a famous person. In groups, agree on a name and prepare the speech for the official opening of the classroom.

3 The apple of your eye

WB P.45

CD2 PISTE 29

Learn more about the history of Apple's logo and turn to your Workbook for help.

Help!

breakthrough: *avancée / percée*
pioneer
hardware (*indénomb.*)
software (*indénomb.*)
genius / prodigy

time-saving
innovative /ˈɪnəveɪtɪv/ˈɪnəvətɪv/

be ahead of: *être en avance sur*
revolutionise
design: *concevoir*
launch a product / a device: *lancer un produit*
release /rɪˈliːs/ (a software programme): *mettre sur le marché*
mark a turning-point: *marquer un tournant*

5 Makers

1 Silicon Valley

A high-tech El Dorado

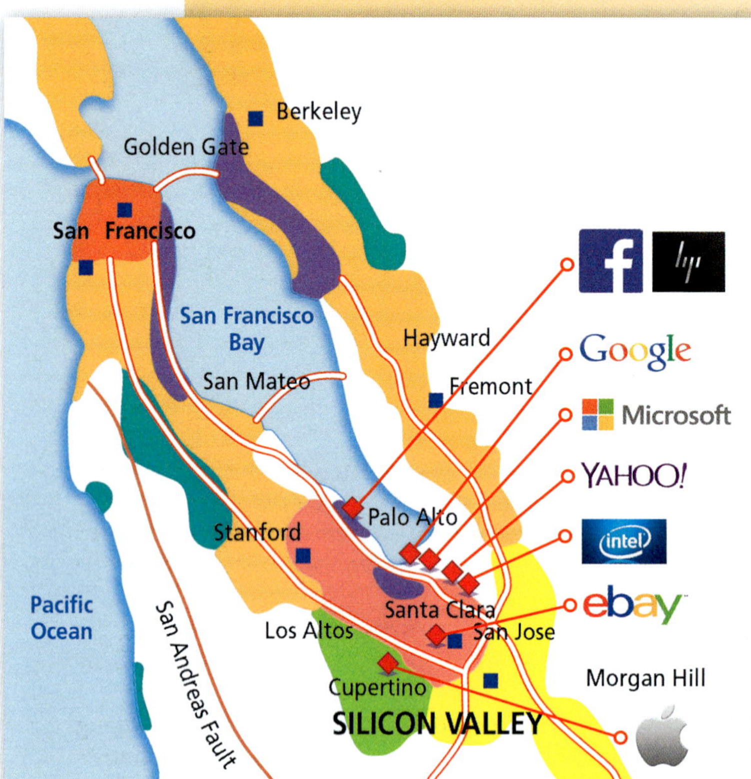

Silicon Valley, also called the Santa Clara Valley, is situated at the southern end of the San Francisco Bay Area in Northern California. This high tech hub[1] comprises several dozen cities, including San Jose.
Back in the 1970s, Silicon Valley gave birth to the computer and information technology industries. This area is the home of most of today's giant computer companies like Yahoo, Hewlett Packard and Apple, etc.
It was named after the silicon which was used in most of the devices created and / or manufactured there such as the microchip.[2] It is now still the heart of the biotech industry, and a place where many young IT[3] entrepreneurs and start-ups come to settle.

1. centre of activity **2.** *puce électronique*
3. information technologies

PREPARE YOUR TASK

a. Read the article and find the origin of the name of the valley.
b. In the text, find a sentence that could be used as a caption for the map above.

CD2 PISTE 30

2 Marissa Mayer

WB p.46

a. Look at the photo. Guess as many things as possible about this woman (age, job…).
b. Listen to learn more about her.
Turn to your Workbook for help.
c. After hearing the interview, post a comment on Marissa Mayer's profile page.
Tell her what you think of her life and work.

Help!

computer science: *l'informatique* engineer corporation / firm skilled: *qualifié* hard-working	talented / gifted daring: *audacieux* hire: *embaucher* compete with

3 David Karp, a prodigy WB p.47

theage.com | June 3rd 2013.

Karp, of course, is the 26-year-old autodidact who founded Tumblr, the social-networking blog site [...]. Karp isn't your typical Internet entrepreneur. He grew up in New York, on the Upper West Side of Manhattan, and attended the Calhoun School, where his mother was a science teacher. [...]

At Calhoun, Karp drove teachers nuts by trying to hack into the school's computer system. After leaving, he spent a year at the Bronx High School of Science, where he studied Japanese. But he fell in with the wrong crowd and dropped out[1] – besting[2] technology giants such as Jobs, Bill Gates, Larry Ellison and Mark Zuckerberg, who all timidly waited until after entering college to abandon their formal education.

By then, Karp had read a book about HTML software and had helped small businesses build websites. As a 14-year-old, he worked at Tekserve, a huge, hipster-laden[3] Apple-repair specialist.

Soon enough, Karp was introduced to Fred Seibert, a former jazz-music record executive who became one of the creative founders of MTV, Nickelodeon and Comedy Central.[4]

"I was so nervous and not sure what to say," Karp said about meeting Seibert. But he remembered being very impressed by Seibert, dressed all in white, hanging out in this cool office space with a bunch[5] of tech geeks, trying to change the world.

He learned so much from Seibert and those around him that Karp's parents allowed him to keep working for [Seibert] while he was home-schooled. He took Japanese classes at the Asia Society and learned maths and English from a tutor.

Eventually, he started working for UrbanBaby [...]. He worked remotely from home, logging into the UrbanBaby servers and cashing his salary cheques. He was nervous that the company's founder, John Maloney, would fire him if he found out he was only 16.

William D. Cohan

1. *abandonna ses études* **2.** = doing better than **3.** *hyper branché* **4.** TV channels **5.** a group of

PREPARE YOUR TASK

a. Use the title at the top of the page and the photo to imagine who this young man is (job, activity...).

b. Read the text and turn to your Workbook for help.

c. Group Work:

Pick out information in the text about David Karp and share your findings with your class. Each group is in charge of one key point.

- Identity and background
- Skills (what he can do)
- Professional life

Help!

self-made man: *autodidacte*
career /kəˈrɪə/
innovator

rebellious
clever / smart / intelligent
determined = strong-willed

be afraid of
lie about: *mentir au sujet de*
quit school
support: *encourager*

4 Act it out!

A journalist comes to interview Marissa Mayer and / or David Karp.
Prepare your questions if you are the journalist or list the elements you consider important if you are one of the two interviewees.

6 New Apps

1 Group 1

a. What applications (apps) do you use? What for?
b. Find more information about the apps you are not familiar with.

2 Group 2

a. Describe the situation.
b. What are the cartoonist's goals?

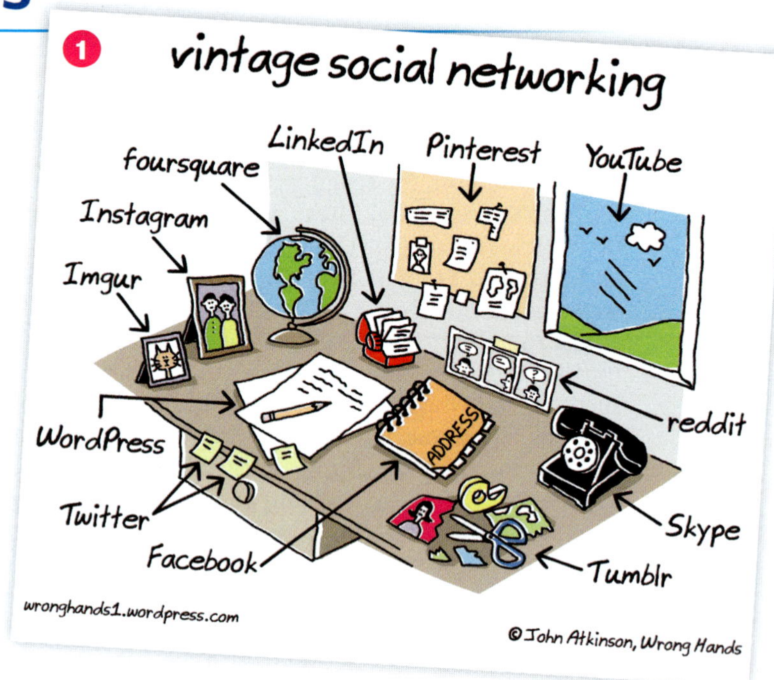

Help!

Nouns
desktop: *bureau*
tape: *ruban adhésif*
face-to-face conversation
shovel /ˈʃʌvəl/ : *pelle*

Adjectives
user-friendly / easy to use
old-fashioned/ outdated
handy / convenient: *pratique*
real ≠ virtual

Verbs
replace
have access to
stay/keep in touch with ≠ lose touch
clear the snow

3 Class Work

- What is the message in each cartoon?
- In your opinion, which cartoon is the most critical of technologies / the funniest / the most and the least true-to-life?
- Compare your opinions with those of the rest of the class.

4 Role play

Your grandmother wants to use one of the apps featured in cartoon 1. You explain to her what you can do with it and how to use it. Imagine your conversation.

7 In My Shoes

Google clearly wants to change every aspect of our lives, from cars that drive themselves, to glasses that superimpose data[1] on our vision, to its most recent effort, shoes that talk to you. Yes, at South By Southwest, Google announced talking high-topped sneakers that react to your activity. [...] Like, "I love the feel of wind in my laces" when you're pounding pavement, and "This is boring" when you're not. Because, you know, what we've been missing in life are shoes that talk. After all, it's important to know what our feet are thinking. [...]

Becoming a Google cyborg

A cyborg is a blend[2] of man and machine, which appears to be the goal that Google aspires to. Once you don[3] Google Glass and Google shoes, you are well down the path of[4] being an integrated part of Google's mobile solution. Google can – conceivably anyway – track every step you take, see everything you see, and likely hear everything you hear. Google will know everything, and I mean everything, about you while you sport your Google fashions.

Fun with Google Shoes

[...] You could end up with:
Shoes: "Damn I'm tired, do you think you might want to get off me for a moment?"
Belt: "Stop complaining, this guy has me set at 38 and he is more like a 42, I'm about to explode."
Hat: "You think you've got it bad! His pin head is trying to poke out[5] the top." [...]
Date:[6] "Ah, you can let me out here, I'll be fine walking home."

▲ Rob Enderle, March 13, 2013

1. *données*
2. a mix of
3. = wear
4. on the road to
5. *crever*
6. *personne avec laquelle on sort*

Help!

state of the art: *dernier cri*
brand new
sophisticated
shocked
ridiculous

warn sb about
alert sb to
track sb: *suivre qqn*
spy on: *espionner*

PREPARE YOUR TASK

1 Main Facts

WB p.49

a. Present the new device and its advantages.
b. Is the narrator for or against these new shoes? Justify with elements from the text.
c. Is the tone: • ironic • enthusiastic • joyful?
d. Would you be ready to buy such shoes? Why? Why not?

2 Become an innovator!

Which object of your daily life would you change? Imagine the characteristics of that high-tech innovation. Present it and convince the committee in charge of Google's innovations.

LANGUAGE AT WORK

+ WORKBOOK
→ Apprendre à apprendre
p. 111 - 112

A La forme V-ING

Précis, p. 269

Observez

1 Observez ces phrases.

a. *He **keeps** (on) surfing the Internet even if he is tired.*

b. *He **enjoys** playing video games.*

c. *I **can't stand** hearing cell phones ring in a restaurant.*

Qu'expriment les verbes soulignés: une activité? un sentiment? La continuation ou la fin d'une action ?

Déduisez

Le gérondif (V-*ing*) se forme à partir d'un...... Après des verbes exprimant ... ou ... on utilise un ....

2 Observez.

a. *She is fed up **with** arguing with her parents about her cell phone bill.*

b. *Parents are used **to** disagreeing with their children.*

c. *I'm looking forward **to** chatting on the Internet this evening. I can't wait.*

d. *He is fond **of** reading the news on the Internet.*

e. *My parents want to prevent me **from** browsing on the Internet late at night.*

With, *to*, *of*, *from* introduisent un complément : ils relient ce complément au groupe de mots qui suit. Ce sont des prépositions. De quoi sont suivies ces prépositions?

Déduisez

Les .... (comme ...., ..., ..., ..., ..., ...) sont suivies de V-ing (gérondif). Attention au cas de to, qui n'est pas toujours une préposition.

3 Observez.

a. Quelle est la nature et la fonction de *books* et la nature et la fonction de *reading* ?

b. Un gérondif peut parfois être remplacé par un nom sans changement de sens. Faites le remplacement dans les phrases suivantes :

- *He can't stand living without his cell phone.*

➜ *He **can't stand** ...*

- *Creating a profile is the first step into a social network.*

➜ *... is the first step into...*

Déduisez

Le gérondif (V-ing) peut être .... ou ..... dans une phrase. Un gérondif peut parfois être remplacé par un nom sans changement de sens.

4 Tweet challenge!

La classe est répartie en équipes. Chaque équipe tire 5 cartes de verbes. Le professeur propose un *tweet* de départ et chaque équipe prépare sa réponse (140 caractères maximum) qui doit contenir au moins un verbe figurant sur une de ses cartes et un gérondif.
(L'équipe gagnante est celle qui aura utilisé tous ses verbes imposés et le plus de gérondifs).

Entraînez-vous

1 **Formez des phrases complètes en utilisant un des verbes ci-dessous :**

argue / be tagged / buy / chat / speak / try

a. *I'm looking forward to … with you on the Internet tonight.*

b. *I feel like … the latest tablet.*

c. *This brand new app is worth … .*

d. *They can't stand ... on a Facebook post.*

e. *She is fed up with people … too loud on their phones on the train.*

f. *She can't help … with her parents about her cell phone.*

2 **Traduisez ces phrases en anglais.**

a. Si tu continues à passer autant de temps devant ton ordinateur, tu vas avoir mal à la tête.

b. Au lieu de sortir avec ses amis, elle surfe sur internet tous les soirs.

c. Je déteste entendre un portable sonner quand je suis dans le métro.

d. Il adore inventer des jeux pour ordinateurs.

e. Avoir un ordinateur dans ta chambre t'empêche de faire tes devoirs.

f. J'ai hâte de découvrir de nouvelles applications.

3 **Traduire**

a. Avoir un ordinateur dans ta chambre t'empêche de faire tes devoirs.

b. Sélectionner ses amis sur Internet est important.

c. Créer un profil m'a permis de rester en contact avec mes amis à l'étranger.

B Improve your vocabulary

Trouvez le contraire de ces mots :

vulnerable - reliable - useful - sensitive - visible - tiring - usual - pleasant - obedient - powerful

Aidez-vous des suffixes et des préfixes négatifs en gras. Vérifiez les mots obtenus à l'aide d'un dictionnaire.

Exemples :

nom + *-**less***/les/ → *defence**less***

un + adjectif → ***un**happy*

in + adjectif → ***in**valid*

dis + adjectif → ***dis**satisfied*

ON YOUR OWN!

Décrivez et commentez ce *cartoon*.

Aidez-vous des expressions suivantes :

The mother:
- *stop* • *be busy*
- *it's not worth V-ING*
- *can't stand/bear*
- *prevent (from) / stop sb (from)*
- *be used to*

The children:
- *it's worth V-ING* • *be fed up with*
- *look forward to V-ING*
- *instead of V-ING*

IMPROVE YOUR READING SKILLS

1 Développez vos stratégies : Inférez le sens des mots inconnus

Part 1

Twitter.com is a Website where you can broadcast very short messages – 140 characters max – to anyone who's signed up to receive them. It's like a cross between a blog and a chat room.

Your "followers" might include six friends from high school, or, if you're movie star Ashton Kusher, 2.5 million faithful fans. At the same time, you can sign up to follow the "tweets" of other people, which scroll up[1] your screen in a big column, all mixed together […].

I'll be the first to admit that I was a Twitter-skeptic. Like most of the first-timers, I found Twitter to be filled with confusing conventions, rules and shorthand. […] But that's the thing about Twitter, it takes a week or so to get it. And all the possibilities slowly began to blow my mind.[2]

1. *faire défiler vers le haut* **2.** amaze me

a. Dérivation

Observez les mots en rose.
- Trouvez la racine de ces mots.
- Quels sont les suffixes utilisés ?
- Déduisez le sens.

b. Mots composés

Observez les mots en jaune.
- De quels mots sont-ils formés ?
- Vérifiez leur sens dans un dictionnaire.

c. Transparence

Observez les mots en vert et devinez leur sens en vous appuyant sur leur ressemblance avec le français.

d. Inférence d'après le contexte

- Observez les mots en turquoise.
Utilisez le contexte pour deviner leur sens.

e. Utiliser un dictionnaire (cf. p. 242) Trouvez le sens des mots en rouge dans le dictionnaire.

f. Relevez tous les mots composés à partir de la racine Twitter. Quelles stratégies allez-vous utiliser pour trouver leur signification ?

Part 2

My transformation into a full-blown[3] Twitterphile began the day I served as a judge on a grant committee. I watched as a fellow judge asked his Twitter followers if a certain project had been tried before. In thirty seconds, his followers replied with Web links to the information he needed. I was amazed by the quality and the quantity of the responses. […]

This wasn't like anything else on the Internet. No Web page, chat room, or e-mail could have achieved the same effect, in real time, with this many participants. […]

It was rapidly becoming apparent that people on Twitter are not the same people who populate MySpace, Facebook, or YouTube. Twitterers are a different breed[4] altogether. […] About 80 percent of us are over 25, and two-thirds of us have college degrees.

3. *averti / expérimenté*
4. *type / race*

▲ David Pogues, *The World According To Twitter*, 2009

2 Qu'avez-vous compris ?

a. Quel est le thème général abordé dans ce texte ?
b. Quels sont les avantages et les inconvénients de Twitter selon le narrateur ?
c. Résumez les deux parties de ce texte en quelques phrases (en français ou en anglais).

YOUR TASK

You are surfing the internet when an article catches your attention. After reading it, choose the best illustration or write a letter to the editor.

Scenario 1

You are a publisher and you have to choose the best illustration for this text (among the three illustrations on p. 112 and on p. 113). Justify your choice.

Scenario 2

You have just read the article on p. 113 and you want to give your opinion. Write a letter to the editor or post a comment on the newspaper website (150 - 180 words).

ETAPE 1

Préparation

Revoyez tout ce que vous avez appris au cours de l'unité (vocabulaire, grammaire, stratégies de lecture, …)

ETAPE 2

Lecture

- Lisez attentivement l'article p. 113.
- Mettez en œuvre les stratégies de lecture étudiées au cours de l'unité (voir *Improve your Reading Skills* p. 110) pour comprendre les mots inconnus et repérer les informations essentielles.
- Complétez la fiche que votre professeur va vous distribuer et évaluez votre compréhension.
- Sélectionnez les points auxquels vous désirez réagir dans votre lettre.
- Imaginez les contre-arguments et des exemples.

ETAPE 3

Rédaction

- Tout d'abord, expliquez que vous réagissez à un article. *I wish to react to your article entitled "…" and published in … on March 7th 20.*
- Dès le début de la lettre, donnez votre opinion.
- Organisez votre discours (utilisez des mots de liaison, faites des paragraphes).
- Reprenez les arguments de l'article et expliquez votre point de vue en l'illustrant avec des exemples.
- Restez clair et concis (pas plus de 4 paragraphes).
- Relisez-vous bien ! (voir Relire son devoir p. 226)

TIPS

Forget me Not!

- ***Vérifiez la mise en forme d'une lettre (voir p. 208).***
- ***Utilisez des formules de politesse (Dear editor…)***
- ***N'écrivez pas en lettres capitales (c'est très agressif) et n'utilisez pas d'abréviations***
- ***Pensez à signer votre lettre.***

Reading Corner

ROBOT DREAMS

At the start of the story, a new employee at US Robots, Linda Rash, informs Dr Susan Calvin, a robotics expert, that one of the company's robots, Elvex, had a dream. They interview the robot to learn more about it.

Part 1

"I dream always very much the same dream, Dr Calvin. Little details are different but always it seems to me that I see a large panorama in which robots are working."
"Robots, Elvex? And human beings, also."
"I see no human beings in the dream, Dr Calvin. Not at first. Only robots."
"What are they doing, Elvex?"
"They are working, Dr Calvin. I see some mining in the depths of the earth, and some laboring[1] in heat and radiation. I see some in factories and some undersea." [...]
"What else did you see, Elvex?"
"I saw that all the robots were bowed down[2] with toil[3] and affliction,[4] that all were weary[5] of responsibility and care, and I wished them to rest."
Calvin said, "But robots are not bowed down, they are not weary, they need no rest."
"So it is in reality, Dr Calvin. I speak of my dream, however. In my dream, it seemed to me that robots must protect their own existence."

1. working **2.** *pliés* **3.** hard work **4.** *détresse* **5.** tired

Part 2

[...] "What of Elvex?"
"I'm still not certain." [...]
Linda said, "But surely Elvex is important to our research. He must not be destroyed."
"Must not, Dr Rash?" That will be my decision, I think. It depends entirely on how dangerous Elvex is." [...]
She said, "Elvex, do you hear me?"
"Yes, Dr Calvin," said the robot.
"Did your dream continue? You said earlier that human beings did not appear at first. Does that mean they appeared afterward?"
"Yes, Dr Calvin. It seemed to me, in my dream, that eventually one man appeared."
"One man? Not a robot? "

"Yes, Dr Calvin. And the man said 'Let my people go!'"[6]
"The man said that?"
"Yes, Dr Calvin."
"And when he said 'Let my people go!', then by the words 'my people' he meant the robots?"
"Yes, Dr Calvin. So it was in my dream."
"And did you know who the man was in your dream?"
"Yes, Dr Calvin. I knew the man."
"Who was he?"
And Elvex said, "I was the man."

▲ Isaac Asimov, *Robot Dreams*, 1986

6. call of Moses to the Pharaoh to free the Jews and allow them to go to Israel, and reference to the Negro Spiritual "*Go down Moses*"

▲ *Real Humans*, Lars Lundström

Japan is banking on friendly robots to save its economy

Here are a few examples of how robots are infiltrating everyday life in Japan:

By Lily Kuo | @lilkuo June 27, 2013

As friends

[...] Friendly robot research is part of the government's plan to put millions of dollars into building robots that will care for the elderly. Because of Japan's aging population, it faces a manpower shortage[1] in multiple industries.

As a robot rock band

Earlier this month, a band of robots playing guitars, drums and a keyboard—engineered by researchers at Tokyo University—accompanied pop group Amoyamo in Tokyo.

As manpower

Early developers of automated industrial robotics, the Japanese government has plans to install one million robots in factories across the country by 2025. In 2005, Japan's robots already numbered over 370,000 and made up about 40% of the world's total.

As first responders

A robotic "safety crawler"[2] in Japan can carry a person of up to 250 pounds (113 kg). Originally created for a police department in Yokohama, the robot is intended to help transport people hurt after disasters like earthquakes.[3] It's controlled remotely[4] and has sensors to detect a victim's vital signs.[...]

1. *pénurie de main-d'œuvre* **2.** *(ici) un robot sur chenille* **3.** *tremblements de terre* **4.** from a distance

Unit 8

SENTIMENT D'APPARTENANCE • MÉMOIRE

Go West!

YOUR TASK AT THE END OF THIS UNIT

You are working on a children's book. Read the short story (from p.124 to p.127), then adapt it for young readers. Don't forget to illustrate it.

p. 123

1 Tune In!

Help!

Landscape

- scenery: *paysage*
- bucket list: list of things you want to do before you die
- stunning = amazing
- breathtaking: *à couper le souffle*
- enormous = huge /hjuːdʒ/
- desert /ˈdezət/

Target and goals

- attract visitors / tourists
- make sb do sth
- be worth V-ING: *valoir la peine de*
- take a break from: *s'évader*
- spend time V-ING
- experience sth

1 The Mighty Five

a. What are your immediate reactions (atmosphere, landscape, colours, ...)?
b. What do the names at the top correspond to? Locate them on a map.
c. What is the slogan? What are the poster's goals?
d. Who is the target?

2 Play with words
WB p. 50

Turn to your Workbook to improve your vocabulary.

video

3 Watch a video

a. What type of outdoor activities are suggested?
b. Which of the following adjectives best describe the experiences shown in the video?
monotonous • unique • unforgettable • tiresome • inspiring • uninteresting • thrilling
c. Would you like to visit The Mighty Five? Why or why not?

4 A walk with death

Tightrope master Nik Wallenda crosses the Grand Canyon with NO safety harness[1] and even manages to RUN the final few feet.

He is planning a tightrope walk between the Empire State building and Chrysler building in New York.

Daredevil[2] Nik Wallenda has completed a breath-taking tightrope walk that took him a quarter mile over the Little Colorado River Gorge in northeastern Arizona.

Wallenda performed the stunt[3] late on Sunday on a 2-inch-thick steel cable, 1,500 feet above the river on the Navajo Nation near the Grand Canyon.

He took just more than 22 minutes.

'It was way more windy, and it took every bit of me to stay focused the entire time,' he said.

The first couple of steps are always the worst, he says. But he doesn't like being called a daredevil.

'I do consider what I do an art,' he says.

[Some] local residents said that the Navajo Nation shouldn't be promoting the gambling of one man's life for the benefit of tourism.

Discovery's two-hour broadcast showcased the Navajo landscape that includes Monument Valley, Four Corners, Canyon de Chelly and the tribal capital of Window Rock. 'When people watch this, our main thing is we want the world to know who Navajo people are. Our culture, traditions and language are still very much alive,' Geri Hongeva, spokeswoman[4] for the tribe's Division of Natural Resources, said before the walk.

▲ Adapted from *The Daily Mail*, 24 June 2013

1. *harnais de sécurité* **2.** *casse-cou*
3. *(ici) a fait de la haute voltige* **4.** *porte-parole*

PREPARE YOUR TASK

a. Main facts WB p. 51

Read the text and turn to your Workbook for help.

b. Breaking News

You are a journalist and work for the Discovery Channel.

• You report live from the Grand Canyon. Describe what is going on, give your feelings and reactions.
• You interview Nik Wallenda after his tightrope walk.

2 On the Lewis and Clark Trail

PREPARE YOUR TASK

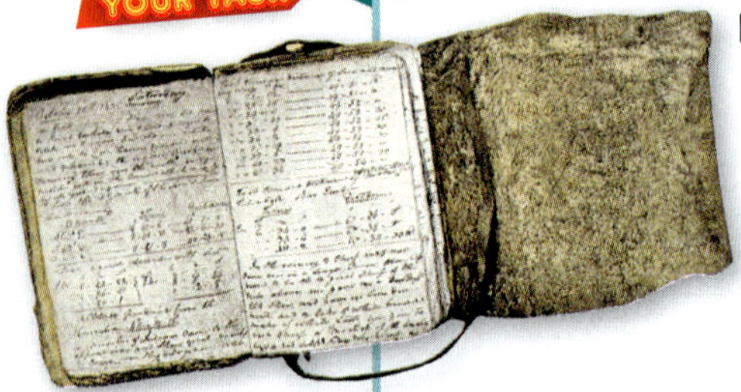

1 Jefferson's mission

Read the first text on the page opposite. Find the key points and justify:

a. Who sent the expedition west? What for?
b. Who are the men in the two portraits?
c. When did the expedition take place?
d. Did they accomplish their mission (see bottom of p. 117)?

CD2 PISTE 32

2 The members of the expedition WB P. 52

Listen to the recording. Turn to your Workbook for help.

a. How many people were part of the expedition? Who is mentioned in particular?
b. What did Lewis and Clark have in common?
c. What were Lewis's particular qualities? And what were Clark's strong points?

3 Focus on Sacagawea WB P. 53

Look at the photo and read the text opposite to find out who Sacagawea was.
Why did Lewis and Clark bring a pregnant woman along? Turn to your Workbook for help.

4 A who's who game

Select a member of the expedition and use the information you have learnt to explain his or her role in the expedition. The rest of the class will guess who it is.

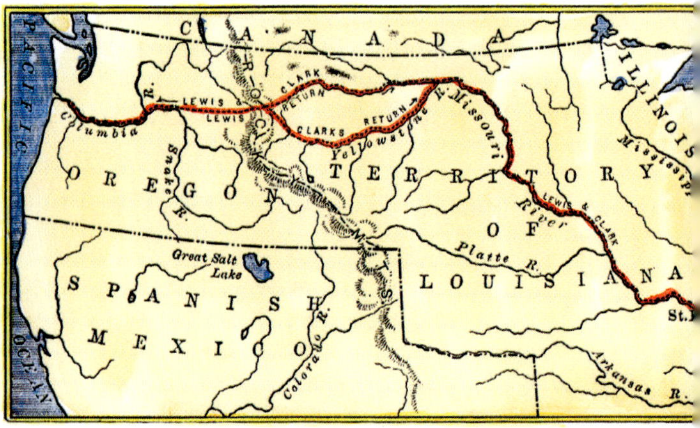

5 Westward ho!

Are you up to the challenge to explore the West with Lewis and Clark? Go on the Internet and take this interactive journey:
www.nationalgeographic.com west/

6 Creative writing

You are a member of the expedition. You have just returned to St. Louis. Write a short letter to your parents in which you recap the major events of your journey. (120 words)

Jefferson's mission

After the Louisiana Purchase[1] in 1803, Thomas Jefferson[2] commissioned his private secretary Captain Meriwether Lewis and Lewis' close friend Lieutenant William Clark to form the Corps of Discovery.

The primary objectives of this group were to explore and map the new territory and try to find a northwest passage: a water route linking the Mississippi River to the Pacific Ocean. Jefferson hoped they would find: "the most direct & practicable water communication across this continent for the purposes of commerce". In addition to studying the plants, animal life and geography and listing all the natural resources, Jefferson wanted the expedition to establish an American presence in this area and to set up trade and diplomatic relations with local Indian tribes.

In September 1806, the expedition returned to St. Louis to report their findings and information to Jefferson.

1. /'pɜːtʃəs/ The United States of America bought the Louisiana territory from the French in 1803.
2. Thomas Jefferson (1743 - 1826), third US President.

> Great joy in camp. We are in view of the ocean, this great Pacific Ocean which we have been so long anxious to see, and the roaring or noise made by the waves breaking on the rocky shores (as I suppose) may be heard distinctly.
>
> CAPTAIN CLARK, 7 NOVEMBER 1805

Sacagawea

Sacagawea was born to the Shoshone Indians in the Rocky Mountain (in what is now Idaho) in about 1788.

In 1804 Lewis and Clark hired Charbonneau and asked him to bring his wife. Sacagawea was then 16 years old and 6 months pregnant[1]. She was the only woman member of the expedition. It is likely that the expedition was viewed as friendly and peaceful by Native American tribes because Sacagawea had her infant son with her. Clark later noted in his journal: "No woman ever accompanies a war party of Indians in this quarter."

Sacagawea spoke both Native American languages, Shoshone and Minitari, and the captains realized that she could be a valuable interpreter if the party encountered the Shoshones. Her ability to speak and negotiate with the Native tribes allowed the expedition to have fresh horses along the way.

On top of her work as a translator she foraged for[2] roots, nuts and berries[3] when food was scarce[4]. She also taught Lewis and Clark the medicinal value of the native plants. In the journals kept by the expedition she is described as a smart and resourceful woman. In one key incident recorded[5] in Clark's journals, she saved records and instruments from being lost overboard during a storm[6].

Although she was largely responsible for the success of the expedition, she wasn't paid for her contributions.

1. *enceinte* 2. *cherchait* 3. *baies* 4. *rare* 5. = narrated 6. *tempête/orage*

- ***Destination:*** Pacific Coast
- ***Departure:*** May 21, 1804 from Saint Louis, Minnesota
- ***Arrival at Pacific:*** November 15, 1805
- ***Return to St. Louis:*** September 23, 1806
- ***Mission accomplished?***
  - explore and map Louisiana ✓
  - establish trade with Indians ✓
  - study plants, animals, geography ✓
  - find water route to Pacific ✗

3 Native Americans Today

CD2 PISTE 33

1 Past and present

a. Listen to the recording. What happened to Native Americans during the 19th century?
b. What is the situation today?
c. Use the information collected to write a short entry for an encyclopaedia on Native Americans, past and present.

2 On the reservation

A young boy has just discovered that the textbook he is holding had belonged to his own mother—so the book is over 30 years old! He is so disappointed with the education he is being given, he throws the book at his teacher.

Part 1

Mr. P grabbed me by the shoulders and leaned so close to me that I could smell his breath.
Onions and garlic[1] and hamburger and shame and pain.
"All these kids have given up," he said. "All your friends. All the bullies. And their mothers and fathers have given up, too. And their grandparents gave up and their grandparents before them. And me and every other teacher here. We're all defeated."
Mr. P was crying.
I couldn't believe it.
I'd never seen a sober[2] adult cry.
"But not you," Mr. P said. "You can't give up. You won't give up. You threw that book in my face because somewhere inside you refuse to give up."
I didn't know what he was talking about. Or maybe I just didn't want to know.
Jeez, it was a lot of pressure to put on a kid. I was carrying the burden[3] of my race, you know? I was going to get a bad back from it[4].

1. *ail* **2.** *qui n'a pas bu* **3.** *fardeau / poids* **4.** *(ici) tout ceci allait être lourd à porter*

Part 2

"If you stay on this rez[1]," Mr. P said, "they're going to kill you. I'm going to kill you. We're all going to kill you. You can't fight us forever."

"I don't want to fight anybody," I said.

"You've been fighting since you were born," he said. "You fought off that brain surgery[2]. You fought off those seizures[3]. You fought off all the drunks and drug addicts. You kept your hope. And now, you have to take your hope and go somewhere where other people have hope."

I was starting to understand. He was a math teacher. I had to add my hope to somebody else's hope. I had to multiply hope by hope.

"Where is hope?" I asked. "Who has hope?"

"Son," Mr. P said. "You're going to find more and more hope the farther and farther you walk away from this sad, sad, sad reservation."

1. Indian reservation **2.** *tu t'es battu lorsque tu as été opéré du cerveau* **3.** *crises d'épilepsie*

▲ Sherman Alexie, *The Absolutely True Diary of a Part-Time Indian*, 2007

PREPARE YOUR TASK

a. Read the text and turn to your Workbook for help. WB p. 54

b. What does the teacher advise the young boy to do? Why? Is he optimistic or pessimistic? Explain with your own words.

CD2 PISTE 34

3 My choice

a. Listen to Native American teenagers.

b. What type of document is this?

c. What do the following numbers refer to?

8 times less likely • 6 times more likely • 9/10 • 33

number of Native American colleges on reservations

fraction of Native Americans who finish college on reservation

to drop out of college

to transfer to university

d. What is the goal of the document? Is the message optimistic or pessimistic?

e. React to what you heard and post a short comment on the website.

f. What are the similarities and the differences between the text and the recording?

4 Act it out!

Your best friend is a Native American. You are talking about your plans for after high school. He/she wants to stay on the reservation, you try to convince him/her to leave. You both give your arguments.

Help!

Life on the reservation

needy
jobless
low standard of living
disillusioned
miserable: *très malheureux*
be stuck: *être bloqué*

The teacher

(a better) income: *revenu*
(better) prospects: *(meilleures) perspectives d'avenir*
opportunities
available: *disponible*
urge sb to do sth: *inciter qqn à faire qch*

The young boy

amazed = very surprised
expect sb to do sth: *s'attendre à ce que qqn fasse qch*
realise: *prendre conscience de*
succeed: *réussir*
fulfil one's dreams: *réaliser ses rêves*

LANGUAGE AT WORK

+ WORKBOOK
→ Apprendre à apprendre
p. 113 - 114

Le passé (prétérit simple / *past perfect*)

Précis, p. 260, p. 265

Observez

1 *Why **did** some people **want** to travel to Oregon?*

*Back in the 1840s people **heard** about Oregon by reading newspapers or hearing stories from travellers. This is how people **learned** of a land to the west of the Rocky Mountains. There **was** plenty of land that you **could** get for free. There **were** big forests, and rivers filled with fish. The word Oregon **made** people think of adventure. In 1843 a thousand people **started** out for Oregon. It **was** one of the biggest groups that ever **travelled** west. It **took** them six months to go from Missouri to Oregon nearly two thousand miles away. The trip **was** not always easy. Many people **did not reach** Oregon and **died** on the way.*

a. Relevez les formes verbales au prétérit simple, et classez-les en trois colonnes: forme affirmative, négative et interrogative. Comment sont formées ces trois formes ?
b. Classez ensuite les verbes en deux colonnes : verbes réguliers et irréguliers. Donnez l'infinitif à chaque fois.

Déduisez

Le prétérit simple est utilisé dans une narration de faits ..., il sert à parler d'événements situés dans le ... et il exprime une ... avec le présent.

2 Au prétérit, l'événement doit être **repéré dans le temps**, par l'indication d'une heure, une date, une période ou tout autre repère temporel.

Heure, date, période
at: at eight o'clock
in: in July, in the summer, in 1843, in the nineteenth century, in the 1840s / 1850s / 1860s
on: on Sunday, on July 4th

Autres repères temporels
ago
at the / that time
in those days
then / back then

3 Qu'expriment les expressions soulignées ci-dessous : un repère temporel ou un marqueur de durée ? A quel temps grammatical sont-elles associées ?
a. *The pioneers lived in a covered wagon for six months.*
b. *Out on the plains they walked for days without seeing any trees or woods.*

Observez

4 *At the end of the day the children were tired: they had travelled miles, had helped their parents, had found water and collected wood for the fire.*

De quels éléments sont composées les formes verbales soulignées ?
Sur papier libre, situez sur cette ligne les événements correspondant aux formes soulignées :

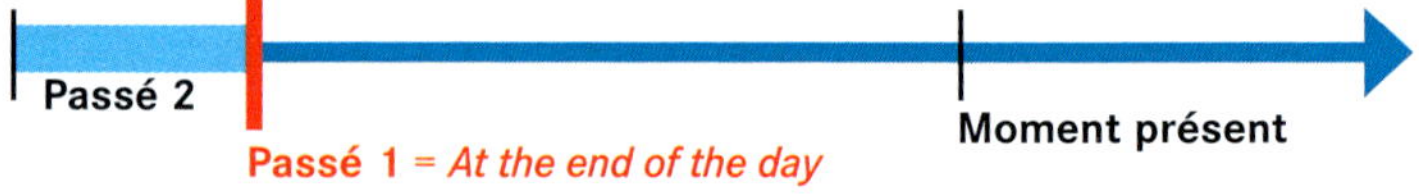

Traduisez ces formes verbales en français.

Déduisez

Le *past perfect* permet de parler d'événements antérieurs à (= situés avant) un autre événement, exprimé au ... . Il exprime un "retour en arrière" par rapport à un moment ... . Il est formé de ... + ...

Entraînez-vous

1 **Remettez les questions dans l'ordre.**

a. *was* | *the journey* | *Oregon* | *how long* | *to* | *?*

b. *the* | *time of year* | *the* | *trip* | *to* | *start* | *what* | *was* | *best* | *?*

c. *travel* | *to* | *people* | *some* | *why* | *want* | *did* | *all the way* | *to* | *Oregon* | *?*

d. *happened* | *if* | *you* | *Indians* | *met* | *what* | *the way* | *on* | *?*

e. *a long time* | *the* | *buffalo meat* | *last* | *how* | *did* | *make* | *Indians* | *?*

2 **Recopiez le texte suivant en complétant les phrases avec les formes verbales qui conviennent.**

The US government (*encourage*) people to settle in Oregon. Half a million people (*cross*) the Rocky Mountains, deserts and rivers to settle there. They (*have*) to leave the Mississippi River in spring to arrive before the first snows. Approximately twenty thousand people (*die*) along the way. They (*endure*) extreme weather, illness, and attacks by Native Americans. The construction of the railroad (*bring*) an end to (mettre fin à) the wagon trains.

3 **Traduisez les phrases suivantes :**

a. Quand l'expédition fut terminée (*be over*), Lewis and Clark avaient parcouru 3700 miles.
b. Ils avaient découvert 122 animaux et 178 plantes inconnues à cette époque-là.
c. Ils avaient exploré un immense territoire et fait des cartes détaillées.
d. Jefferson fut ravi car ils avaient atteint *(reach)* tous les objectifs qu'il leur avait donnés.

4 **Rédigez un paragraphe à partir des éléments suivants.**

Crazy Horse

a visionary Indian chief, a brilliant leader, a man of supreme courage / a brave warrior
fight for freedom all his life
goal in life: defence of the values and traditions of the Lakota tribe
1849: date of birth
steals horses before the age of 13
1865-1868: fight against settlers in Wyoming
1867: destruction of W. J. Fetterman's brigade at Fort Phil Kearny
1873: attack of troops of G.A. Custer
1876: leader of the resistance, alliance with the Cheyenne
June 17, 1876: victory of Little Bighorn
June 25, 1876: destruction of Custer's seventh Cavalry
May 6, 1877: surrender; last important chief to yield (*céder*)
September 1877: arrest by General George Crook; resistance on the way to jail (struggle against the guards); a soldier stabs (*poignarde*) him in the back

IMPROVE YOUR READING SKILLS

1 Lisez le texte suivant

The Mormons were a people with different religious beliefs who experienced persecution from the authorities and many of their neighbors in Missouri and Illinois. In 1844 their founding leader, John Smith, was killed by a mob while he was in jail. The new leader, Brigham Young, decided to guide his followers west in search of a new home.

In 1846 Young led a group of 5,000 followers from a Mormon settlement in Nauvoo, Illinois, across what is now Iowa to Winter Quarters, a camp he established on the Missouri River in Nebraska. He moved on to Wyoming, and northern Utah to the Great Salt Lake Valley where he established a new settlement. Young organized permanent campsites along the route to help future emigrants. Thousands of Mormons followed the trail from Nauvoo, Illinois, to the Great Salt Lake. Some farmers were wealthy enough to own wagons, oxen, and many possessions. Many less fortunate Mormons loaded all their possessions into handcarts which were pulled and pushed for 1,200 miles across the plains, along and across the Platte River, and over the Rocky Mountains to the new settlement. Between 1846 and 1869, more than 70,000 people used the Mormon Trail.

▲ Rachel Dickinson, *Great Pioneer Projects You Can Build Yourself*, 2007

2 Repérez

> Les dates clés :
- 1844
- 1846
- Between 1846 and 1869

> Les noms propres :
- John Smith
- Brigham Young

> L'événement essentiel relaté :
Opportunities and dreams

> Les lieux suivants, à l'aide d'une carte :
- Missouri and Illinois
- Nebraska, Wyoming, and northern Utah
- Great Salt Lake
- Rocky Mountains

> Les chiffres clés :
- 5,000
- 1,200
- 70,000

3 Utilisez le dictionnaire

a. Identifiez la nature des mots en bleu.
b. Trouvez pour chacun de ces mots la traduction correspondant au contexte.

4 Devinez le sens des mots

- Appuyez-vous sur les mots proches du français.
- Inférez le sens des mots en
• jaune à l'aide de la dérivation et la composition.
• vert à l'aide du contexte.

5 Résumez ce que vous avez compris

YOUR TASK

You are working on a children's book. Read the short story (from p.124 to p.127), then adapt it for young readers. Don't forget to illustrate it.

Lecture de la nouvelle (p.124)

- Lisez une première fois la nouvelle partie par partie.
- Ne restez pas bloqué(e) sur les mots inconnus.
- Utilisez les stratégies étudiées p.122.
- Repérez les informations clés:

Qui sont les personnages principaux ?

Que se passe-t-il ? Quelles sont les conséquences ?

A quelle époque l'action se déroule-t-elle ? Où ?

Remplissez ensuite la fiche que votre professeur vous distribuera.

Scénario 1

> **Vous participez à l'adaptation de la nouvelle.**
Résumez-la en partie ou en entier pour la publier dans un recueil pour enfants.
Pensez à vos jeunes lecteurs et soignez votre style.

❗ Réfléchissez aux **formes verbales** que vous allez utiliser pour rédiger votre récit.

Rappel
- Le **prétérit simple** s'emploie pour faire un récit (succession d'événements passés).
- Le **prétérit BE + V-*ing*** s'emploie pour décrire une scène qui se déroule et faire un « arrêt sur image ».
- Le ***past perfect*** s'emploie pour évoquer une action passée qui précède une autre action déjà située dans le passé, ou pour effectuer un bilan par rapport à un point de repère passé.

❗ Utilisez des **verbes introducteurs variés.**

feel, think, realise, believe, wonder ...

❗ Utilisez un **vocabulaire précis**

- **adverbes** (*angrily, nastily, hurriedly ...*)
- **adjectifs** (*terrified, horrified, puzzled ...*) afin d'évoquer les **réactions** et les **sentiments** des personnages.
- **le lexique** étudié dans l'unité

❗ **Structurez votre récit**

- **marqueurs chronologiques** : *first ..., then ..., after a while ..., later / a few minutes later ..., little by little, suddenly / all of a sudden ..., eventually / finally ....*
- **phrases complexes** : *...when ... ,...while ..., ...as ..., ...because ...*

Scénario 2

En dehors de la classe, illustrez votre résumé : choisissez des images (décor, personnages, objets importants, moments clés) ou dessinez vous-même pour illustrer les moments clés. Intégrez tous ces éléments à votre récit et reliez-le sous forme de petit livre.

Reading Corner

This is my land

Part 1

Henry Page and his family set off with their wagon train across wide prairies of the Middle West. He learned to ride a horse, to drive a team of horses, and to mend[1] the wagons when they broke down. He never saw an Indian until he reached Black River Bend. He wondered what all the fuss was about, the Indians there were thin and unhappy people, living on scraps[2] of food and working for the white settlers, doing the worst jobs and spending what little money they got on cheap whisky. Most of the time they were drunk, they never looked anything like Henry had been expecting. They were poor, ignorant savages. Henry felt sorry for them.

At Black River Bend Henry heard about the land which was being given to settlers. The best pieces had already gone but if you would take a risk and settle your family in the wilds[3] you could have as much land as you wanted. All you had to do was to take a horse and a bundle of marker posts[4] and set off at dawn. You put down a marker post every hour and you could have as much land as you could mark off in twenty-four hours.

Henry rode out way beyond the furthest settlement and picked out a beautiful valley for himself. There was a clear river running through it, masses of trees on the slopes of hills all around and good grassland on both sides of the river. He set out at sunrise one morning and rode like the wind for the rest of that day. He did not stop to eat and only drank in the saddle as he raced along. By dawn the next day he had managed to mark off the whole valley. He rode back to Black River Bend and claimed[5] the valley as his own, naming it Valley Page. His claim was marked off on the map of the State and Henry Page was now a landowner.

From Charles Murray he got an axe and a saw, a sack of nails, and a hammer. He set to work to clear a space by the river and built himself a small log cabin. Mary fished the river and turned the cabin into a home. They were still very poor but they were very happy.

1. *réparer*
2. *des restes*
3. *territoires inhabités*
4. *piquets*
5. *revendiqua*

Henry worked like a demon. He worked every hour there was in the day and went to his homemade bed tired and aching all over. Slowly he made his farm, with axe and saw and hammer he built his fences[6] and cleared the ground. As much as possible he made with his own hands, other things he had to pay for at Murray's store in Black River Bend and to get money he cut timber[7] and floated it down the river into the little town.

He and his family kept to themselves[8]. When winter came he went hunting in his valley and came back with deer and wild birds to eat. The little log cabin was warm and snug. Henry and his family were happy.

The years passed. Page Six arrived, a girl who was given the name of Ruth. The little cabin was no longer big enough and Henry set to work to build a really nice house, with a garden and stables[9] and a barn[10]. He began to farm the land and the soil was good. He cleared more ground and got horses to draw the plough. He sowed corn and maize and raised good crops[11]. He was beginning to make money at last. His crops sold for a good price and he was able to buy cattle[12].

More ground was needed and so more trees came down, more fences went up and more ploughing was done. After ten years Henry Page could look out on his farm and feel pleased with himself.

6. *clôtures*
7. *du bois*
8. *s'isolèrent*
9. *écuries*
10. *grange*
11. *récoltes*
12. *bovins*

Part 2

And then one day he went riding down to the far end of his valley. Mary had told him that the fish hadn't been coming down the river lately, that something must be blocking their run. He rode along the river's edge and came at last to the waterfall where the river ran into the valley.

There, just below the tumbling waters where the river was narrow, sat an Indian family. They had nets[1] slung across the river from bank to bank and a heap of shining silvery fish lay on the grass.

Henry went up to them. They stood up as he reached them and Henry saw that the man had an old shotgun in his hand. His wife and three children hid themselves behind a skin tent. The man waited until Henry was facing him.

"This is my land," said Henry. "And those are my fish."

The Indian's eyes glittered. He looked at Henry for a long time before he spoke. He raised a hand and swept it all around him[2] at the wooded slopes of the valley.

"This my people's land. Not your land. All this belong my people."

Henry frowned. How could you tell an Indian savage about the white man's laws?

"Listen! You take your family and clear out of it, see? You not take any more fish, understand? You go ..."

Henry had a Winchester rifle in his saddle-holster[3].

He looked at the Indian and felt the man's hatred[4] blazing in his eyes. Henry walked away and made his way back to his house feeling rather sad. He wasn't a hard man, he didn't want to drive the Indian family ... and yet he'd spoken to them like all the other whites. He told Mary what had happened.

"We are all alone out here," she said. "There's no helping us if we're attacked. And there's the children."

1. *filets de pêche*
2. *balaya d'un geste large*
3. *étui sur sa selle*
4. *haine*

Henry went into Black River Bend and bought two more Winchesters and a large amount of ammunition. He told the storekeeper about the Indian family on his land.

"Give me ten dollars," said the storekeeper. "You won't be bothered[5] by them varmints[6] any more." Then, seeing that Henry was still worried he went on. "There's a trapper I know ... he'll move 'em on, nice and peaceful like."

Henry paid the man, glad to have someone else to do the job for him. Next morning he heard the sound of shots from the far end of the valley. He saddled his horse and rode out there. He met the trapper, Luke, coming back.

Luke grinned[7] at him. "Guess you won't be having any more trouble from them," he said. And laughed.

5. *embêtés*
6. *animaux nuisibles*
7. *regarda avec un large sourire*

Part 3

Henry rode past the man. He reached the waterfall and the first thing he saw was a blazing[1] tent. There was blood on the ground and the fishing net was ripped into pieces. The Indian woman stood some way off, the three children huddled around[2] her. She faced him as he walked up to her and Henry saw that she was standing in front of the man's body.

Henry felt ashamed. He held out both hands to show that he carried no weapon. He knelt beside the fallen Indian and saw that the man had a gaping wound[3] in his side. But he was not dead, though he had lost much blood.

Henry ripped[4] the sleeve from his own shirt and bound the wound as best he could. The woman watched him silently while he did his clumsy best to stop the bleeding. He was shaking like a leaf[5] as he helped the Indian to his feet and he walked him across to his horse. Gently he lifted the man into the saddle[6] and then walked off down the river's edge towards his house. Looking back he saw the woman and her children following him at a distance. The woman was carrying the old shotgun but she didn't know how to use it. Henry was thankful for that.

Mary rushed out to meet him as he came to the house. Henry snapped at her, told her to get a bed ready, to get herbs and bandages. He took the Indian off the horse and carried him in his arms into the house.

The Indian made a slow recovery[7]. Almost three weeks went by before he was on his feet again. Henry tried his best to be friendly but the man uttered not one word[8] in all that time. When at last the time came for him to go Henry offered the man a new fishing net and ten dollars in money.

The Indian turned his back on Henry and walked into the sunshine without a word.

▲ William Charles Henry Chalk, *Jim Silent*, 1971

1. *en feu*
2. *blottis contre elle*
3. *blessure béante*
4. *arracha*
5. *tremblait comme une feuille*
6. *mit l'homme en selle*
7. *se remit lentement*
8. *ne prononça pas un mot*

Unit 9

Free at Last

YOUR TASK AT THE END OF THIS UNIT

You are an artist and you have been asked to illustrate a story. Read it carefully and create a "Wanted" poster or write speech bubbles for a storyboard. p. 139

1 Tune In!

1 Amistad

Look at this still and react. What can you guess about the man's situation?

▲ *Amistad*, Steven Spielberg, 1997

Help!

Slaves
- labour force: *main d'oeuvre*
- cattle: *bétail*
- naked /ˈneɪkɪd/: *dévêtu, nu*
- enslave = reduce to slavery
- be captured
- be tied up / chained
- drag sb away from sth: *arracher qqn à qqch*

Reactions
- anxious
- desperate
- powerless: *impuissant*
- degrading
- humiliating
- inhumane
- (be) heart-broken: *qui a le coeur brisé*

2 Learn more about the slave trade

WB p. 57

CD 2 PISTES 35-36-37

Turn to your Workbook for help.

a. Listen to three short recordings and define the following terms.

1. What is a slave? **2.** The slave trade **3.** A slave ship

b. Report to the class.

3 Play with words

WB p. 59

Turn to your Workbook to improve your vocabulary on slavery.

2 The Middle Passage

Cinque was captured by African slave-hunters in his village in Western Africa. He was then transported aboard a slave ship with hundreds of other people. The owners of La Amistad *bought him for $450.*

It was June 29, 1839, and the Amistad was being thrown about off the coast of[1] Cuba. [...] He would probably be sold as a field-worker in the sugarcane fields there. He was bound to live the rest of his life that way, in service to his white master. But he was fighting it with everything he had. [...] He held onto his wife's image in his head. He remembered the sound of his children as they played in the yard[2]. He would not forget. He would do what he had to do to try to get back to them. And so as he lay in his narrow[3] space in the slave decks of the Amistad, as he had done nearly every minute since his capture, he thought desperately about ways of escape. Of finding a way out. He'd seen people kill themselves to keep from becoming slaves. He didn't want to die that way. But he would not resign himself either. He'd seen that too. People who just got so tired of fighting the cruelty and violence that they gave up. And then they let other people decide for them who they were. That would not be him either. If he died, it would be while trying to escape. No one really knew, but Cinque, regardless of[4] the chains and the distance he was from his homeland[5], was determined to return there.

1. *au large de*
2. *cour*
3. *étroit*
4. *malgré*
5. *terre natale*

▲ David Pesci, *Amistad*, 1991

PREPARE YOUR TASK

1 Read and understand

WB p. 59

Turn to your Workbook for help.

a. Pick out information about the slaves' conditions of travel.
b. What have you learnt about Cinque's past life?
c. What are the different alternatives for him?
d. Explain what the Middle Passage is.

2 Cinque's speech

Cinque wants to comfort his fellow prisoners who feel desperate. Imagine his speech. Use elements from the text.

3 Role play

You are a guide for the Liverpool Slave Museum and you tell students about the Middle Passage.

Help!

The Crossing

bunk beds: *lits superposés*
shelf, shelves: *étagère(s)*
locked: *enfermé*

be crammed: *être entassé*
transport below deck: *transporter à fond de cale*

Feelings

(dis)obedient
determined
strong-willed: *volontaire*
hopeful ≠ hopeless

give up: *abandonner*
refuse one's fate: *refuser son destin*

3 Sorrow Tales

1 Auction

PREPARE YOUR TASK

a. Group work:

Group 1 will deal with the poster. Group 2 will work on the text.
- Look at your document to find out key elements. (Who? What? Where? When?)
- Is the author of your document for or against slavery?

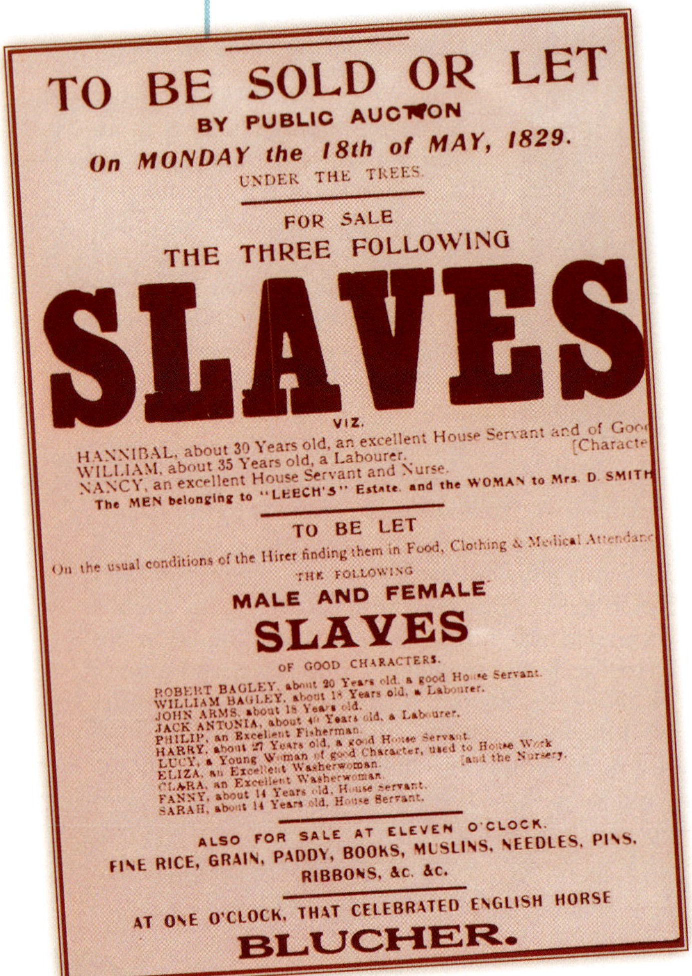

I saw a mother lead seven children to the auction-block. She knew that *some* of them would be taken from her; but they *took all*. The children were sold to a slave-trader, and their mother was bought by a man in her own town. Before night her children were all far away. She begged the trader to tell her where he intended to take them; this he refused to do. How *could* he, when he knew he would sell them, one by one, wherever he could command the highest price? I met that mother in the street, and her wild, haggard face lives to-day in my mind. She wrung[1] her hands in anguish, and exclaimed, "Gone! All gone! Why *don't* God kill me?" I had no words wherewith to comfort her. Instances[2] of this kind are daily.

▲ Harriet A. Jacobs, *Incidents in the Life of a Slave Girl*, 1861

1. *se tordit* **2.** examples

b. Class work:

What are the similarities and the differences between the two documents above?
- Compare the events described.
- Oppose the two points of view on slavery.
- Which one do you find the more striking? Why?

Help!

Life on the plantation	Slave market	The narrator
sugar cane, rice, tobacco cabin: *case*	auction block: *vente aux enchères* for sale: *mis en vente*	compassion = sympathy
obedient	heart-rending (moment): *déchirant*	outraged / shocked / horrified
work from sunrise to sunset pick cotton harvest: *récolter* obey sb = do as one is told complain about	be on display: *être exposé* consider sb an object burst into tears: *fondre en larmes* split up / tear apart families	stand up against / rebel denounce condemn side with: *prendre le parti de*

PREPARE YOUR TASK

2 Aunt Sue's Stories

WB p.61

Read the poem and turn to your Workbook for help.

Aunt Sue has a head full of stories.
Aunt Sue has a whole heart full of stories.
Summer nights on the front porch
Aunt Sue cuddles[1] a brown-faced child
in her bosom[2]
And tells him stories.

Black slaves
Working in the hot sun,
And black slaves
Walking in the dewy[3] night,
And black slaves
Singing sorrow songs on the banks
of a mighty river[4]
Mingle themselves[5] softly
In the flow of Aunt Sue's voice,
Mingle themselves softly
In the dark shadows that cross and recross
Aunt Sue's stories.

And the dark-faced child, listening,
Knows that Aunt Sue's stories are real stories.
He knows that Aunt Sue never got her stories
Out of any book at all,
But they came
Right out of her own life.

The dark-faced child is quiet
Of a summer night
Listening to Aunt Sue's stories.

▲ Langston Hughes, *The Collected Poems*, 1921

1. *câline* **2.** *poitrine* **3.** *couverte de rosée*
4. *fleuve puissant, ici le Mississippi* **5.** *se mélangent*

3 Writing workshop

Choose one of the two assignments.

a. Twenty years later, the child describes these evenings spent with Aunt Sue to his/her own child. Write their conversation. Imagine:
- The narrator's life as a child
- Aunt Sue (place where she lived, status...)
- The stories (subject of the stories, impact on the child, the atmosphere then...)

b. You are one of the children who listen to Aunt Sue's stories. Write one story she told you. Use the illustration below and the documents studied (100-120 words).

4 Resistance

1 I want to break free WB p.62

Martin is a runaway slave. He meets two white teenagers, Laura and Bert, who are ready to help him out.

"Lots of folks[1] hid me, black folks and white ones. They could've sent me back to my master for the big reward[2], but they didn't."

"So lots of people helped you," Laura said thoughtfully.

"Yes'm[3]. I couldn't even count how many. Moses, she said people who helped the poor runaway slaves are the kindest people in the world."

"*Moses*?" Bert laughed. "Moses was a *man* and he lived hundreds of years ago."

Martin shook his head. "Not the Moses I mean. She's a woman, all right, and she's as black as I am, and she led a whole lot of slaves to the Promised Land."

"Oh!" Bert looked delighted. "I know who you mean. Her name is Harriet Tubman, isn't it? She was a slave, herself, and she escaped to Canada. Then she went back down south[4] and helped other slaves to get away."

"Miss Tubman, that's her name. Only everybody call her Moses. My pappy talked to her and he told her how his master was going to sell him down south and split up our family. So when Miss Tubman was ready to go north, she came outside our cabin and sang, '*Go down, Moses*.' My pappy heard her, and he said, "There's Moses. It's time for us to go."

"Can you sing it?" asked Bert. "Let's hear that song, 'Go down, Moses.' "

Martin appeared glad to oblige. He rocked back and forth as he sang softly:

Oh, go down Moses,
Way down into Egypt land,
Tell old Pharaoh,
To let my people go.

Laura's eyes felt misty. Martin's high, sweet, young boy's voice was appealing. Though she had heard Uncle Jim's slaves sing the same song, she had never guessed its hidden meaning. [...]

"Moses leads the slave to the promised land?" she asked, wondering.

"That's right, Miss Laura. She takes them to Canada. That's the Promised Land where we can be free."

▲ Margaret Goff Clark, *Freedom Crossing*, 1980

1. people **2.** *récompense* **3.** yes, madam **4.** slavery was legal in the southern American states

PREPARE YOUR TASK

a. Read the text. Turn to your Workbook for help.

b. Make a one-minute oral report of the story. Include these points:
- Martin's family and escape, his destination, the people who helped him
- Harriet Tubman's life, her role and her tactics to help slaves out

c. Creative writing: The following day Laura writes about the meeting with Martin in her diary (120 words).

video

2 Watch a video

Learn more about Harriet Tubman. Turn to your worksheet for help.

a. Where was she brought up?
b. What happened to her when she first rebelled?
c. What was her role?

Harriet Tubman by numbers

4: years she worked for the Union army (the Northern Army) as a scout and spy

5: age when she started her first job making clothes

10: number of her brothers and sisters, all slaves

19: times she went south to lead slaves to freedom

29: age when she escaped slavery

93: age when she died

3 Role play

You are in a newly-built school in the USA. A name for this school has to be found. You suggest Harriet Tubman and justify your choice. Use what you have learnt in the video and the numbers and dates above to draw her portrait.

Help!

Admiration
astonishing = amazing
incredible: *incroyable*
How courageous!
iconic figure: *personnage emblématique*

look up to sb = admire sb
thanks to: *grâce à*

On the way
conductor = *(ici) guide*
shelter: *abri*
escape route

run away = escape = flee
hide, hid, hidden: *(se) cacher*
save sb from sth
rescue

Trackers
bounty hunter: *chasseur de primes*

determined / resolute
mean: *méchant*
pitiless / merciless

track down: *traquer*
be driven by money: *être motivé par l'argent*

5 Abolitionists

PREPARE YOUR TASK

1 Who's who?

The biographies of two abolitionists, Abraham Lincoln and William Wilberforce, have been jumbled. Re-order the paragraphs.

a. He was born in 1809 in Kentucky, USA. He worked on his father's farm and attended school for less than a year, but taught himself to read and write.

b. He was born in 1759 in Hull (Britain). He was the son of a wealthy merchant. He studied at Cambridge University.

c. He did different types of jobs before he settled as a highly successful lawyer. He was gradually drawn to politics.

d. In 1780, he became Member of Parliament for Yorkshire. He was interested in social reform, particularly the improvement of factory conditions in Britain and the prevention of cruelty to animals.

e. He was shocked by the conditions of slaves on ships going from Africa to the West Indies as goods to be bought and sold. The West Indies were British colonies at that time.

f. He was elected President in 1860. At that time the USA was divided over the practice of slavery. The white men owned large farms in the southern states. People in the north were against slavery and wanted to abolish it.

g. Finally, the Civil War broke out between the northern and southern states. He fought the war bravely and declared: "A nation cannot exist half free and half slave." He won the war and kept the country united.

h. For 18 years he regularly introduced anti-slavery motions in Parliament in London.

i. He made people aware of the situation with pamphlets, books, meetings and petitions. In 1833 an act was passed giving freedom to all slaves.

j. He was assassinated on April 15, 1865.

k. He died on 29 July, 1833 and was buried in Westminster Abbey.

2 Be creative

With the help of the information given in the text, create a timeline of Lincoln's or Wilberforce's life. Illustrate it with a collage or an online poster.

6 Slavery in Films

1 Match each title with the corresponding synopsis and still. Justify your answers.
- *Django Unchained*, Quentin Tarantino, 2012
- *Roots*, the TV mini-series based on Alex Haley's 1977 novel
- *Jefferson in Paris*, James Ivory, 1995

A A saga of African-American life, starting with Kunta Kinte being kidnapped from his African village, sold into slavery, and taken to America. He makes several escape attempts until he is finally caught. He marries Bell, his plantation's cook, and they have a daughter, Kizzy, who is eventually sold away from them. Kizzy has a son by her new master, and the boy grows up to become Chicken George, a legendary cock fighter who leads his family into freedom.

B Two years before the Civil War a freed slave meets a German bounty hunter. Together they arrest some of the worst outlaws in the country. But he cannot forget his wife who is still in bondage and they decide to come back to Mississippi to set her free. She now lives in the Candyland plantation and belongs to a cruel, brutal and sadistic planter.

C The American ambassador to the court of Louis XVI befriends French politicians, writers and artists. During his stay in France his wife dies. His daughters blame their father for having an affair with his 15-year-old slave Sally Hemings. What will happen to the beautiful black girl? Will she get her freedom for being a famous man's lover and giving him a son?

2 Watch the trailer of *Twelve Years a Slave*, Steve Mc Queen, 2014. Convince a friend to go and see the film with you.

LANGUAGE AT WORK

+ WORKBOOK
→ Apprendre à apprendre
p. 115 - 116

A L'infinitif avec *to*

Précis, p. 256

Observez

1 Lisez les phrases suivantes.

a. *Every slave wanted to be free and decided to leave the plantation forever.*

b. *Lincoln expected to meet difficulties.*

c. *Harriet Tubman intended to save as many people as she could.*

d. *William planned to escape during the night.*

Comment sont construits les verbes dans les énoncés ci-dessus ? De quoi sont-ils suivis ?
Ces verbes sont-ils tournés vers le passé ou l'avenir ? Quelle idée commune trouve-t-on dans tous ces verbes ?

2 Repérez les expressions du but dans les énoncés ci-dessous :

a. *The father left the South in order to escape from slavery.*

b. *He went to Canada so as to have better opportunities.*

c. *He left his family to start a new life.*

Laquelle de ces trois expressions appartient à la langue courante?

3 Associez chaque question à sa réponse :

1. *The boy came to Canada to have a more pleasant life.*
2. *He ran away because they dreamt of a more pleasant life.*

a. *Why did the slave run away?*
b. *What did he come to Canada for?*

Observez

4 Observez.

a. *The mother* ***wanted*** *her son* ***to stay*** *with her.*

b. *The father* ***expected*** *his children* ***to have*** *better opportunities.*

c. *The father* ***expected*** *them* ***to have*** *better opportunities.*

d. *The parents* ***would like*** *their children* ***to be*** *happy.*

Quelle est la structure commune à ces trois verbes ? Verbe + ... + ...
Dans la phrase **c.** : le pronom est-il utilisé sous sa forme sujet ou sa forme complément ?
Traduisez en français les quatre énoncés ci-dessus. Que remarquez-vous ?

B Obligation, permission et interdiction dans le passé

Précis, p. 258

Incapacité / interdiction dans le passé :
• *could not* /kʊd nɒt/ + BV

Permission dans le passé :
• *was / were allowed to* + BV /əˈlaʊd/

Obligation dans le passé :
• *had to* + BV

Interdiction dans le passé :
• *was / were forbidden to* + BV /fəˈbɪdn/

Capacité dans le passé :
• *was / were able to* + BV

Entraînez-vous

1 **Rédigez des phrases à l'aide des éléments proposés. Utilisez les formes verbales qui conviennent et ajoutez des mots grammaticaux si nécessaire (déterminants, pronoms, prépositions) :**

a. *The runaway - expect - people - give him - food - along the way.*
b. *Both Lincoln and Wilberforce - want - everybody - be treated - fairly.*
c. *They both - expect - people - evolve - get rid of - prejudices.*
d. *The slaves - would have liked - new master - be - more - understanding.*

2 **Traduisez :**

a. William a l'intention de quitter les États-Unis pour commencer une vie nouvelle au Canada.
b. Il a décidé de tout quitter pour vivre en (*as a*) homme libre.
c. Harriet Tubman s'attendait à avoir beaucoup de difficultés quand elle aidait les fugitifs.
d. Elle voulait mourir plutôt que de vivre en esclave.
e. Beaucoup d'esclaves avaient pour projet de s'installer au Canada.

3 **Sur papier libre, recopiez les phrases suivantes. Puis complétez-les en exprimant une obligation, une incapacité, une interdiction ou une permission au passé, selon le sens.**

a. *Slaves … defy their master, refuse hard work or work too slowly. They… use their native language, names or practise their religion. Of course, they … complain.*

b. *Field slaves … work from sunrise to sunset every day. On some plantations some slaves … relax one day a month or … have their Sundays off.*

c. *When a slave rebelled, the other slaves … watch the punishment as an example.*

d. *Slaves … live in the slave quarters. They sometimes … share a one-room cabin. No black person … be on the roads at night. That's why the local sheriff … shoot them dead.*

e. *Slaves … own a house or objects. They… use the furniture, cooking and eating objects and clothing the owner gave them. House servants … have much better clothes. When sold, a slave … leave everything behind and start again in the new place.*

C Improve your vocabulary

1 **Reconnaître la nature d'un mot.**

a. Sur papier libre, classez les mots suivants selon leur catégorie grammaticale : nom, adjectif, participe passé, verbe (deux de ces mots peuvent entrer dans deux catégories).

dead • death • die • life • live • lived • born • birth work • worked • belief • believe • succeed • success successful

b. Réécrivez le paragraphe suivant en complétant les espaces numérotés à l'aide d'un mot de la liste ci-dessus. Rétablissez la bonne forme grammaticale si nécessaire.

Abraham Lincoln was 1 in 1809. He 2 all his 3 first on his father's farm, then as a lawyer, and eventually he became the 16th American President. He 4 all men were equal and consequently made slavery illegal in 1863. His biggest 5 was winning the Civil War. He was shot in Washington where he 6. His 7 in 1865 was a real shock for the nation.

2 **Composition**

a. Sachant que le suffixe *-ful* signifie "plein de" et que *-less* signifie "sans", "dépourvu de", fabriquez des adjectifs à partir des mots suivants et associez-les à leur traduction française :

beauty • *care* • *dread* (redouter) • *fear* • *help* • *hope* • *joy* • *mercy* (pitié) • *pain* • *power* • *pity* • *price* • *use*

- sans pitié / impitoyable		- désespéré
- épouvantable	- douloureux	- indolore
- prudent	- négligent	- utile
- inutile	- intrépide	- craintif
- joyeux	- puissant	- impuissant
- sans défense	- inestimable	- beau

Vérifiez vos réponses à l'aide d'un dictionnaire.

b. Retrouvez la racine des mots suivants pour comprendre leur sens, puis traduisez-les :

- disobedient *- enslaved* *- unknown*

IMPROVE YOUR READING SKILLS

1 Lisez l'extrait suivant et utilisez les stratégies données ci-contre

The scene takes place in the 18th century. Mack McAsh has been arrested and bought by Jay Jamison, a plantation owner. He meets Kobe Tambala, a middle-aged black man who works for Mr. Jamison.

"You speak English well."

"I've been here nearly forty years." A look of bitterness came over his face. "I was just a boy when they stole me."

Peg and Cora were on Mack's mind.

"There were two people on the ship with me, a woman and a girl," he said. "Will I be able to find out who bought them?"

Kobe gave a humourless laugh. "Everybody's trying to find someone they were sold apart from. People ask around all the time. When slaves meet up, on the road or in the woods, that's all they talk about."

"The child's name is Peg," Mark persisted. "She's only thirteen. She doesn't have a mother or a father."

"When you've been bought, nobody has a mother or father."

Kobe has given up, Mack realized. He had grown accustomed to his slavery and learned to live with it. He was bitter, but had abandoned all hope of freedom. I swear I'll never do that, Mack thought.

▲ Ken Follet, *A Place Called Freedom*, 1995

Appuyez-vous sur les **mots transparents** = **les mots proches du français** ainsi que les mots connus.

Devinez le sens des mots inconnus.
Déduisez le sens des mots :
- en vert **à l'aide du contexte**.
- en jaune **en les décomposant** (dérivation, composition).

Repérez les **marqueurs de temps** importants.

Identifiez la **situation de départ**, le nombre de **personnages présents** dans la scène, les **personnages mentionnés.**

Identifiez le référent.
A qui ou à quoi se réfèrent les pronoms encadrés dans le texte ?

Trouvez les idées clés, les sentiments dominants de chaque personnage.

Repérez le **type de texte** (roman, article, pièce de théâtre,...)

2 Résumez le texte en quelques phrases clés

YOUR TASK

You are an artist and you have been asked to illustrate a story. Read it carefully p.140 and create a "Wanted" poster or write speech bubbles for a storyboard.

Les étapes à suivre

Lisez l'extrait p.140 et mobilisez les stratégies de lecture étudiées dans l'unité.
- Aidez-vous des mots transparents (= proches du français).
- Déduisez le sens des mots inconnus à partir des indices contenus dans le texte et des procédés de dérivation et de composition.

Repérez :
- Les personnages principaux (noms, les liens entre eux)
- Les lieux mentionnés dans le texte
- Le(s) moment(s) où se passe l'histoire
- Les événements clés et leur enchaînement

Complétez la fiche que votre professeur va vous distribuer et approfondissez votre compréhension.

Scénario 1

Créez une affiche ("*Wanted*" *poster*) en utilisant les éléments clés donnés dans le texte : nom, délit, circonstances (date, lieu...) description physique, portrait, nom du maître et son adresse, montant de la récompense ...

Scénario 2

Écrivez les bulles d'une planche de BD
- Repérez les moments clés (narration).
- Résumez-les en phrases courtes.
- Créez les dialogues entre les personnages. Transformez les passages narratifs en dialogue et vice versa.
- Utilisez la planche de dessins que votre professeur va vous fournir.

Relisez-vous avec soin. (cf. Relire son devoir p. 226)

Reading Corner

Linda has just learnt that her son Benjamin has had trouble with his master.

My first thought was that Benjamin was killed. "Don't be frightened, Linda," said William; "I will tell you all about it."

It appeared that Benjamin's master had sent for him, and he did not immediately obey the summons. When he did, his master was angry, and began to whip him. He resisted. Master and slave fought, and finally the master was thrown. Benjamin had cause to tremble; for he had thrown to the ground his master — one of the richest men in town. I anxiously awaited the result.

That night I ran to my grandmother's house; and Benjamin also ran away from his master's. My grandmother had gone to spend a day or two with an old friend living in the country.

"I have come," said Benjamin, "to tell you good bye. I am going away."

I inquired where.

"To the north," he replied.

I looked at him to see whether he was serious. I saw it all in his firm, set mouth. I implored him not to go, but he paid no attention to my words. He said he was no longer a boy, and every day made life unbearable. He had raised his hand against his master, and was to be publicly whipped for the offence. I reminded him of the poverty and hardships he must encounter among strangers. I told him he might be caught and brought back; and that was terrible to think of.

He grew vexed, and asked if poverty and hardships with freedom, were not preferable to our treatment in slavery. "Linda," he continued, "we are dogs here; foot-balls, cattle, everything that's mean. No, I will not stay. Let them bring me back. We don't die but once."

It is not necessary to state how he made his escape. He was on his way to New York when a violent storm overtook the vessel. The captain said he must put into the nearest port. This alarmed Benjamin, who was aware that he would be advertised in every port near his own town. His embarrassment was noticed by the captain. To port they went. There the advertisement met the captain's eye. Benjamin so exactly answered its description, that the captain laid hold on him, and bound him in chains. The storm passed, and they proceeded to New York. Before reaching that port Benjamin managed to get off his chains and throw them overboard. He escaped from the vessel, but was pursued, captured, and carried back to his master.

▲ Adapted from Harriet A. Jacobs, *Incidents in the Life of a Slave Girl*, 1861

▲ *Jazz Village, 1967*, Romare Bearden

A Negro Spiritual

Sometimes I feel like a motherless child
Sometimes I feel like a motherless child
Sometimes I feel like a motherless child
Long way from my home
Sometimes I wish I could fly
Like a bird up in the sky
Oh, sometimes I wish I could fly
Fly like a bird up in the sky
Sometimes I wish I could fly
Like a bird up in the sky
Closer to my home
Motherless children have a hard time
Motherless children have a such a hard time
Motherless children have such a really hard time
A long way from home
Sometimes I feel like freedom is near
Sometimes I feel like freedom is here
Sometimes I feel like freedom is so near
But we're so far from home

A Work Song

Gonna jump down, turn around
Pick a bale[1] of cotton
Gonna jump down, turn around
Pick a bale a day

Oh, lordy[2], pick a bale of cotton
Oh, lordy, pick a bale a day
Oh, lordy, pick a bale of cotton
Oh, lordy, pick a bale a day

I said me and my buddy[3] gonna pick a bale of cotton
Now me and my buddy gonna pick a bale a day
I said me and my buddy gonna pick a bale of cotton
Now me and my buddy gonna pick a bale a day

Oh, lordy, pick a bale of cotton
Oh, lordy, pick a bale a day
Oh, lordy, pick a bale of cotton
Oh, lordy, pick a bale a day

Gonna jump down, turn around
Pick a bale of cotton
Gonna jump down, turn around
Pick a bale a day

1. *ballot* **2.** *Seigneur* **3.** *mon copain*

▲ Traditional holler (work song)

Évaluation sommative
Reading

J'évalue mes progrès

Je revois les stratégies apprises dans les unités précédentes (*Improve Your Reading Skills* p.110, p.122 et p.138) afin de faire le bilan de mes compétences.

1. Je fais les premiers repérages

a. Identifiez le type de texte (site internet, presse, roman).

b. Relevez les noms propres.

c. Les mots répétés vous aideront à trouver les idées clés du texte.

Is it time to stop teaching cursive handwriting[1]?

More and more teachers are choosing not to teach cursive handwriting, focusing instead on keyboarding and other computer-based communication.

In today's Internet-driven world, do kids still need to be taught cursive in school? Is there any point in learning a skill[2] that fewer and fewer of us are using? Or is it still important for kids to learn to write?

George Couros, the principal of innovative teaching for Parkland School Division in Edmonton, thinks the days of formally teaching handwriting are coming to an end. [...]

"Technology and literacy are continuously developing ... and I think we need to really focus on what we do in school to help kids connect with the world," he told CTV's Canada AM this week.

But Jim Brand, principal of Toronto's Maria Montessori school, says it would be a shame to do away with teaching cursive altogether.

He says in the Montessori program, writing is taught very early, even before reading, because it's thought that it's a skill that kids can pick up earlier and that helps to speed up the reading process.

Brand says while he has no problem with teaching kids about current technology, cursive should still be taught as well. He says it's a skill that helps develop hand-eye coordination, fine motor skills and even creativity.

▲ February 10, 2013, CTVNews, Canada

1. *écriture cursive = à la main* 2. *compétence*

2. J'utilise les stratégies de lecture pour mieux comprendre

a. Appuyez-vous sur les mots transparents en vert ainsi que sur les mots connus.

b. Décomposez les mots et expressions soulignés afin de trouver leur sens :
computer-based communication • *Internet-driven world* • *speed up* • *hand-eye coordination*

c. Retrouvez la racine des mots suivants : - *fewer* - *earlier*. Qu'indique le suffixe ?

d. Devinez le sens des mots en bleu à l'aide du contexte.

e. En vous appuyant sur le contexte, choisissez la bonne traduction :
- *formally* (l. 12) : ❑ fortement ❑ formellement ❑ systématiquement ❑ finalement
- *literacy* (l. 14) : ❑ alphabétisation ❑ littérature ❑ lecture ❑ illettrisme

3. Je réponds aux questions

a. Quel est le thème général abordé dans ce texte ? .... (3 pts)
b. Quelles personnes sont concernées par ce problème ? .... (2 pts)
c. Qui sont les deux hommes interrogés (noms, métier, lieux de travail). .... (3 pts)
d. Faites la liste des arguments de chacun d'entre eux. Sont-ils d'accord ? Pourquoi ? .... (6 pts)
e. Résumez les deux parties du texte en quelques phrases (en français ou en anglais). .... (6 pts)

4. Je me corrige

Corrigez vos réponses à l'aide de la fiche que vous trouverez sur le site compagnon.

Je fais le bilan

Analysez vos résultats à l'aide des critères de cette grille d'évaluation où sont définis les différents niveaux de compétence de compréhension de l'écrit. Le niveau attendu en classe de seconde est B1.

Je peux...	Niveaux
... repérer des personnes, des mots isolés, des noms de lieux, des dates, des moments de la journée, des phrases simples	**En route vers A2**
... lire des textes courts, très simples et trouver une information particulière. ... comprendre des textes courts et simples si les mots appartiennent à un domaine familier et sont d'un usage fréquent. ... suivre le déroulement d'un texte dans une langue simple. ... identifier la nature d'un texte (dialogue, récit, description).	**A2**
... deviner le sens des mots inconnus à l'aide du contexte. ... deviner le sens des mots inconnus à l'aide de la formation des mots. ... comprendre les arguments /événements principaux d'un texte narratif. ... comprendre les descriptions d'un sentiment ou d'un souhait.	**B1**
... comprendre l'implicite d'un texte.	**En route vers B2**

Évaluation

Votre professeur va vous distribuer un texte que vous devrez lire attentivement avant de remplir la fiche d'évaluation correspondante.

Unit 7 Geeks

Unit 8 Wild West

Unit 9 Slavery

Une fois l'évaluation terminée, votre professeur pourra ainsi déterminer à quel niveau vous vous situez par rapport à la grille d'évaluation du Cadre Européen Commun de Référence pour les Langues.

▲ *Twelve Years a Slave*, Steve McQueen, 2013 (starring Chiwetel Ejiofor, Lupita Nyong'o and Michael Fassbender)

Speaking interaction

Unit 10 Green Art

VISION D'AVENIR • SENTIMENT D'APPARTENANCE

- How do street artists react to environmental problems? Discover a mural in Chicago and works by Banksy.
- Read a poem written by a young poet.
- What could our future be like? Turn to the passage from a science fiction book in the Reading Corner.

YOUR TASK Your school is preparing an event for Earth Day. You have to decide on the best design for the T-shirts you are going to wear.

p. 155

Unit 11 On Stage

VISION D'AVENIR • SENTIMENT D'APPARTENANCE

- Discover an important institution in the 19th century: marriage.
- Learn and interpret a famous scene from a play by Oscar Wilde.
- Read an extract from a graphic novel, *Jane Eyre*.

YOUR TASK In groups, put on stage a scene you have studied from *The Importance of Being Earnest*, or imagine a modern version of the interview between Lady Bracknell and Jack.

p. 167

Unit 12 Pop Goes my Art

VISION D'AVENIR • SENTIMENT D'APPARTENANCE

- What is Pop Art? Discover some major Pop Artists: Warhol, Lichtenstein, Rosenquist, Hockney, Haring…
- Learn more about their techniques and subject matter.
- Understand the movement and become an art critic.

YOUR TASK The school board has decided to buy two life-size posters of Pop Art to be displayed in your high school. You are on the Selection Committee that will debate and choose the artworks.

p. 181

Unit 10

VISION D'AVENIR • SENTIMENT D'APPARTENANCE

Green Art

YOUR TASK AT THE END OF THIS UNIT

Your school is preparing an event for Earth Day. You have to decide on the best design for the T-shirts you are going to wear. *p. 155*

1 Tune In!

1 Danger ahead

a. What elements immediately strike you in the mural below (setting, places, objects, colours, contrasts ...)?
b. List the problems which are illustrated by the artist.
c. Find in the mural what causes climate change.

▲ Mural in Chicago, Illinois

Help!

waste: *déchets* (indénombrable)
fumes
chimney stack: *cheminée d'usine*
factory = plant: *usine*
carbon footprint: *empreinte carbone*

hands (of the clock): *aiguilles*
scales: *balance*
drought /draʊt/: *sécheresse*
sea level
scream
rise, rose, risen

ice cap: *calotte polaire*
endangered species /ˈspiːʃiːz/
bear /beə/
seal: *phoque*
penguin
threaten /ˈθretn/: *menacer*
melt, melt, melt: *fondre*

2 Play with words
WB p. 64

Turn to your Workbook to learn more vocabulary on the environment and environmental problems.

PREPARE YOUR TASK

3 Observe and react

a. Group Work: Choose one picture and react. Report to the class.

b. Class Work:

• What do the cartoons and the mural have in common? Which picture has the strongest impact on you? Which one is the most effective? Why?

• Find a title for each picture and justify it.

Help!

Cartoons

barrel: *tonneau/barril*
sewage /sjuːɪdʒ/: *eaux d'égoût*
rubbish (GB) / garbage (US)
tyre (GB) = tire (US) /taɪə/: *pneu*
oil spill: *marée noire*
shore: *rivage*

filthy = very dirty

dump: *déverser*
die out: *disparaître*

Reactions

realistic
scary: *effrayant*
disgusting
humorous: *humoristique*
shocking

become aware of: *prendre conscience de*
realise: *se rendre compte*
warn /wɔːn/: *avertir*
prevent from + V-ING

4 A burning issue
WB p. 65

CD3 PISTE 1

a. Listen to a recording on global warming. List the different problems mentioned: causes, consequences.

b. Go on the Internet and find information about Earth Day.

c. You are the person who painted the mural. Give an interview and explain your message and your goals.

Global Warning!

Part 1

Tsunamis sweeping across the deep seas
Hurricanes howling with deafening breeze
Earthquakes shaking our tectonic plates
Volcanoes erupting 'round Earth as it breaks

Dinosaurs died and allowed man to stand
Millions of years changed the face of the land
A new world was born and with life it did flourish
Enough natural resources to keep us all nourished

For a long time the man and the Earth were as one
We drank from its rivers, bathed in light from the sun
The soil was rich, and ideal for seeds[1]
The planet attended to[2] all of our needs

But Earth for its pleasures could not comprehend
The mentality of its so newly found friend
We used and consumed without fear, or care
We scarred and we butchered[3] a beauty so rare

Poisoning oceans and chopping down trees
Re-laying landscapes to build as we pleased
Taking for granted[4] our grand evolution
Seeds that were planted, replaced by pollution

Part 2

Have we not wondered why it's so called "*Mother Earth*?"
Throughout all of history it has *given birth*!
This bluish-green ball, gently floating through space
Has potential for life, quite like no other place

It gives and it gives and has nothing to ask
To treat it with love and respect is our task
For the moment the future we can't comprehend
Is the world that we know, may soon come to an end

But there is still some time to undo what's been done
Requiring our species to *all act as one*
With wind turbines turning and running on air
Solar panels sourcing our sun's constant glare

We could cut our emissions and clean up with care
Make it our mission to heal and repair
Salvage[5] and save for all that it's worth
Secure our existence as people of Earth

1. *graines*
2. *s'occupait de*
3. *Nous avons mutilé et massacré*
4. *Nous avons considéré comme normal*
5. *(ici) aller à la rescousse*

▲ Poem used to open the CNN / YouTube Debate on Climate Change (2009)
www.martinpowellpoetry.com/p/poet.html

1 Read and understand the poem

WB p. 66

Turn to your Workbook for help.

2 Act it out

Martin Powell tells a journalist who has just asked him why he wrote his poem. Imagine what he says. Include the following elements and use the vocabulary below:

- Catastrophes /kə'tæstrɒfiz/
- Man's life in the past
- Measures to take
- Impact on nature
- Poet's goals
- Explanations given

Help!

Situation	Explanation	Measures
mankind: *humanité* natural disaster deforestation extent of the damage: *étendue des dégâts* threaten: *menacer* dump: *déverser*	careless available: *disponible* unaware of: *inconscient de* destroy use up = exhaust resources: *épuiser les ressources* be responsible for upset nature's balance: *bouleverser l'équilibre de la nature*	alternative sources of energy sustainable development warn: *avertir* prevent / stop from V-ING cope with a problem: *s'attaquer à* become aware of realise: *se rendre compte* live closer to nature

3 Prepare for an audition

a. Go on the Internet and watch the video of Martin Powell reciting his poem.
b. Choose the stanza you like best then train to read it aloud.
c. Enter the contest for the best interpretation of the stanza.

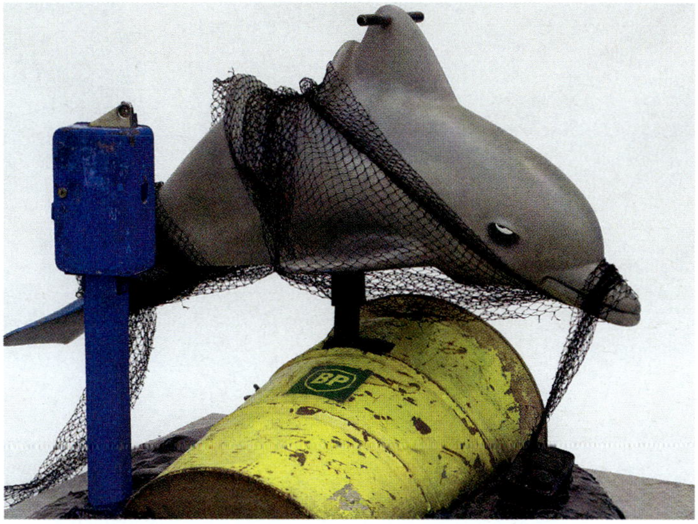

Sculpture by Banksy ▶

PREPARE YOUR TASK

4 Be creative

Choose one of the two activities below:
a. You are working on an anthology on modern poetry that will include Martin Powell's poems. Which of the visuals on this double page best illustrates the poem *Global Warning?* Why?
b. Create your own work of art.
- In groups: discuss what elements you want to illustrate in the poem.
- Make a painting, drawing, collage, slideshow (select pictures on the Internet or in magazines). You can also add a musical background.
- Present your work to the class. Justify your choices.

video

5 A commercial

Turn to your worksheet for help.

3 Going Green

PREPARE YOUR TASK

1 Observe and react

Group Work: Identify the issues raised in the ads below. Who is the target? What measures can be taken? What are the advertisers' goals? Say which ad you prefer and explain why.

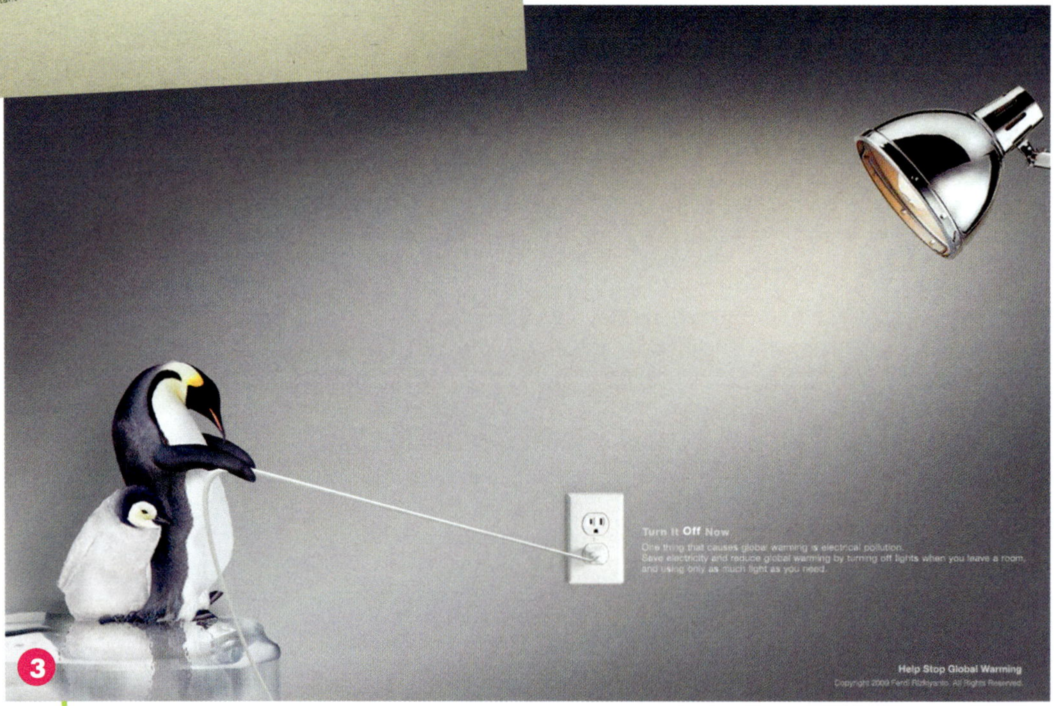

video

2 Discover reverse graffiti

a. Watch Moose, a graffiti artist who works in San Francisco and speaks about his technique and his goals.
Turn to your worksheet for help.
b. React to this visual.

3 Song corner

OUTSIDE SCHOOL

a. Go on the Internet and read the lyrics of the following songs:

Earth Song, Michael Jackson
In the year 2525, Ten Years After

My City Was Gone, The Pretenders
Blackened, Metallica

Big Yellow Taxi, Joni Mitchell
Nothing but Flowers, Talking Heads

Unsustainable, Muse

Choose your own song.

IN CLASS

b. In groups, work on the lyrics: what do they have in common? What do they denounce?
c. Vote for the song you prefer. Explain why and rank your playlist.

4 Creative writing

a. Read the following lines.

Affirmations

I swear to take care of the air that I breathe
I declare to fight for what I believe
I guarantee to be the best I can be
I vow[1] to help others to be just as free
I promise to never be consumed by greed[2]
I pledge my allegiance[3] to all those in need
I assure my assistance so suffering may cease
And I give my word to speak only of peace

▲ Martin Powell, *The Power of Young People*, 2010

1. /vaʊ/ *jure*
2. *cupidité*
3. *(ici) je m'engage à aider*

b. Choose one of the two topics:

Write a short poem with five personal resolutions to save the environment.

Write a song entitled *"One Earth, One Future"*.

LANGUAGE AT WORK

+ WORKBOOK
→ Apprendre à apprendre
p. 117 - 118

A Structures causatives : « faire faire » et « laisser faire »

Précis, p.253 -p.257

Observez

1. *This ad* [*makes*] *me* <u>*laugh*</u> *because it is humorous.*
2. *The authorities* [*let*] *people* <u>*drink*</u> *that water although it is polluted.*
3. *The government* [*made*] *the oil company* <u>*pay*</u> *for the damage of the oil spill.*

Quel est le sujet des verbes encadrés (qui est responsable de ce qui se passe) ?
Quel est le sujet des verbes soulignés?
Quel verbe utilise-t-on pour le sens de « déclenchement d'une action » ?
Quel verbe utilise-t-on pour le sens de « laisser faire » ?
Quel verbe indique une pression exercée ?
De quoi sont suivis les deux verbes encadrés?

Make / Let + …

Entraînez-vous

1 ***Make*** **ou** ***Let*** **? Complétez les phrases suivantes.**

a. *The new boss won't … us leave our offices without making sure our computers are switched off. The goal is to … us save energy and reduce gas emissions.*

b. *The price of oil will soon … people walk or bike or take public transport to go to work.*

c. *It's important to … people realise that it takes hundreds of years for plastic bags to degrade.*

2 **Traduisez avec** ***make*** **ou** ***let*****.**

a. Le but de cette loi est de ne pas laisser les bateaux continuer de polluer.

b. Cet article m'a fait réfléchir et changer mes habitudes.

c. La ville a laissé l'artiste faire sa peinture murale pour sensibiliser les citoyens au réchauffement climatique.

B Expression de l'hypothèse

Précis, p.255

Observez

1. *If we* ***go*** *on doing nothing, many species* <u>***will soon be***</u> *extinct.*
2. *If we* ***bought*** *locally grown produce, we* <u>***would reduce***</u> *our carbon footprint enormously.*

Comparez les formes verbales en gras puis les formes verbales soulignées.
- Laquelle des deux subordonnées en *If* exprime une **hypothèse irréelle** portant sur un **fait présent** ?
- Laquelle des deux subordonnées en *If* exprime une **hypothèse possible** portant sur un **fait présent ou futur** ?

Déduisez

Hypothèse possible :	*If* + verbe au …	… + …
Hypothèse irréelle portant sur un fait présent :	*If* + verbe au …	… + …

Entraînez-vous

3 **Complétez les phrases à l'aide de** ***will*** **ou** ***would*****.**

a. *If nothing is done against pollution, the world … soon run out of drinkable water.*

b. *People … not waste so much water, if it was more expensive.*

c. *If we turned down the heat in winter, we … save a lot of energy and money.*

d. *If you leave your TV on overnight, it … use as much electricity as four hours' viewing time.*

e. *If we use electric cars, we ... cut oil use and save money.*

f. *We ... reduce air pollution only if we burn less gas.*

g. *If governments invested in clear energy, it ... create new jobs.*

h. *We could all help, if each of us ... made an effort.*

C Improve your vocabulary

**Complétez les textes avec les mots proposés dans les listes.
Effectuez les changements grammaticaux nécessaires.**

1 *crisis - clean - coal - gas - greenhouse effect - oil - oil consumption - renewable solar - wind*

We will soon be confronted with an energy [1]. The world's demand for energy –[2], [3], [4]– is rising. More [5] sources of energy like [6], [7] and hydro power will be used in the next two decades. Governments want to develop public transport and [8] energy sources to reduce [9] and the [10].

2 *destroy - dump - Earth - fight - garbage can/dustbin - health hazard - man - recycle - threaten - waste disposal*

We are immediately struck by the fact that the Earth has been turned into something that looks both like a [1] and a cooking pot. The cartoonist's goal is to make us aware of the enormous amount of waste we produce every day but also of the [2] that waste represents. The problem of [3] is acute (*aigu*) because litter is [4] everywhere, and is polluting rivers and oceans. Our waste should be [5] or burnt. The message is clear: our blue planet is [6] with extinction because [7] is [8] the environment. We should all [9] for the protection of the [10].

D Improve your pronunciation

CD3
PISTE 2

Listen to a passage from a speech delivered by a teenager at the UN. Work on the pronunciation with the help of your Workbook, then read it aloud.

ON YOUR OWN!

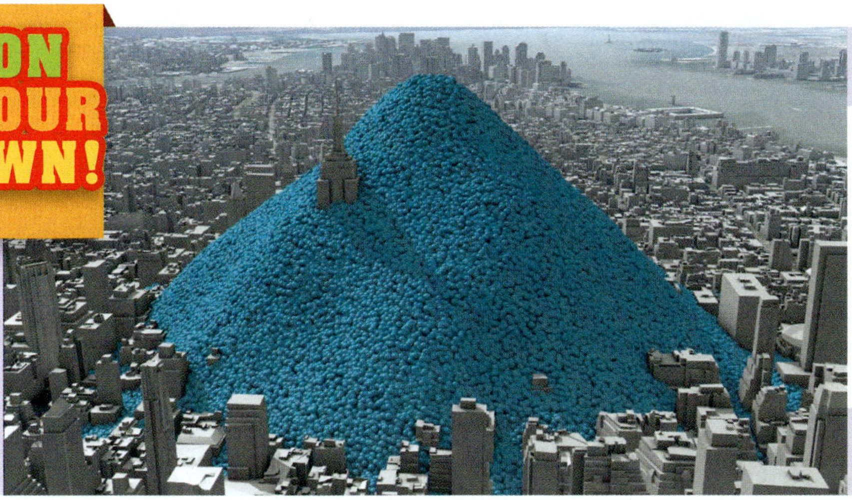

video

You are in charge of writing the captions or recording the voice-over to explain the goals of the video. Use what you have learnt on p. 230-231.

MP3 PISTE 27 CD3 PISTE 3

How to express feelings and reactions

Look at the two pictures and read the mind map carefully, then listen to two people's reactions. Use a piece of paper to write down the words and phrases from the mind map used below.

Reacting

- I am puzzled *(perplexe)* by this cartoon.
- I find this ad quite (+) / rather surprising.
- To my mind this advertisement is useless / pointless.

Goals of the artist

- He / She wants to make us react / feel
- He / She would like us to feel concerned.
- He / She wants us to feel / think ...

MP3 PISTE 28 CD3 PISTE 4

Defending choices/opinions

Positive comments

- humorous
- moving
- disturbing *(troublant)*
- striking
- amazing *(étonnant)*
- convincing
- effective
- realistic
- optimistic

Negative comments

- plain *(simple)*
- banal
- stereotyped /ˈsteriəʊtaɪpt/
- puzzling
- weird /wɪəd/= strange
- frightening
- scary
- pessimistic
- pointless = useless
- It leaves me cold.

Comparing

- It is more forceful / amusing than all the others.
- It is scarier than the other.
- I like it better / best.
- Compared to the first one, this ad is really clever.
- To my mind the message is (not) as ... as ...

YOUR TASK

Your school is preparing an event for Earth Day. You have to decide on the best design for the T-shirts you are going to wear.

Step by step

- Give your personal reaction to the ads below. What first caught your eye? What impact did it have on you?
- Compare the ads. Which is the most effective ad and message? Why? Justify your choice.
- Choose one of these ads, or design your own T-shirt with a picture and a slogan of your own.
- Defend your choice in front of the class: explain what aspect of the problem the photo and the slogan tackle *(s'attaquer à)*, why this aspect is important and why your choice is the best for the Earth Day T-shirt.
- Vote for the best print(s).

Reading Corner

8/01/15

UK to commence 60% Carbon Rations

In a historic parliamentary speech the Prime minister announced the date of the full UK entry into a nationwide carbon rationing system. [...]

Sat, Jan 3rd

Dad sat us all down again and took us thru a disgusting government online form to work out what our family CO allowance actually is. Basically we've got a carbon allowance of 200 Carbon Points per month to spend on travel, heat and food. All other stuff like clothes and technology and books have already got the Carbon Points built into the price.

At first they set up a free trading system so that if you were rich you could just buy up carbon in cash and live how you wanted - but after the riots last September the Gov backed down and changed the rules so that no one was allowed to buy more than 50 extra points a month.

And the worst thing is, on top of all this, me and Kim have to give up loads of our points for the family energy allowance, which leaves us some pathetic amount for travel, college, going out ... The car's gonna be cut way back, all of us get access to the PC, TV, HD, stereo for only 2 hours a day, heating is down to 16°C in the living room and 1 hour a day for the rest of the house, showers max 5 minutes, baths only at week-end.

Tues, Jan 20th

We had a powercut in the night. The house is so cold now, it feels like 200 years of evil chill creeping into my bones. Reminds me of the Great Storm. Cuts give me the creeps - You know when you go to switch the light on and it's dead? It was freezing I went shopping to Waitrose with Mum and Dad just to keep my blood moving.

Super-strange experience. It was all dark in there cos they'd switched off loads of lights and aircon and those fans that waft baking-bread smells around. It was just like a big warehouse. It was pretty funny, all the nice middle-class people pretending they were not panic buying and that it was completely normal for them to be pushing six trolleys bulging with stuff. The staff kept making people put things back at the checkout cos they'd gone over their CO points.

▲ Saci Lloyd, *Carbon Diaries 2015*, 2010

Observe and react

▲ *Crude Oil*, Banksy

▲ *Camera, Man & Flower*, Banksy

Unit 11

VISION D'AVENIR • SENTIMENT D'APPARTENANCE

On Stage

YOUR TASK AT THE END OF THIS UNIT

In groups, put on stage a scene you have studied from *The Importance of Being Earnest*, or imagine a modern version of the interview between Lady Bracknell and Jack. *p. 167*

1 Tune In!

1 Time out

a. Read this review of *West Side Story*, a musical based on the film by Robert Wise (1961).

Don't miss *West Side Story*! This musical is a thrill! The cast on stage are brilliant and give wonderful performances. The director has managed to give life to this well-known plot. The characters are moving. The costumes are amazing. The props and stage set are perfect, they realistically recreate the setting: the West Side of New York City. The actors sing beautifully. What a joy to hear an entire audience react to the most memorable songs! All the hard work put into the rehearsals is rewarded. It's simply wonderful.

b. In the review, find the words that correspond to the following definitions:

- a fictional person in a play
- a representation
- a person who gives instructions to actors and actresses
- practice before playing in public
- accessories used on stage
- people who come to watch a play
- all the actors in a play
- platform on which actors appear
- clothes actors and actresses wear
- story of a play
- place where the action happens
- a play with songs and dances

c. List all the positive adjectives and adverbs used in the review. Use a dictionary to find their opposites. Write the same review from the point of view of someone who hated the play.

PREPARE YOUR TASK

2 A quarrel

a. Look at this photo. Work in pairs and imagine what the man and the woman are arguing about.
b. Choose a role and act out the scene.

Prompts

How dare you!
How could you?
This is the limit!
I'm not having that!
Let me speak!
I don't believe it!
Just you wait!

3 Play with words

CD3 PISTE 5 · MP3 PISTE 29 · WB P.68

Improve your vocabulary with the help of your Workbook.

2 Wedlock

1 First impressions

Look at the poster. What strikes you?

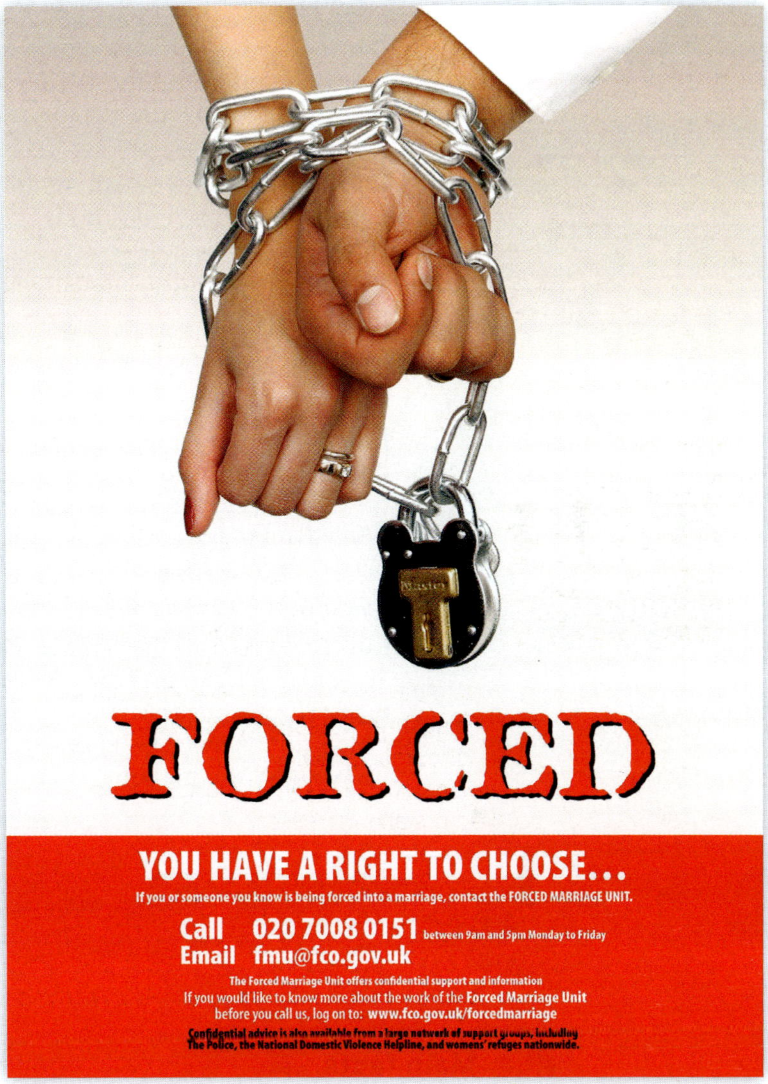

2 Group work

PREPARE YOUR TASK

Analyse the poster. Each group will focus on one of the following aspect:

- A. Characters? Objects?
- B. Dominant colours? Why?
- C. Message? Target audience?
- D. Reactions?

3 Radio spot

Prepare a one-minute radio spot for an awareness campaign on the same issue.

Help!

Who? What?

bride /braɪd/: *mariée*
bridegroom: *marié*
wedding ring: *alliance*
suit /suːt/: *costume*
padlock: *cadenas*

be locked
marry sb = get married to sb
be forced / obliged / compelled to do sth

What for?

arranged marriage
obedient / submissive

impose sth on sb
urge sb to + BV: *inciter fortement qqn à*
support
warn sb about sth
prevent sb from V-ING : *empêcher qqn de*
against sb's will: *contre la volonté de qqn*

3 A Suitable Boy - Part I

CD3 PISTE 6 MP3 PISTE 30

Jack: Gwendolen, will you marry me? *(Goes on his knees.)*

Gwendolen: Of course I will, darling. How long you have been about it! I am afraid you have had very little experience in how to propose[1].

Jack: My own one, I have never loved anyone in the world but you.

Gwendolen: Yes, but men often propose for practice. [...] What wonderfully blue eyes you have, Ernest! They are quite, quite, blue. I hope you will always look at me just like that, especially when there are other people present. *(Enter Lady Bracknell.)*

Lady Bracknell: Mr Worthing! Rise[2], sir, from this semi-recumbent[3] posture. It is most indecorous[4].

Gwendolen: Mamma! *(He tries to rise; she restrains him.)* I must beg[5] you to retire. This is no place for you. Besides, Mr Worthing has not quite finished yet.

Lady Bracknell: Finished what, may I ask?

Gwendolen: I am engaged[6] to Mr Worthing, mamma. *(They rise together.)*

Lady Bracknell: Pardon me, you are not engaged to anyone. When you do become engaged to someone, I, or your father, [...] will inform you of the fact. [...] And now I have a few questions to put to you, Mr Worthing. While I am making these inquiries, you, Gwendolen, will wait for me below[7] in the carriage[8].

Gwendolen: *(Reproachfully.)* Mamma!

Lady Bracknell: In the carriage, Gwendolen! *(Gwendolen goes to the door. She and Jack blow kisses to each other behind Lady Bracknell's back. Lady Bracknell looks vaguely about as if she could not understand what the noise was. Finally turns round.)* Gwendolen, the carriage!

Gwendolen: Yes, mamma. *(Goes out, looking back at Jack.)*

▲ Oscar Wilde, *The Importance of Being Earnest*, 1895

1. make an offer of marriage **2.** stand up **3.** *à moitié allongée* **4.** improper, not dignified
5. *je vous supplie* **6.** *fiancée* **7.** *en bas* **8.** *calèche*

1 Main facts

WB p.69

Read this extract. Turn to your Workbook for help.

2 Creative writing

Gwendolen writes an entry in her diary about Jack's attitude, and gives her feelings and reactions to the the scene that has just happened. (100 - 150 words)

Help!

Gwendolen	Jack	Lady Bracknell
impatient	hesitant	shocked / outraged
assertive: *sûr de soi*	earnest /ˈɜːnɪst/	cross = angry
self-confident = self-assured	submissive	authoritative = domineering
straightforward: *direct*	propose to sb: *demander qqn en mariage*	contemptuous = scornful: *méprisant*
vain: *vaniteux*	in love with	haughty = arrogant
obedient		
rather / quite : *plutôt / assez*	he looks / sounds + *adjectif*	belong to the aristocracy / the upper class
she seems to ...		
challenge = defy sb		

3 Meet my parents

a. Compare the cartoon and the text you have just read. Is the situation similar or different?

PREPARE YOUR TASK

b. Imagine the advice Jack could have been given before he met Lady Bracknell. Act out the dialogue.

4 You are the stage director

a. Describe the tone used by each character at the beginning of the scene. Use the adjectives from the *Help* p. 160.

b. Write the stage directions at the end of each line (text p. 160) . Use an adverb as well as one of the following verbs:
add - announce - assert - ask - answer - declare - explain - order - reply

Examples:

GWENDOLEN: I am engaged to Mr Worthing, mamma.
(Gwendolen announced loudly / defiantly.)
LADY BRACKNELL: Pardon me, you are not engaged to anyone.
(She answered drily.)

PREPARE YOUR TASK

c. Imagine Lady Bracknell and Jack on stage:

- What is Lady Bracknell's attitude at the beginning of the scene? How does she look at Jack and Gwendolen? What is her attitude when Gwendolen leaves the room?

- Does Jack stay where he is or does he step back? Does he look at Lady Bracknell or does he avoid her eyes? Is he confident or embarrassed?

d. Mime the whole scene: use gestures only.

Useful words
- sit comfortably
- take one's time
- purse: *porte-monnaie*
- look sb up and down = look at sb fixedly

5 How to pronounce WB P. 70

CD3 PISTE 7 MP3 PISTE 30

Work on your pronunciation with the help of your Workbook, then read the dialogue aloud.

4 A Suitable Boy - Part II

CD3 PISTE 8 MP3 PISTE 31

Lady Bracknell: *(Sitting down.)* You can take a seat, Mr Worthing. *(Looks in her pocket for note-book and pencil.)*

Jack: Thank you, Lady Bracknell, I prefer standing.

Lady Bracknell: I feel bound to[1] tell you that you are not down on my list of eligible young men[2], although I have the same list as the dear Duchess of Bolton has. We work together, in fact. However, I am quite ready to enter your name[3], should your answers be what a really affectionate mother requires[4]. Do you smoke?

Jack: Well, yes, I must admit I smoke.

Lady Bracknell: I am glad to hear it. A man should always have an occupation of some kind. [...] How old are you?

Jack: Twenty-nine.

Lady Bracknell: What is your income[5]?

Jack: Between seven and eight thousand a year.

Lady Bracknell: In land, or in investments?

Jack: In investments, chiefly.

Lady Bracknell: That is satisfactory. [...] Now to minor matters. Are your parents living?

Jack: I have lost both my parents. [...] It would be nearer the truth to say that my parents seem to have lost me... I don't actually[6] know who I am by birth. I was... well, I was found.

Lady Bracknell: Found! [...]

Jack: In a hand-bag.

Lady Bracknell: A hand-bag?

Jack: Yes, Lady Bracknell. I was in a hand-bag - a somewhat large, black leather[7] hand-bag, with handles to it - an ordinary hand-bag in fact. [...] In the cloakroom[8] at Victoria Station.

Lady Bracknell: [...] I confess I feel somewhat bewildered[9] by what you have just told me. [...]

Jack: May I ask you then what you would advise me to do? I need hardly say I would do anything in the world to ensure Gwendolen's happiness.

Lady Bracknell: I would strongly advise you, Mr Worthing, to try and acquire some relations as soon as possible, and to make a definite effort to produce at any rate one parent, of either sex, before the season is quite over. [...] You can hardly imagine that I and Lord Bracknell would dream of allowing our only daughter - a girl brought up with the utmost care[10] - to marry into a cloak-room, and form an alliance with a parcel[11]? Good morning, Mr Worthing!

▲ Oscar Wilde, *The Importance of Being Earnest*, 1895

1. *je me sens obligée de* **2.** *fiancés possibles* **3.** *Je suis tout à fait prête à faire figurer votre nom* **4.** *si vos réponses correspondent à ce que peut exiger une mère pleine d'affection* **5.** *revenus* **6.** *en réalité* **7.** *cuir* **8.** *consigne* **9.** a little perplexed **10.** *élevée avec le plus grand soin* **11.** *paquet*

1 Key information

WB p.71

Read the dialogue, then turn to your Workbook for help.

a. What do we learn about Jack's origins?
b. How does Lady Bracknell react in this scene? Why?
c. Imagine how Jack feels after Lady Bracknell leaves.
d. What questions should a really affectionate mother ask her future son-in-law?

Help!

Jack	**Lady Bracknell**
orphan: *orphelin* prospects: *perspectives* polite = well-mannered careful = cautious honest /ˈɒnɪst/ straightforward = frank = direct wealthy = well-off miserable: *très malheureux* gain sb's approval disappoint	curt: *cassant* inquisitive = indiscreet astonished / amazed = very surprised snobbish stunned: *stupéfait* outraged: *scandalisé* inquire into be prejudiced against: *avoir des préjugés envers* approve of ≠ disapprove of sb / V-ING What shocks her most is that…

2 Define the tone

Finish the sentences with one of these adverbs:

hesitatingly — *contemptuously* — *hopefully* — *impatiently* — *proudly* — *sincerely*

"I will do anything," Jack said…
"I can produce the handbag," Jack said…
"I would strongly advise you, Mr Worthing, to try and acquire some relations as soon as possible," Lady Bracknell replied…
"Well, yes, I must admit I smoke," Jack answered…
"Gwendolen received a very good education," Lady Bracknell said…
"Good morning, Mr Worthing," Lady Bracknell said…

CD3 PISTE 9 — MP3 PISTE 32

3 How to pronounce

WB P.73

Work on your pronunciation with the help of your Workbook, then read the dialogue aloud.

PREPARE YOUR TASK

4 After the interview

Act out one of the two conversations below. Include comments, reactions, feelings and emotions.

a. Lady Bracknell meets her best friend and tells her what has just happened.
b. Jack narrates the scene to Gwendolen.

5 You are the stage director

Work on the following points:

- Are the two characters far from or close to each other? What does Lady Bracknell do during the interview? What is Jack's attitude?
- How does Lady Bracknell walk off stage? Does she give Jack a final look or not?
- How should Jack act at the end of the scene?
- What song or music could accompany this scene? When would you play it?

video

6 Watch a video

Watch an extract from the film *The Importance of Being Earnest* by Oliver Parker, 2002. Turn to your worksheet for help.

LANGUAGE AT WORK

+ WORKBOOK
→ Apprendre à apprendre
p. 119 - 120

Le style indirect (*il dit que...*)

Précis, p. 252

Observez

1 Style direct ou indirect ?

a. Repérez les énoncés au discours direct, et ceux qui sont au discours indirect. Puis associez chaque énoncé au discours direct avec son équivalent au style indirect.

"I am engaged!"

Lady Bracknell answered **she** was surprised by what **he** had told **her**.

Gwendolen said that / ø **she** was engaged.

"Are your parents living?"

Lady Bracknell asked **Jack** if **his** parents were living.

"I'm surprised by what you have told me"

2 Ordre des mots

– "*Where is it playing?*" → He wonders where it is playing.
– "*How much does a ticket cost?*" → He wants to know how much a ticket costs.

3 Correspondances

a. "***Do you smoke?***" *Lady Bracknell asked.*	*Lady Bracknell asked if Jack smoked.*
b. "***Where did Mr Cardew find*** *you?" Lady Bracknell asked.*	*Lady Bracknell asked where Mr Cardew had found him.*
c. "***I will speak*** *to Lady Bracknell tomorrow," Jack said.*	*Jack said he would speak to Lady Bracknell the following day.*
d. "***I have lost*** *both my parents," Jack answered.*	*Jack answered he had lost both his parents.*
e. "***Wait for me*** *outside!" Lady Bracknell ordered.*	*Lady Bracknell ordered Gwendolen to wait for her outside.*
f. "***Try and acquire*** *some relations before next week," Lady Bracknell advised Jack.*	*Lady Bracknell advised Jack to try and acquire some relations before the following week / before the coming week.*

a. A quel temps sont tous les verbes introducteurs dans la deuxième colonne du style indirect ?
b. Expressions de temps : relevez les deux expressions de temps au style direct et trouvez leur équivalent au style indirect passé avec un verbe introducteur au passé. Que remarquez-vous ?

Déduisez

- Les paroles rapportées sont introduites par … ou … .
- Lorsque l'on rapporte les paroles de quelqu'un, certains pronoms représentant des personnes doivent … .

Lorsqu'on rapporte une question au style indirect on rétablit l'ordre de la phrase … .

Déduisez

Au style indirect, lorsque le verbe introducteur est au …, on doit opérer les changements suivants dans le groupe verbal de l'énoncé rapporté :
- le présent devient un … . De même, *will* devient … .
- le prétérit qui désigne une action antérieure au moment où l'on parle devient un …
- pour un impératif, le verbe introducteur sera un verbe indiquant ... , par exemple : ...

Entraînez-vous

1 **Rapportez les questions de Gwendolen et Lady Bracknell en utilisant un verbe introducteur au passé.**

a. **Gwendolen:** *"Why do I have to go into the carriage?"*
b. **Lady Bracknell:** *"Have you told your father you were engaged?"*
c. **Lady Bracknell:** *"Are you speaking seriously?"*
d. **Gwendolen:** *"How do you know Jack was found?"*
e. **Gwendolen:** *"Isn't there a solution?"*

2 **Rapportez cet échange au style indirect passé à l'aide de verbes introducteurs variés.**

Example: Lady Bracknell: Found!
Lady Bracknell asked where he had been found and wondered if Jack had really been found.

Jack: The late Mr. Thomas Cardew, an old gentleman, found me, and gave me the name of Worthing, because he happened to have a first-class ticket for Worthing in his pocket at the time. Worthing is a seaside resort[1] in Sussex.
Lady Bracknell: Where did the charitable gentleman find you?
Jack: In a hand-bag.

1. *station balnéaire*

3 **Réécrivez le passage suivant au style direct. N'oubliez pas les guillemets.**

Jack announced to Lady Bracknell that he was an orphan. He added that he had no parents because they had abandoned him. Lady Bracknell asked if he was joking, and Jack answered that it was the absolute truth. Lady Bracknell was surprised and advised Jack to find a family if he wanted to marry her daughter. Jack replied that he only wanted to make Gwendolen happy. He thought that his family background was of no importance. Lady Bracknell exclaimed that she would never marry her daughter to a man without a respectable family.

4 **Find the perfect match!**

Votre professeur va vous distribuer une liste de phrases au style indirect. Le maitre du jeu va tirer une carte contenant une phrase au style direct. A vous de voir si vous avez la phrase correspondante au style indirect !

ON YOUR OWN!

Racontez cette histoire au style indirect passé. Variez les verbes introducteurs :
tell, answer / reply, ask, declare, explain.

▲ Bill Watterson, *Calvin and Hobbes, It's a magical world,* 1996

IMPROVE YOUR SPEAKING SKILLS

1 Écoutez et repérez

MP3 PISTE 33 CD3 PISTE 10

a. le mot plus particulièrement accentué dans ces phrases.

- *Pardon me, you are not engaged to anyone.*
- *While I am making these inquiries, you, Gwendolen, will wait for me below in the carriage.*

b. comment se prononcent les mots soulignés :

- *I was in a hand-bag. In the cloak-room at Victoria Station.*
  /wɒz/ ou /wəz/ ? /æt/ ou /ət/ ?
- *We would never dream of allowing our only daughter to marry you.*
  /ɒv/ ou /əv/ ? /tuː/ ou /tə/ ?

c. les liaisons consonne - voyelle :

- *I must admit I smoke.*
- *What is your income? In land, or in investments?*

d. Les pauses dans des phrases longues.

You can hardly imagine that I and Lord Bracknell would dream of allowing our only daughter - a girl brought up with the utmost care - to marry into a cloak-room, and form an alliance with a parcel?

e. Lisez toutes ces phrases à haute voix en imitant le modèle fourni.

2 Jouez avec votre voix

MP3 PISTE 34 CD3 PISTE 11

a. Entraînez-vous à dire cette phrase doucement, puis de plus en plus fort, n'hésitez pas à exagérer :

Good morning, Mr Worthing!

b. Utilisez différents tons de voix. Dites :

"Good morning, Mr Worthing!"

- d'un ton surpris
- avec colère
- avec mépris
- avec joie

Vérifiez à l'écoute si votre intonation était correcte.

c. Déterminez le ton de voix pour chaque phrase de l'extrait suivant.

Gwendolen: I am engaged to Mr Worthing, mamma.

Lady Bracknell: Pardon me, you are not engaged to anyone. When you do become engaged to someone, I, or your father, will inform you of the fact. And now I have a few questions to put to you, Mr Worthing. While I am making these inquiries, you, Gwendolen, will wait for me below in the carriage.

d. Deux personnes joueront le rôle de Lady Bracknell et Gwendolen, une troisième sera le metteur en scène et les guidera.

Have more confidence in yourself.

Exaggerate much more. Emphasise with your voice.

You should be much more nervous / anxious / uncomfortable…

Make a gesture to indicate…

You need to speak much louder / to be clearer and slower.

Bring more energy to the scene.

Look at him/her when you … The audience must see your face, not your back.

YOUR TASK

In groups, put on stage a scene you have studied from *The Importance of Being Earnest*, or imagine a modern version of the interview between Lady Bracknell and Jack.

Scénario 1

1. Répartissez les rôles

Si vous décidez de jouer la scène d'Oscar Wilde dans son entier, Lady Bracknell et Jack peuvent être joués par une personne différente dans chaque partie.

a. Désignez :
- un metteur en scène
- un souffleur
- une personne en charge de la musique
- un accessoiriste

b. Synthétisez les besoins à l'aide d'un tableau.

c. Répartissez les rôles des comédiens.

2. Apprenez votre rôle

- Vérifiez que vous comprenez bien tout ce que vous allez dire.
- Aidez-vous des pages de votre *Workbook* sur la prononciation des scènes ainsi que de vos enregistrements MP3.
- Marquez les groupes de souffle, les sons qui vous posent problème, les accents de mots, les liaisons d'une couleur, et barrez les formes réduites d'une autre couleur sur votre photocopie personnelle.
- Mémorisez votre rôle à la perfection en vous déplaçant chez vous, pour vous donner l'habitude d'occuper l'espace.

3. Travaillez votre scène

- Commencez par mimer la scène.
- Puis réfléchissez :
  - au ton de voix à utiliser,
  - à la façon dont vous allez regarder votre partenaire ou vos partenaires,
  - aux gestes que vous allez faire, marquez-les sur votre photocopie personnelle,
  - aux pauses, les silences doivent aussi être prévus,
  - à vos différents mouvements sur scène.
- Parlez fort, sans accélérer.
- Écoutez attentivement votre/vos partenaire(s), regardez-le(s).

Scénario 2

Imaginez les questions que Lady Bracknell poserait à Jack aujourd'hui.
Écrivez la scène en incluant les didascalies. Puis jouez-la devant la classe.
Appuyez-vous sur les conseils donnés ci-dessus pour mettre en scène votre dialogue.

Reading Corner

Jane Eyre is a governess at Thornfield Hall where she teaches a little girl named Adèle. Her employer, Mr Rochester, is a mysterious and passionate man whom Jane secretly loves. Mr Rochester soon falls in love with her and proposes to her. Jane accepts. The scene takes place on their wedding day.

THIS GIRL KNEW NO MORE THAN YOU OF THE DISGUSTING SECRET: SHE THOUGHT ALL WAS FAIR AND LEGAL, AND NEVER DREAMT SHE WAS GOING TO BE ENTRAPPED INTO A FEIGNED UNION WITH A DEFRAUDED WRETCH, ALREADY BOUND TO A BAD, MAD, AND EMBRUTED PARTNER!
BRIGGS, WOOD, MASON, I INVITE YOU ALL TO COME UP TO THE HOUSE AND VISIT MRS. POOLE'S PATIENT, AND MY WIFE!
YOU SHALL SEE WHAT SORT OF BEING I WAS CHEATED INTO ESPOUSING, AND JUDGE WHETHER OR NOT I HAD A RIGHT TO BREAK THE COMPACT, AND SEEK SYMPATHY WITH SOMETHING AT LEAST HUMAN.
GOOD MORNING, MRS. POOLE! HOW ARE YOU AND YOUR CHARGE TO-DAY?
WE'RE TOLERABLE, SIR, THANK YOU.
RATHER SNAPPISH, BUT NOT 'RAGEOUS.
EE-AHH-AHHH!
SHE HAS NO KNIFE NOW, I SUPPOSE?
ONE NEVER KNOWS WHAT SHE HAS, SIR.
FOR GOD'S SAKE, TAKE CARE!
We had better leave her.
GO TO THE DEVIL!

Unit 12

VISION D'AVENIR • SENTIMENT D'APPARTENANCE

Pop Goes My Art

YOUR TASK AT THE END OF THIS UNIT

The school board has decided to buy two life-size posters of Pop Art to be displayed in your high school. You are on the Selection Committee that will debate and choose the artworks. p. 181

1 Tune In!

PREPARE YOUR TASK

1 Life is Art

a. Group Work: Focus on one painting and report on it.
- What is represented?
- What colours are used?
- What are your reactions?

b. Class Work: Discuss.
- What do these paintings have in common?
- What techniques are used?
- Which painting do you find closer to the reality of everyday life? Justify your answer.

▲ Andy Warhol, *Campbell's Soup Cans*, 1962

◄ James Rosenquist, *Dishes*, 1964

2 Play with words
WB P.74

Turn to your Workbook to improve your vocabulary on art.

3 Listen and draw
WB P.75

CD3 PISTE 12

a. You will hear the description of a Pop Art painting by Tom Wesselmann.
b. Turn to your Workbook to draw the objects in the right places. You will get a complete picture of the room.

video

4 Watch a video: Young prodigy

a. Outside school, go on the Internet and find out who the prodigy is.
b. Write a short newspaper article about her (who / what her work consists of / who influenced her).
c. Do a little research on the artists mentioned, find other Pop Artists and share your findings.

Help!

Techniques
repetition
silkscreen: *sérigraphie*
realistic ≠ abstract
geometrical
similar
recognisable

Subject matter
in rows /rəʊz/: *en rang*
advertising
brand name: *marque*
mass consumption
uniformity
everyday life

Reactions
universal
original ≠ uninteresting
attracted by ≠ indifferent to
fascinated by
it leaves me cold

5 Art concept
WB P.75

PREPARE YOUR TASK

a. Discuss in pairs / groups the 'everyday life' object(s) / situation(s) you would represent if you were a Pop Artist. Explain your choice and be ready to answer questions from the other groups.
b. Write a definition of the Pop Art movement in an online encyclopedia using what you have seen and learnt on this double page. Turn to your Workbook for help.

2 Fame

1 President Elect

Who is portrayed? What other elements are represented?

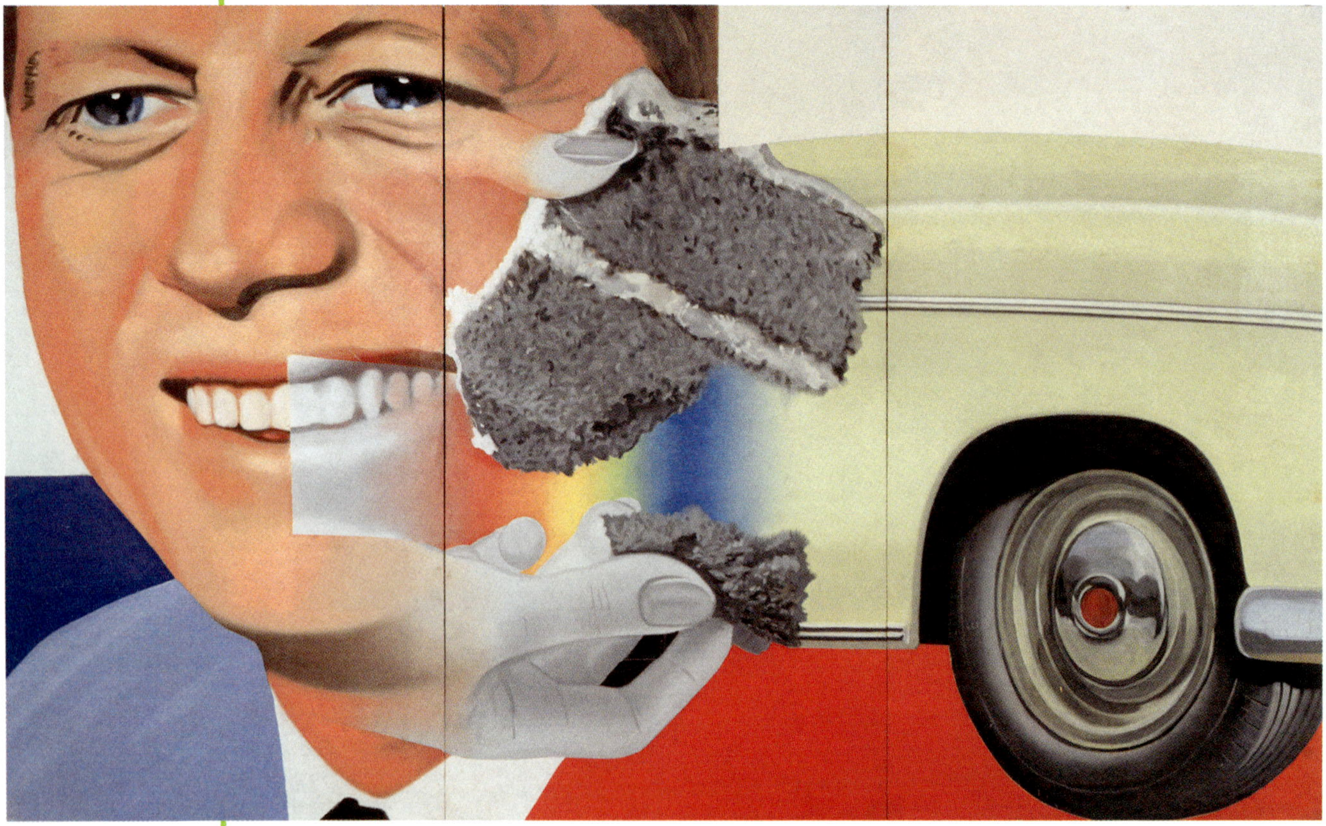

▲ James Rosenquist, *President Elect*, 1960-1961

CD3 PISTE 13

2 The Swinging Sixties WB P.75

a. Listen to a history teacher who will give you more information about the Sixties. Turn to your Workbook for help.
b. What characterized that decade in the United States? What were the main events?
c. To what extent does the painting above illustrate this period of American history?

CD3 PISTE 14

3 Kennedy's assassination WB P.77

a. Read the following article. Sum up the event in a few words.

President Kennedy is slain by assassin in Dallas

Dallas, Texas, November 22, 1963

President John F. Kennedy was killed today when a sniper fired three rifle shots at the presidential limousine as it drove along Elm Street in downtown Dallas. The nation was in shock at the loss of its elegant, dynamic and popular young president.
The shooting occurred at 12:35.

"Oh no! Oh no!" Jacqueline Kennedy cried over and over, cradling his head in her lap as the limousine raced to the Parkland Memorial Hospital three miles away. At 1 p.m., John F. Kennedy, America's youngest elected President, was pronounced dead.

▲ *Chronicle of America*, 1989

b. Observe the painting below and listen to the audioguide of *Sixteen Jackies* by Andy Warhol /'wɔːhəʊl/ (UK), /'wɔːrhoʊl/ or /'wɔːrhɔːl/(US).

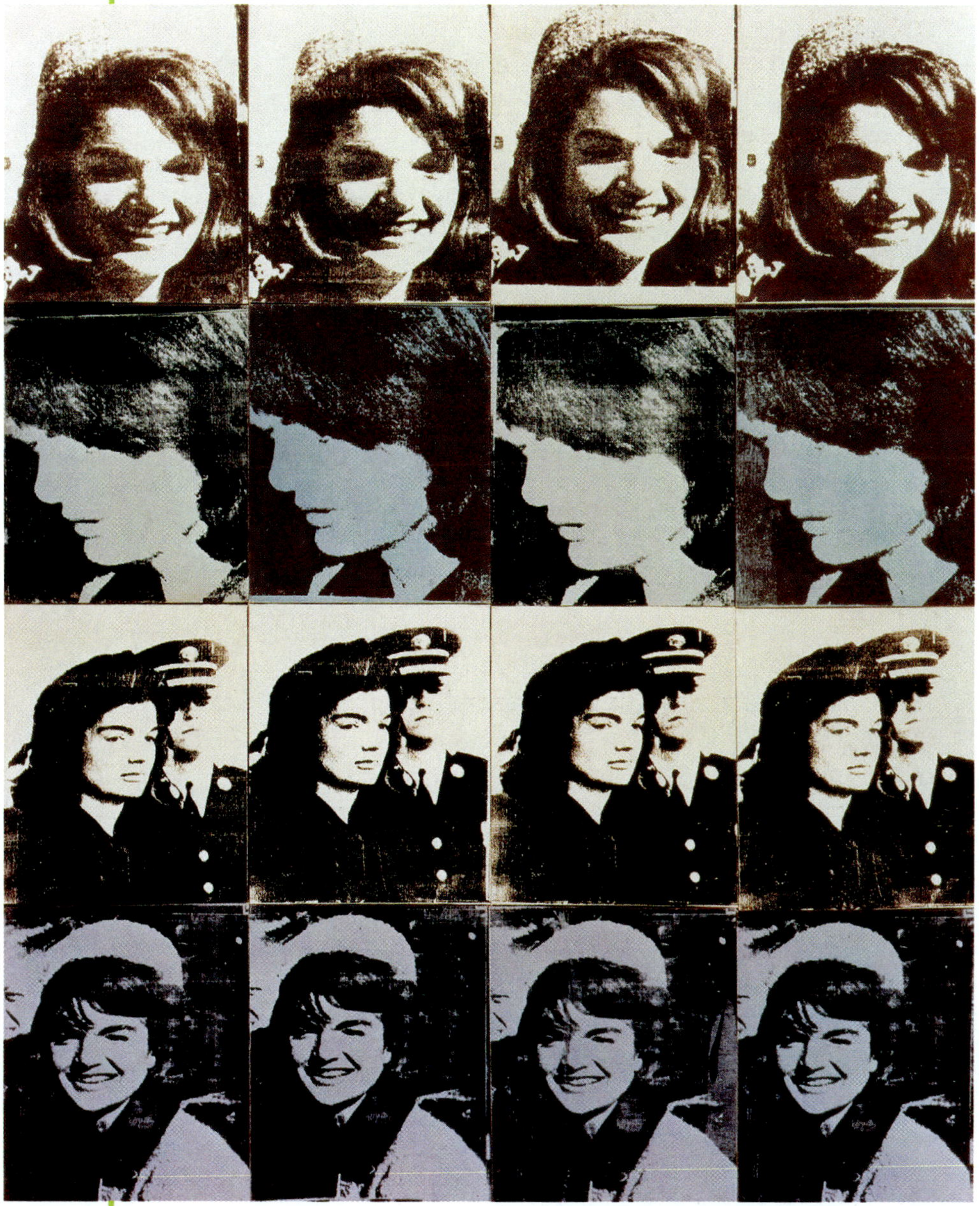

▲ Andy Warhol, *Sixteen Jackies*, 1964

PREPARE YOUR TASK

c. Be creative: In pairs or groups:
- Decide what key figure you would choose today.
- Select significant moments of his / her life.
- In the style of Warhol, make your own poster / piece of art and present it to the class.
Justify your choice and be prepared to answer your classmates' questions.

Help!

Jackie Kennedy's life
first lady
widow: *veuve*
funeral: *enterrement*
grief /griːf/: *chagrin*
in mourning /'mɔːnɪŋ/: *en deuil*
beaming: *très souriante*

Techniques
device: *procédé*
collage /kə'lɑːʒ/
(a) photograph: *(une) photographie*
close /kləʊs/ up: *plan rapproché*
similar
replicate: *reproduire*

Interpretation
fame: *renommée*
public figure
icon /'aɪkɒn/: *figure emblématique*
haunted /'hɔːntɪd/ by death
mortal
embody = personify

3 I want

1 Down in the Mall

There's a brand new shopping center seven
Storeys[1] high
There's bound to be a sale or two--something
We can buy
There's four floors of parking and we're sure
To find a space
We'll spend all the money that the government
Doesn't take

Chorus
Down in the mall
I'll be your man
We'll go shopping, babe
It's something we can stand
Down in the mall

We will abide[2]
Up on the escalator
Darling, we will ride

Shopping for a pair of shoes, shopping for a hat
We're buying some of this and we're buying
Some of that
We'll shop up a storm 'til we can't shop no more
Then we're stopping off at the video store

Chorus

We'll be alright
Monday through Saturday
Til nine o'clock at night

We're buying CDs and we're buying lingerie
We'll put it on a charge account[3] we're never
Gonna pay
Department store, camera store, tobacco store,
Appliance[4] store
Sporting goods, oriental imports,
You buy everything you want and then you
Want more

Chorus

We will abide
Up on the escalator
Darling, we will ride
Down in the mall

▲ Written by Warren Zevon c. 1989 Zevon Music BMI (© EMI Music Publishing)

1. (US) storey = floor **2.** (formal) stay **3.** *compte à crédit*
4. /əˈplaɪəns/ *électro-ménager*

◄ Keith Haring, *Andy Mouse*, 1986

2 Understanding the song

a. Read the lyrics, then close your book. What words, or lines are repeated?
b. List the different places and various objects that are referred to in the song.
c. - Who is the narrator? Who is the other character mentioned?
- What are they planning to do?
d. What characterises these two people? Justify your choices by quoting lines. They are:
• reasonable • successful • careful • strange • responsible • excessive
• shopaholics (= addicted to shopping)
e. In your opinion, what is really important in the life of these people?

PREPARE YOUR TASK

3 Big splash!

Group A

- What immediately strikes you? What does this setting remind you of?
- What are the dominant colours? What is the atmosphere like?

Group B

- What type of house is this? Where could it be located?
- What can you deduce about the owner (social background, job/occupation, living conditions, lifestyle, hobbies, etc.) ?

Recap

- Does this painting make you dream? Why or why not?
- You pass-by this house with a friend (you can be the two people from the song). Imagine the conversation.

▲ David Hockney, *A Bigger Splash*, 1967

4 Cover flow

PREPARE YOUR TASK

A friend of yours has chosen this painting to illustrate the song by Warren Zevon on a playlist for his MP3 player. Discuss his choice. You can suggest another illustration. Give arguments to support your views.

Help!

The couple	Big Splash !	Interpretation
up-to-date: *récent* trendy = fashionable superficial /ˌsuːpəˈfɪʃəl/ materialistic /məˌtɪəriəˈlɪstɪk/ (be) bored to death (be) into sth = (be) interested in	movie setting / film scene palm tree diving board: *plongeoir* luxurious /lʌɡˈʒʊəriəs/ privileged wealthy = well-off = rich show off: *vouloir impressionner*	consumer society emptiness sanitised /ˈsænɪtaɪzd/: *aseptisé* exaggerate denounce / expose imitate brainwash sb into V-ING

4 Please

1 Observe and speak

▲ Roy Lichtenstein, *Eddie Diptych*, 1962

a. What does this painting remind you of? Why?
b. What strikes you? What are the dominant colours?
c. In groups, focus on one of the characters. Can you imagine what the problem is?
Group A: On the left-hand side
- Who is speaking? Justify by quoting from the text.
- Who is she thinking about? What can we guess about her feelings?
- What is happening in her life?

Group B: On the right-hand side
- How does the blond woman react to the other person's words?
- What can you guess about their relationship?

2 Role play

Discuss what the girl and her parents might say to each other after this scene and act the dialogue out.

3 At the Tate Modern

a. Do a little research on Roy Lichtenstein, find paintings you particularly like.
b. You are in charge of the exhibition **'Lichtenstein, a Retrospective'**. Discuss which painting you will print on the exhibition flyers.

PREPARE YOUR TASK

Help!

comic strip: *bande dessinée*
print: *reproduction*
canvas //ˈkænvəs/ : *toile*
frame: *cadre, vignette*
speech balloon
thick outline: *contour épais*
dot: *point*
parody
ordinary = everyday life situation
enlarge /ɪnˈlɑːdʒ/: *agrandir*

5 Pop Icon

1 **a.** Look at the painting. What immediately strikes you: colours • figures • actions • attitudes?

b. In groups, work on the interpretation:
- Decide which text best corresponds to the painting.
Justify your answer.

A. Radically opposed to unrestrained mass consumption, Keith Haring criticized capitalism and the consumer society by showing individuals were crushed down by the dominant, never-ending desire for possessing more products.

B. Keith Haring was concerned by all forms of discrimination, best represented by racism and colonization. That's why he denounced the slavery and oppression or plunder[1] in colonized countries that led to the birth of poverty.

1. *pillage*

▲ Keith Haring, *Untitled*, 1982

C. A number of Keith Haring's paintings showed his revolt against institutions. He defended individuality and freedom against the invasive, strong power of the state, for example.

- Do you think Keith Haring's criticism is still valid today? Give precise examples to illustrate your point of view.
Give a title to the painting.

c. Log on http://www.haring.com and find information about the artist.

Help!

Situation

wolf: *loup*

vivid colours
garish: *criard*
careless: *peu soucieux de*
pitiless = merciless

crush: *écraser*
throw into the air

Interpretation

pawn: *pion*
dictatorship: *dictature*

strong ≠ weak
powerful ≠ powerless

be considered an object
get rid of: *se débarrasser de*
fire = sack: *licencier*

PREPARE YOUR TASK

2 **Work in pairs**

One of you is Keith Haring, the painter of this work. The other is a journalist giving the interview. In your conversation, give a brief description of the painting, then talk about the artist and his technique, and the message he wants to convey.

LANGUAGE AT WORK

+ WORKBOOK
→ Apprendre à apprendre p. 121 - 122

Le quasi certain, le possible et l'impossible: *must, may / might, can't*

Précis, p.257

Les modaux sont utilisés par l'énonciateur :
- soit pour évaluer les chances qu'un événement a de se produire (degré de probabilité)
- soit pour exprimer la contrainte, l'absence de contrainte ou la "capacité".

Observez

1 **Dans quel énoncé must n'exprime-t-il pas une quasi-certitude ?**

a. *She started painting at 8. She must be talented.*

b. *I must tell him the museum is closed today!*

c. *The girl is crying. She must be miserable.*

d. *They must be really irresponsible to spend so much money on gadgets.*

e. *She doesn't want to speak to him anymore. She must be very angry with him.*

2 **Quelle est la valeur de *can't* dans ces phrases ?**

The woman was doing her shopping with her rollers on.

*It **can't** be true. Are you kidding me?*

The girl is eighteen.

*She **can't** be that young!*

3 **Quasi-certain ou possible / peu probable?**

a. Classez les énoncés suivants en deux colonnes en fonction de la valeur du modal :
Quasi-certain • Possible/Peu probable

- *Her shopping-cart is full. She must have a large family.*
- *They may be bored to death to spend a whole day in a mall.*
- *The girl looks quite young – she must be in her twenties.*
- *She may change her mind and call him.*
- *The girl has not spoken a word for days. Her parents must be worried.*
- *They might make it up* (se réconcilier) *one day, but I doubt it.*

b. En fonction du sens de la phrase, reformulez chacun des énoncés ci-dessus à l'aide de *perhaps* ou *certainly*. Puis, traduisez-les.

Entraînez-vous

1 **Repérez l'expression française qui indique le degré de probabilité puis trouvez le modal correspondant en anglais.**

a. Elle est sans doute fâchée.
b. Elle aura peut-être un avenir brillant.
c. Elle ne sait pas trop si elle va le revoir.
d. Elle va peut-être le revoir.
e. Il se peut qu'ils achètent une nouvelle caméra.
f. Ce tableau ne peut pas être à la Tate Modern, il est trop ancien.
g. Ce tableau est sûrement très cher.

2 **Réécrivez les phrases suivantes en employant *may* + base verbale ou *must* + base verbale, *can't* + base verbale.**

a. I'm sure he is lonely.
b. Her parents are supportive for sure.
c. Perhaps her parents will manage to cheer her up.
d. It's impossible for her to be so naive.
e. Perhaps they know the truth.
f. I'm positive they know the truth.
g. Perhaps he will tell her the whole truth.
h. It's impossible for them to be so foolish.

3 **Traduisez ces énoncés en français.**

a. He must be a film director.
b. She can't be so stupid!
c. He may write to her and apologize.
d. He can't be so rude and not phone her to say he won't come.
e. She might forgive him.

ON YOUR OWN!

▲ Roy Lichtenstein, *M-Maybe*, 1965

a. Who is the painter? How do you know?
b. Where is the girl? What is she doing? Who is she thinking about?
c. Imagine why she is wearing gloves/glʌvz/ *(gants)*?

Don't forget to use modals in your answer!

d. What can we guess about her age, her social background and her feelings?
e. What can we guess about the man's job?
f. Imagine reasons why he is late.
g. What might happen next?

SAVOIR DÉBATTRE

1 Apprendre à écouter MP3 PISTE 35 CD3 PISTE 15

Écoutez le dialogue.

a. Identifiez le point de vue de chaque interlocuteur. Quels arguments chacun d'eux avance-t-il ?
b. Sur papier libre recopiez la grille ci-dessous et complétez-la.

Mots, expressions, structures utilisés pour…	…réagir…	…donner son opinion…	…argumenter / commenter…
…positivement			
…négativement			

2 Apprendre à parler MP3 PISTE 35 CD3 PISTE 15

Lisez la fin de la conversation.

- WOMAN: Don't you like Warhol's Campbell Soup?

- MAN: That painting! Hang on! What is the point of this? I'm, I'm just trying to understand.
It's a can of soup; I can open my cupboard and look at that.

- WOMAN: You can, yes, but you wouldn't look at it that way if it hadn't been painted. You'd just, you'd just take it down and not see that it has a shape, it has dimensions, it has colour. You wouldn't look at the object in itself, you know. It would be a can of soup. That's, that's the way, eh, that's the way I understand it.

- MAN: Nonsense.

a. Classez les arguments en deux colonnes : pour et contre.
b. Par groupe de deux : Choisissez un rôle et répétez les répliques enregistrées à haute voix en suivant le modèle donné.

Veillez à respecter :
- la réduction des voyelles dans un grand nombre de syllabes non accentuées (cf. p. 237).
- les liaisons consonne - voyelle
- les intonations (pour donner l'impression d'être sûr(e) de vous, utilisez des intonations descendantes. Une intonation montante implique doute et incertitude).
- les mots mis particulièrement en relief.

Puis inversez les rôles.

3 Your turn!

Practise giving your point of view and reacting to the quotes below: do you agree or disagree? Why? Prepare three arguments and discuss them in groups of 3 or 4.

"No great artist ever sees things as they really are. If he did he would cease to be an artist."
OSCAR WILDE

"Art is not what you see, but what you make others see."
EDGAR DEGAS

"Art is for everybody."
KEITH HARING

YOUR TASK

The school board has decided to buy two life-size posters of Pop Art to be displayed in your high school. You are on the Selection Committee that will debate and choose the artworks.

Before the debate

1. Choose your role:

- a member of the school board
- a student
- a student's parent
- a member of the school administration
- a(n) (art) teacher

2. Choose a work of art: it can be one of the pieces of art in your book (p. 182-183) or another artwork you have found somewhere else. Prepare your arguments to support your choice.

Brush up on your debating vocabulary using p.180 and page 232.

TIPS
Why did you choose this particular work? What will it bring to your school? What does it mean? How much will it cost?

On the day

3. Bring a copy of the artwork you want to see displayed in your school. Defend your choice in front of the Selection Committee: explain why the artwork you have chosen should be in the top three. Be convincing!

TIPS
Stress the important words; keep eye contact with the others; express your opinions....

Your presentation must not be longer than 1 minute. You will have extra time to defend your project in the exchange with the rest of the class.

4. After everyone's presentation, the Selection Committee will discuss the pros and cons of the various pieces.

TIPS
Listen to one another, add arguments. You may object to the others' suggestions but always remain calm and polite!

5. Proceed to the vote: you may vote for your piece or for someone else's work you finally find more appropriate… but in the end you will all have to agree on the 2 final choices.

◄ Claes Oldenburg, *Pastry Case 1*, 1962

YOUR TASK

▲ Roy Lichtenstein, *"Ohhh...Alright..."*, 1964

▲ Andy Warhol, *Ten Marilyns*, 1967

▲ Tom Wesselmann, *Still Life*, 1962

▲ Keith Haring, *Untitled*, 1982

Évaluation sommative
Speaking interaction

J'évalue mes progrès

Je revois les stratégies apprises dans les unités précédentes (*Improve Your Speaking Skills* p.154, 166 et 180) afin de faire le bilan de mes compétences.

1. Je me prépare

Vous vous promenez dans la rue avec un(e) ami(e). Vous voyez cette affiche et vous réagissez : mobilisez le lexique que vous connaissez.

a. Vous exprimez votre opinion : donnez trois amorces de phrase.
b. Vous voulez donner des exemples, comment les introduisez-vous ? (trois expressions)
c. Vous souhaitez récapituler ce que vous venez de dire. Donnez deux exemples d'expressions à utiliser.
d. Vous ne comprenez pas votre ami(e), vous lui demandez des explications supplémentaires. Quelles phrases allez-vous utiliser ? Donnez trois exemples.
e. Trouvez deux structures pour exprimer votre accord avec ce qu'il/elle a dit.
f. Listez trois expressions pour exprimer votre désaccord avec les propos de votre ami(e).
g. Vous voulez couper la parole poliment à votre ami(e). Utilisez deux expressions.

2. Je prends la parole

Exprimez vos réactions face à ce document et commentez-le.

3. Je me corrige

CD3 PISTE 16 MP3 PISTE 36

Écoutez l'enregistrement correspondant à cette affiche et comparez vos réponses à celles d'Emily et de Ben qui ont été interviewés.

Je fais le bilan

Analysez vos résultats à l'aide de cette grille d'évaluation où sont définis les différents niveaux de compétence en production orale en interaction. Le niveau attendu en classe de seconde est B1.

Je peux...	Niveau
... participer à une conversation simple à condition que mon interlocuteur parle lentement et m'aide à trouver mes mots.	**A2 en cours d'acquisition**
... discuter sur des sujets simples de la vie quotidienne même si je n'arrive pas à comprendre toute la conversation dans les détails. ... exprimer mes goûts, mon opinion, mes sentiments au cours d'une conversation. ... participer à des conversations avec des jeunes de mon âge et parler de sujets qui nous concernent (musique, sports, jeux vidéos, environnement...).	**A2**
... discuter de divers sujets en exprimant mes sentiments. ... interroger quelqu'un pour connaître son opinion et exprimer mon opinion poliment. ... couper la parole à quelqu'un poliment si je n'ai pas compris ce qu'il disait ou pour exprimer mon désaccord. ... reformuler mes propos si mon interlocuteur ne me comprend pas. ... réagir pour exprimer mon désaccord. ... être à l'origine d'une discussion (aborder un sujet qui m'intéresse).	**B1**
... être à l'origine d'une discussion, la poursuivre en relançant la conversation et la conclure. ... participer activement à une conversation (sans avoir préparé mon intervention). ... défendre mes idées en les argumentant. ... résumer les idées suggérées, peser le pour et le contre de ces arguments.	**En route vers B2**

Évaluation

Votre professeur va vous demander de réagir par groupe de deux à partir de la situation figurant sur votre fiche. Plusieurs jeux de rôles seront proposés sur chacune des unités travaillées en cours.

Unit 10 **Green Art**

Unit 11 **On Stage**

Unit 12 **Pop Goes My Art**

Vous devez prendre connaissance de la situation proposée, puis en discuter avec un autre élève. Donnez votre opinion, défendez votre point de vue et illustrez vos propos par des exemples concrets.

Temps de préparation individuel : 5 minutes

Temps de parole : 1 à 2 minutes

⚠ Ne rédigez pas votre texte, vous n'aurez droit qu'à des notes.

Une fois l'évaluation terminée, votre professeur pourra ainsi déterminer à quel niveau vous vous situez par rapport à la grille d'évaluation du Cadre Européen Commun de Référence pour les Langues.

▲ *Becoming Jane*, Julian Jarrold, 2007 (starring Anne Hathaway)

Writing

Unit 13 City in the Sky

SENTIMENT D'APPARTENANCE • MÉMOIRE

- Explore New York City, visit the monuments and different districts.
- Read about the experience of immigrants when they landed at Ellis Island.
- Discover the culture (past and present) and atmosphere of a vibrant city.

YOUR TASK You work for a travel agency. Write the script of a slideshow promoting New York City or a flyer advertising a three-day break to the Big Apple.

p. 197

Unit 14 Summer Rocks

SENTIMENT D'APPARTENANCE • MÉMOIRE

- Discover the tradition of summer festivals in Great Britain:
  - the Edinburgh Fringe in Scotland
  - Wakestock on the Welsh coast
  - the Notting Hill Carnival in London
  - Glyndebourne and Glastonbury

YOUR TASK You want to go to one of Britain's famous festivals. Exchange emails with a British travel agency to prepare for your trip.

p. 209

Unit 15 Masters of Suspense

SENTIMENT D'APPARTENANCE • MÉMOIRE

- Meet Alfred Hitchcock and learn his techniques for creating suspense.
- Who is the father of the detective story? *Elementary, my dear Watson!*
- Use your powers of observation and deduction to solve murder mysteries.

YOUR TASK Creative writing contest: write a short extract for a detective story or create a short film based on several pictures. Which story or film script will be published in the school newspaper or on the school website?

p. 221

Unit 13

City in the Sky

YOUR TASK AT THE END OF THIS UNIT

You work for a travel agency. Write the script of a slideshow promoting New York City or create a flyer advertising a three-day break there.

p. 197

1 Tune In!

1 Take a bite of the Big Apple! WB p. 78

a. Read the description of each building and match it with the picture it corresponds to. Justify your answers by quoting key words from the paragraphs.

b. With the help of your Workbook find more details about each building, then locate them on the map of Manhattan.

c. Take part in a 'Treasure Hunt' and learn more about New York City.

A The Freedom Tower claims top spot in the city's skyline. With its patriotic 1,776 feet and 104 floors, this super-tall skyscraper stands on the site of the former World Trade Center and as such reasserts Lower Manhattan's predominance as a business center. This tall, pointed tower on the tip of Manhattan has a cubic base and a steel frame with glass to the outside of the structure. A spire[1] and antenna mast have been added to the top. It rises into the sky in a faceted, crystalline form filled with, and reflecting, light.

1. *flèche*

B The Guggenheim Museum is a modern art museum. It can be found at the corner of 89th Street and Fifth Avenue (overlooking[1] Central Park). Frank Lloyd Wright designed it in 1959. From the street, the building looks like a white ribbon curled[2] around a cylinder[3], wider at the top than the bottom. The round appearance of the building is in contrast with the more typical box-like Manhattan buildings that surround it.

1. *avec vue sur* 2. *ruban enroulé* 3. /ˈsɪlɪndə/

3

4

C **The Chrysler Building** is surely the jewel in the crown of New York City's skyline. The 77-story[1] Art Deco skyscraper was the tallest in the world at the time it was completed in 1930. It quickly became the symbol of big city glamor, excitement, and style. It is recognizable thanks to its spire[2] with the crescent-shaped steps made of steel[3]. The top of the tower reminds us of car radiators, which is perfect for the headquarters of an automaker. You can enter the building from three sides: Lexington Avenue, 42nd and 43rd Streets.

1. *étage* **2.** *flèche* **3.** *acier*

D **The Empire State Building** has been featured[1] in almost a hundred Hollywood films over the years. It is the most famous landmark on the New York skyline. It's a limestone[2] classic built in just 410 days during the Great Depression[3]. The 102-story, 1472ft-high (to the top of the antenna) skyscraper, which is located at 350 5th Avenue, opened in 1931. The view of the vast city from the Empire State Building is just spectacular, but be prepared to queue for a long time to get to the observation decks, found on the 86th and 102nd floors.

1. presented as a special attraction **2.** *(roche) calcaire* **3.** economic and financial crisis in the1930s

2 Play with words

WB P.79

Turn to your Workbook to improve your vocabulary.

CD3 PISTE 17

3 Lady Liberty

WB P.80

a. How much do you know about the statue?
b. Listen to the recording and learn more about it and its symbols.

video

4 Watch a video: New York Overview

PREPARE YOUR TASK

a. Watch the video, then turn to your worksheet for help.
b. Identify the most famous sights of New York: pick out as many key words as you can to characterize them.
c. You are the webmaster of a travel agency website. Write a short paragraph to present the video and encourage people to watch it.

2 The Golden Door

CD3 PISTE 18

1 Ellis Island
WB P.81

a. Listen to the recording and pick out as many stressed words as you can.
b. In groups, recap what you have learnt about:
- **immigrants**: number, period of time, native countries, reasons for leaving, conditions of transportation.
- **Ellis Island**: definition, opening and closing dates, what the immigrants had to go through, percentage of people sent back to Europe.
- **regulations**: goals, periods of time, consequences.

2 Getting through
WB P.82

a. Read the following extracts about the immigrants' arrival at Ellis Island.
b. The paragraphs have been mixed up. Re-organize them in chronological order with the help of the pictures.

A Those who failed[1] to get past both doctors had to undergo a more complete medical exam. The others moved on to the registration clerk[2], who questioned them with the aid of an interpreter: what is your name? Your nationality? Your occupation? Can you read and write? Have you ever been in prison? How much money do you have with you? Where are you going?
Some immigrants were so upset that they could not answer. They were allowed to sit and rest and try again.
About one immigrant out of every five or six[3] was detained for additional examinations or questioning.

1. échouaient 2. employé responsable de l'inscription sur les registres 3. un immigrant sur cinq ou six

B Filing into an enormous inspection hall, the immigrants formed long lines separated by iron railings[1].
Now the examinations began. First the immigrants were examined by two doctors of the United States Health Service. One doctor looked for physical and mental abnormalities. When a case aroused suspicion, the immigrant received a chalk[2] mark on the right shoulder for further inspection: L for lameness[3], H for heart, X for mental defects, and so on.

1. grilles de fer 2. /tʃɔːk/ craie 3. claudication (claudiquer = boiter)

C Immigrants usually crossed the Atlantic as steerage[1] passengers. Because steerage conditions were crowded[2] and uncomfortable, passengers spent as much time as possible on deck[3]. The voyage was an ordeal[4], but it was worth it[5]. They were on their way to America. The great majority of immigrants landed in New York City, at America's busiest port. They never forgot their first glimpse at the Statue of Liberty.

1. *troisième classe* **2.** *(ici) les passagers étaient sérrés les uns contre les autres* **3.** *pont* **4.** *épreuve* **5.** *en valait la peine*

D The second doctor watched for contagious and infectious diseases[1]. Since trachoma caused more than half of all medical detentions, this doctor was greatly feared. He stood directly in the immigrant's path[2]. With a swift movement, he would grab[3] the immigrant's eyelid, pull it up[4], and look beneath[5] it. If all was well, the immigrant was passed on.

1. *maladies* **2.** *sur le chemin* **3.** *attrapait* **4.** *retroussait* **5.** *en dessous*

E When their ship docked[1] at a Hudson River pier[2], the immigrants had numbered identity tags pinned to their clothing. Then they were herded[3] onto special ferryboats that carried them to Ellis Island. Officials hurried them along, shouting "Quick! Run! Hurry!" in half a dozen languages.

1. *se mettait à quai* **2.** *jetée* **3.** *rassemblés comme un troupeau*

▲Adapted from Russell Freedman, *Immigrant Kids*, 1995

3 Role play

Choose a role: • customs officer • doctor • an immigrant family (father, mother and child). List the questions the immigrants were asked and imagine their answers.

Help!

Places and atmosphere

steerage /ˈstɪərɪdʒ/: *troisième classe*
deck: *pont*
pen: *enclos*

stifling /ˈstaɪflɪŋ/: *étouffant*
overcrowded /ˌəʊvəˈkraʊdɪd/

Actions

cry
go through
control
expect

Impressions and feelings

moved: *ému*
impressed
frightened /ˈfraɪtnd/
relieved: *soulagé*

fear that sth / sb might…

PREPARE YOUR TASK

4 Remembering things past

Look at the painting opposite and write the letter the parents sent to their relatives in their native country. Include the following elements: crossing (*traversée*) to the US, landing, inspections, first impressions, feelings and reactions (150 words).

3 The Dream City

Uuuu, New York (x 2)

Grew up in a town
That is famous as a place of movie scenes,
Noise is always loud
There are sirens all around,
And the streets are mean[1]
If I can make it here,
I could make it anywhere,
That's what they say
Seeing my face in lights,
Or my name on marquees[2] found down on Broadway

Even if it ain't[3] all it seems
I got a pocket full of dreams

CHORUS
Baby I'm from New York!
Concrete[4] jungle where dreams are made of,
There's nothing you can't do
Now you're in New York!
These streets will make you feel brand new,
Big lights will inspire you,
Hear it for New York!
(New York, New York)

On the avenue,
There ain't never a curfew[5], ladies work so hard
Such a melting pot
On the corner selling rock
Preachers pray to God,
Hail a gipsy cab[6],
Takes me down from Harlem to the Brooklyn Bridge

Someone sleeps tonight
With a hunger for more than an empty fridge

I'm going to make it by any means,
I got a pocket full of dreams,

CHORUS
One hand in the air for the big city,
Street lights, big dreams, all looking pretty
No place in the world that can compare
Put your lighters in the air,
Everybody say Yeah, Yeah,
Yeah, Yeah!

New York,

CHORUS

▲ Alicia Keys, *Empire State of Mind II, Broken Down*, 2009

1. *(ici) impitoyables* **2.** *portiques d'entrée des théâtres* **3.** (familiar) isn't **4.** *béton* **5.** *couvre-feu* **6.** illegal taxi

1 Empire State of Mind

a. Read the lyrics, then close your books. Which words or phrases can you remember? Which lines are repeated?
b. Pick out the name of a district, a monument, and a famous street.
c. What do you learn about the narrator's origin? Quote the text.
d. Pick out words, phrases (groups of words) or lines related to:

▲ Georgia O'Keeffe, *City Night*, 1926

- Success, opportunities and dreams
- New York City
- A unique place
- A multicultural city
- A competitive and hectic (*trépidante*) life

e. What does the narrator dream of? Why? Does she believe she will achieve her goal?
f. New York is nicknamed 'the city that never sleeps'. Where is this illustrated in the song?
g. *'A place of movie scenes'* (l.3): go on the Internet and find concrete examples that can illustrate what the singer means by this.
www.easynewyorkcity.com/movielocations.htm
h. Would you say the tone is: ironic • funny • sad • enthusiastic • critical • laudatory (*élogieux*) • optimistic?
Justify your answer by quoting key words from the song.

Help!

Description
energy
magic
pulse = beat, throb, vibe
impressive
glamorous
inspiring /ɪnˈspaɪərɪŋ/
on the move

Feelings
excited
fascinated

fulfil one's dreams: *réaliser ses rêves*
achieve one's goals: *atteindre son but*
start from scratch: *repartir à zéro*
praise: *faire l'éloge de*

Comments
subjective ≠ objective

approve of... ≠ object to
I agree with... ≠ I disagree with...
refer to: *faire référence à*
mention
for instance = for example

PREPARE YOUR TASK

2 Action!

You are a fan of this song. Write a comment on the Internet to say why you love it.

3 Karaoke

Sing the song to improve your pronunciation.

CD3 PISTE 19

4 A multicultural city

WB P.84

Listen to Kareem describing his home city.

PREPARE YOUR TASK

5 Writing workshop

You take part in a song contest. Write a stanza or a complete song celebrating New York (100-150 words).

LANGUAGE AT WORK

+ WORKBOOK
→ Apprendre à apprendre p. 123 - 124

A La forme passive

Précis, p. 260

Observez

1. *New York City* ***is divided*** *into five boroughs.*
2. *The Twin Towers* ***were destroyed*** *in the 9/11 attacks.*
3. *The 9/11 attacks* ***will*** *always* ***be remembered*** *as a trauma for America.*
4. *Harlem* ***has been rehabilitated*** *over the last few years.*
5. *The skyscrapers that* ***have been built*** *in New York are in Midtown and Lower Manhattan.*
6. *The Statue of Liberty* ***was designed by*** *Auguste Bartholdi and Gustave Eiffel.*

Quels éléments grammaticaux composent les formes verbales en gras ? Quel élément est conjugué ? A quoi sert *'by'* ?

Déduisez

Sur papier libre, recopiez ce schéma et complétez-le.

Auxiliaire ... conjugué — **+ ... d'un** { **verbe régulier ...** / **verbe irrégulier ...** } **+ *by* introduit le ...**

Observez

a. *The Trump Tower* ***was designed*** *by Polish architect Marta Rudzka.*
b. *The building* ***was*** *much* ***admired****.*

Dans chacune de ces phrases, l'agent est-il mentionné ou non ? Traduisez les énoncés ci-dessus.

Déduisez

Quand le complément d'agent du passif n'est pas mentionné, l'équivalent en français utilise généralement ... .

Entraînez-vous

1 Complétez ce récapitulatif sur Ellis Island en utilisant des formes passives.

Ellis Island ***(locate)*** *in New York Harbor. It* ***(call)*** *Gibbet Island in the early 18th century after pirates* ***(hang)****. Then it* ***(use)*** *to process immigrants before they could enter America, that is why their health and criminal records* ***(check)*** *carefully. It is now an attraction which* ***(visit)*** *by many tourists every year.*

2 Découvrez les origines de la ville de New York.
Reconstruisez les phrases au passif en utilisant les éléments donnés dans l'ordre. Faites les ajustements nécessaires.

a. *The place where New York is located / discover / Giovanni da Verrazano / in 1524.*
b. *That same area / occupy / the Algonquins / in the 16th century.*
c. *In 1624 / a colony named New Amsterdam / establish / the Dutch West India Company.*
d. *It / name / New York / in 1665 / in honor of the Duke of York / when Manhattan / seize / English forces.*
e. *The city / take / George Washington / at the end of the Revolutionary War / in 1783.*

Entraînez-vous

3 Traduisez les phrases suivantes.

a. On a créé Central Park d'après les plans de Frederick Law Olmsted et de Calvert Vaux.
b. Quand on a bâti le Chrysler Building en 1930, il était alors le plus haut gratte-ciel du monde.
c. On connaît le Guggenheim dans le monde entier à cause de sa forme bizarre.
d. On tourne *(shoot)* beaucoup de films à New York parce que l'on y trouve toute la diversité que l'on veut.

4 Guess what?

Individually, write down a few sentences about a monument or landmark in NYC. Describe it using passive forms only and DO NOT give its name! The rest of the class will try to guess which is referred to.

B Improve your vocabulary

1 Classez les mots suivants en deux colonnes: *urban life - fascination*. Utilisez un dictionnaire si nécessaire.

flashy billboards - busy - colorful - impressive -hectic - dizzy - noisy - loud - amazing- vibrant - breathtaking - hypnotized - stunning - astonishing - lively - traffic jam -overcrowded

2 L'ordre des adjectifs

a. Dans chacun de ces groupes nominaux, quel adjectif exprime le point de vue subjectif de l'énonciateur ?

1. *a crazy dark-haired French sculptor* **2.** *an original seventy-five-story skyscraper*
3. *a scary 1776-step staircase* **4.** *an impressive century-old steel building*

Complétez la phrase suivante: Quand on utilise plusieurs adjectifs devant un nom, on place … celui/ceux qui exprime(nt) le point de vue subjectif de l'énonciateur.

b. Observez les mots *story* et *step* dans les énoncés 2 et 3. Que remarquez-vous ?

ON YOUR OWN!

Imagine the teaser you could write for a new disaster film or the radio ad you will record to promote your production. Use the words in the *Help!* box and passive forms when necessary.

Help!

inhabitants
casualties: *victimes*
violent storm
tidal /ˈtaɪdəl/ wave: *raz de marée*
tornado /tɔːˈneɪdəʊ/ = twister (US)
heavy rain
hit
flood /flʌd/: *inonder*
drown /draʊn/: *(se) noyer*
evacuate
injure: *blesser*
knock /nɒk/ down
collapse: *s'effondrer*
submerge
rescue
survive

IMPROVE YOUR WRITING SKILLS

COMMENT ÉCRIRE UN PARAGRAPHE POUR PROMOUVOIR UN LIEU, UN MONUMENT OU UNE ACTIVITÉ ?

THIS IS NOT JUST ANY CITY, IT IS THE CITY, THE BIG APPLE. This is the place to be. This is the port where the immigrants landed and the door to America. It's the center of the world. This is joggers in Central Park and the most fabulous matches you can dream of in Yankee Stadium. This is Times Square on New Year's Eve. This is the best bagels[1] and pizza, pretzel and hot dog stands. Marino's ice creams are the yummiest in the world. This is huge department stores on 5th Avenue, the bull on Wall Street, gospel and red hot jazz in Harlem. Uptown, downtown, shop till you drop, style and design, it's all the rage. It's hailing yellow cabs "Taxi!" or squeezing into a packed subway train. This is five cities in one: Manhattan, Brooklyn, Queens, Staten Island and the Bronx. People moving, pushing, going, always in a hurry. Stress and excitement. A vertical city, skyscrapers tickling the clouds. Elevators and electric lights. Cars and traffic-jams. People and progress. Mingling[2] and mixing. This is so inspiring and intense you can feel it deep in your soul. This is such an exceptional and extraordinary city that you will remember your trip there all your life. One thing and its opposite. MY CITY AND YOURS. This is New York City.

1. a bread roll (*petit pain*) shaped like a ring 2. intermixing

1 Observez

1. Lisez le document ci-dessus. Quel en est le thème principal ?
2. Quels éléments attirent votre attention dans la mise en page ?
3. Repérez la phrase d'accroche. Que remarquez-vous ?
4. Donnez un titre à chaque groupe de phrases. *Ex* : introduction, sport…
5. Sur papier libre, relevez la répétition utilisée, les adjectifs, les superlatifs, les propositions relatives, les phrases plus complexes (subordonnées) et classez-les dans un tableau.

2 À vous

1. Choisissez un des aspects de New York que vous voulez promouvoir : lieu particulier, monuments, gratte-ciels, quartiers, musique, mode, cinéma …
2. Rédigez un paragraphe (8-10 lignes) à l'aide des éléments repérés plus haut qui vous permettront d'attirer l'attention de votre lecteur.

CONSEILS

- Utilisez des adjectifs plus précis que : *good, bad, big, cool.* Réemployez les adjectifs repérés dans l'affiche ou appris p. 193, par exemple : *breathtaking* (à couper le souffle), *innovative, impressive…*
- Chercher des verbes plus précis que *do*, *be*, *have*.
- Utilisez des propositions relatives ou subordonnées.

YOUR TASK

You work for a travel agency. Write the script of a slideshow promoting New York City or create a flyer advertising a three-day break there.

Scénario 1

1. Choisissez au minimum 3 aspects de New York qui vous frappent le plus.

a) Sélectionnez un site de la ville (parc, quartier…) un monument (gratte-ciel, musée…), une œuvre artistique (musique, cinéma…), etc.
b) Complétez vos connaissances sur Internet ou à l'aide d'une encyclopédie.
c) Cherchez des photos représentatives.

▲ *The Wall Steet Bull*, Arturo Di Modica

2. Rédigez le texte qui accompagne chacune des photos.

a) Dépassez la simple description de l'image. Apportez un maximum d'informations et d'idées avec un lexique approprié et précis.
b) Ecrivez un ou plusieurs paragraphes par thème.
c) Mobilisez les stratégies acquises p.196 y compris pour la typographie (mise en page, police, caractères...).
d) Trouvez un titre à chaque diapositive.

Aérez l'ensemble :
- pensez aux alinéas,
- sautez une ligne entre chaque paragraphe.

3. Organisez votre diaporama.

a) Classez les différentes diapositives selon une progression logique (historique, géographique, etc).
b) Trouvez un titre général et accrocheur pour l'ensemble du diaporama.
c) Personnalisez votre diaporama: travaillez les transitions, ajoutez un fond sonore...

Scénario 2

Rédigez une brochure faisant la promotion d'un séjour de 3 jours à New York.
Sélectionnez :
- les différents monuments ou musées à visiter
- les endroits à découvrir (lieux touristiques connus, endroits où des films célèbres ont été tournés, quartiers...)
- les divertissements nocturnes
- les restaurants où goûter les différentes spécialités new-yorkaises

Soyez convaincants ! Trouvez des arguments pour justifier vos choix.

Reading Corner

Find the similarities and differences between the four documents.

1 [Inga] heard on the radio that a plane had hit the tower eight blocks south. She decided to get Sonia out of school and began to walk downtown when she saw the second plane ram[1] the other tower. She had started to run then, against the crowd streaming toward her, but she didn't register what had happened, not really, but raced to Stuyvesant, where she was stopped by a guard. There was another mother, too, whom they wouldn't let in, a woman whose voice reminded her of a squalling[2] cat at night. Inga remembered the woman's contorted mouth, her saliva hitting the man's collar as she wailed[3], 'Let me in! I want my son!' and how the sight of the woman's face had made her strangely quiet, calm, and distant, and how she had waited for them to find her daughter, standing numb[4] in the lobby, and that when she finally saw Sonia's face, she felt it must match her own, a mask of pallid[5] emptiness, and how when they left the building the towers were gleaming red like burning skeletons, and Inga had said to herself, 'I am seeing this. It is true. I must tell myself this is real,' and then they ran north to White Street without saying a word to each other, running with hundreds of other people pushing forward away from the fires.

1. crash into / hit **2.** *hurlant* **3.** *gémit* **4.** *hébétée* **5.** pale

▲ Siri Hustvedt, *The Sorrows of an American*, 2008

2

3

Arkansas Democrat Gazette
ARKANSAS' NEWSPAPER
Printed at Little Rock • Wednesday, Sept. 12, 2011 arkansas Online www.ardemgaz.com 78 pages 12 sections ** 50 ¢

How many dead?

TERRORIST ACTS STUN AMERICA

ARKANSAS DEMOCRAT-GAZETTE STAFF AND WIRE REPORTS

In parallel attacks on the symbols of American financial and military power, terrorists crashed passenger jets into the World Trade Center in New York and the Pentagon[1] outside Washington on Tuesday.

Two planes hit the Trade Center, the first at 8:45 a.m. EDT[2], the other 18 minutes later, leaving huge holes[3] in the twin, 110-story glass and steel towers. An hour later, with ominous rumbles[4] and colossal showers of debris, the towers collapsed. Witnesses described people on fire jumping in terror, including a man and a woman holding hands.

The plane that hit the Pentagon struck with tremendous force, [...] at 9:40 a.m.

Barbara Olson, the wife of U.S. Solicitor General[5] Theodore Olson, was among the passengers on that plane. She used a cell phone to tell her husband that the plane had been hijacked[6] by attackers using knives and sharp instruments.

Another passenger jet crashed 80 miles southeast of Pittsburgh at 10 a.m. A Virginia congressman, Rep. James Moran, said the intended target of that plane was apparently Camp David, the presidential retreat in Maryland, 85 miles away.

Casualties[7] are sure to be in the thousands, but no one had a count Tuesday. The airliners carried 266 people and there were no known survivors. That alone would surpass the death toll[8] of the April 19, 1995 Oklahoma City bombing, which claimed 168 lives in what was the deadliest act of terrorism on U.S. soil.

Fifty thousand people work at the Trade Center, 20,000 at the Pentagon.

1. headquarters of the Department of Defense **2.** eastern daylight time **3.** *(ici) trous béants* **4.** *grondements menaçants* **5.** law officer **6.** *avait été détourné* **7.** victims **8.** *nombre de morts*

4

Unit 14

Summer Rocks

YOUR TASK AT THE END OF THIS UNIT

You want to go to one of Britain's famous festivals. Exchange emails with a British travel agency to prepare for your trip. p. 209

1 Tune In!

1 Get the feel of it

a. Look at this photo and react. (Who? Where? What? Weather? Attitude? Why?)
b. What kind of document is it? What is its aim?

PREPARE YOUR TASK

2 Are you a fan?

Choose topic **a** or **b**. (50 words)
a. You are one of the people in the crowd above. Post a new status on your favourite social network about your experience (positive or negative).
b. React to this photo your friend has just posted and write a comment saying what kind of music event you would like to attend and why.

3 Play with words

WB p. 86

Turn to your Workbook to improve your vocabulary on travelling and holidays.

Help!

enthusiastic /ɪnθjuːziˈæstɪk/
hysterical
overjoyed = thrilled: *fou de joie*
in the open = outdoors ≠ indoors
overcrowded: *plein de monde*

gig = concert

attend: *assister à*
cheer ≠ boo /buː/
scream / yell: *hurler*
go crazy

4 What's your festival?

a. Take the quiz below to find out what kind of festival best suits your personality. Note down the results on a separate piece of paper.

1. For you, going to a festival means going with …

a) your parents, it's a family activity.
b) your best friend, to have a great time together.
c) a big group of friends, the more the merrier[1]!

2. You would like to go to a festival …

a) to discover new artists and enrich your cultural knowledge.
b) to meet new people and have fun.
c) for the atmosphere, the craziness and the loud music.

3. What is the worst thing that could happen to you at a festival?

a) Heavy rain and a wet tent.
b) You injure yourself[2], and as a result you cannot dance.
c) The sound system breaks and your favourite band cannot play.

4. When you're in a crowd you like to …

a) chill[3] at the back on a blanket[4].
b) make sure you get a spot at the front so you don't miss a thing.
c) try to get on someone's shoulders.

5. Where are you going to sleep?

a) You booked a nice, quiet bed and breakfast a few months before.
b) You have found a hotel close to the festival to be back early the next day.
c) You will be camping with your friends or going to a youth hostel[5].

6. What kind of music do you enjoy most?

a) Classical music.
b) Pop, rock, R'n'B.
c) Heavy metal and hard rock.

7. What do you do in your free time?

a) You spend hours listening to music. You need to relax and feel good.
b) You love dancing to the music you listen to.
c) You do a lot of sport.

1. *plus on est de fous, plus on rit*
2. *vous vous blessez* 3. relax
4. *couverture* 5. *auberge de jeunesse*

b. Read the results. To what extent do they correspond to your personality?

If you answered mainly a

You are the quiet type. You do not like large crowds and you love comfort. You are interested in music but you hate it when it is too loud. Do not choose the large crowded festivals. Go for something quieter. There are plenty of excellent literary and classical music festivals around the UK.

If you answered mainly b

You have eclectic[1] music tastes and you enjoy discovering different cultural events. You are sociable and easygoing, and you like to get things organised before you do anything. Go for the world-famous festivals with varied music styles and street performances you will never forget!

1. *varied*

If you answered mainly c

You intend to live life to the full! Gather a big crowd of friends, and set off for a festival where you will listen to loud music at night and discover extreme sports during the day. Looking for adrenalin? There are some amazing British festivals which offer many hair-raising activities!

2 A Taste of Scotland

1 Discover Edinburgh

a. Locate Edinburgh on the map of the United Kingdom.
b. Go on the following website to learn more about the city:
www.edinburghfestivals.co.uk/explore-edinburgh

2 A guidebook review WB p.87

a. Read about the Edinburgh Festival Fringe and turn to your Workbook for help.
b. Select three phrases that best describe the festival in the text below.

http://www.edinburgh.org/see-do/events/festivals/fringe-free

The largest arts festival anywhere in the world, the magnificent and world-famous Edinburgh Festival Fringe hosts a range of outstanding events and performances. [...]

The Edinburgh Festival Fringe is one of several festivals which takes place in Scotland's capital each August. In 2012, the Fringe featured 42,096 performances of 2,695 shows across 279 spectacular and varied venues[1]. With just under 1.9 million tickets sold, there really is something for everyone here, and more. [...] The Fringe has everything from theatre to children's shows, exhibitions, music and comedy. Throughout the summer, the Fringe completely takes over the city's historic Royal Mile [...]. You will soon discover that everything and everywhere in Edinburgh becomes a venue during the Fringe, taking in large theatres, bars, restaurants, churches and even the odd[2] caravan! [...] The Edinburgh Festival Fringe, a truly unique and remarkable experience that has launched the careers of many big stars [...].

1. /'venju:z/ places where the events take place. **2.** occasional

PREPARE YOUR TASK

3 Decision making

Your Scottish host family has written to invite you to Edinburgh.
Read the end of the letter and reply after choosing one of the following roles:

- You love classical theatre
- You never go to the theatre
- You enjoy outdoor performances

...We're so glad you intend to come to visit us next summer.
Why dont you come when the Edinburgh Festival Fringe is on? It presents artists who perform in many different kinds of shows all around the city. It would be a true cultural experience for you!
I'm sure you'd enjoy the varied street performances.
You could come with a friend if you feel like it.
We could all go to the festival together.
We look forward to hearing back from you soon so we can start to organise your stay!
Love,
Jane McAlister
xxx

Help!

performance: *représentation*
audience: *spectateurs*
line-up: *artistes au programme*
front row: *premier rang*
stage: *scène*
show: *spectacle*
exhibition: *exposition*
available: *disponible*
book tickets: *réserver des places*
perform a play

3 Wales

1 How much do you know about Wales?

video

a. Watch the video and react: does it make you want to visit Wales? Why or why not?

b. Visit the following website and prepare ten questions about Wales.
www.bbc.co.uk/wales/culture/sites/aboutwales/pages/geography.shtml

c. Work in pairs and quiz your partner about Wales in turns. Count your points. Who is the winner?

2 Wakestock festival: in for music or in for sports?

WB P.88

CD3 PISTE 20

a. Listen to a recording about Wakestock and wakeboarding.

b. Report to the class.

Help!

camping site
fun/ exciting / thrilling
impressive

experience sth : *vivre qch*

both /bəʊθ/: *les deux, à la fois*
either… or: *ou … ou bien…*

PREPARE YOUR TASK

3 Promote Wakestock

a. Tweet it! Enter the competition to win a weekend at Wakestock. Use what you have learnt about the festival and Wales to write the best possible tweet. (130 to 140 characters)

b. Use your note to create a 30-second radio spot advertising Wakestock.

@WakestockUK

Wakestock @WakestockUK Actually, it is the one festival I really want to go to this summer…

Wakestock @WakestockUK Wakestock seems to be such an awesome music and wakeboarding festival!

4 The Notting Hill Carnival

1 Caribbean London
WB P.89

Read this extract carefully and find as much information as you can about the black Caribbean minority in London.

In 1948 a ship arrived at Tilbury Dock on the north bank of the Thames. Its arrival marked an important moment in the history of modern England. That ship was the Empire Windrush, which brought the first large group of West Indian[1] immigrants to the UK.

Six years of war had devastated Britain's infrastructure. Reconstruction was badly needed, but labour was in short supply. Caribbeans were encouraged to come to Britain and work for the Mother Country[2]. Many of these Jamaicans were young men who had served with the Allied Forces in Europe during the war and were keen to return, because of all the opportunities Britain could offer.

Most stayed on and settled in Great Britain and were later joined by their wives and families. They set up homes and worked mainly for London Transport or for the National Health Service.

Jamaicans tended to settle in the south of the Capital (Clapham, Brixton) whereas people from Trinidad and Barbados tended to move to the areas around Notting Hill.

1. the West Indies: *les Antilles (ou Îles des Caraïbes)* **2.** *(ici)* Britain

2 The carnival
WB P.90

Turn to your Workbook to find out how to get to the Notting Hill Carnival.

Help!

- (beat) a drum: *tambour*
- social event
- steel band
- colourful
- share
- be dressed up as…
  - wear a costume
- promote: *promouvoir*

3 Origins of the festival
WB P.90

CD3 PISTE 21

a. React to this photo (Who? What? Where? Impressions?)
The following words are written phonetically. Read them aloud and write them down.
/ˈkɑːnɪvəl/ /striːt ˈfestɪvəl/ /ˈseləbreɪt/ /ɪnˈvɒlv/ /bænd/ /ˌmʌltiˈkʌltʃərəlɪzəm/
b. Listen and turn to your Workbook for help.
c. Recap what you have understood using the following prompts:
The recording deals with… • The journalist explains the origins / goals….
• He / She gives us the reasons why… • He / She mentions…, interviews…

4 Writing workshop
PREPARE YOUR TASK

You work for a travel guide. Write a paragraph to promote the Notting Hill Carnival. (100-150 words)

5 Worlds Apart

1 Between concerts

a. Compare the two photos. (What? Where? Setting? Clothes?)
b. What social classes do you think the people in the photos belong to?

Glyndebourne[1] Summer Festival

Founded in 1934, Glyndebourne, a small house in the southwest of England, presents opera of the highest quality, developing new talent and reaching new audiences.
Much of the membership[2] consists of serious opera-lovers, and it's usually the cheaper seats (under £100) that are grabbed[3] first.

1. /ˈglaɪndbɔːn/ **2.** members **3.** taken

Glastonbury Festival

It was set up in 1971 and is held annually in the small village of Pilton in the southwest of England. Glastonbury draws in people from many different walks of life[1]. It usually takes place on the last weekend of June to coincide with the summer solstice.

1. *couches de la société*

2 The changing face of Glastonbury

WB p. 91

CD3 PISTE 22

PREPARE YOUR TASK

a. Listen to a radio programme entitled *'Glastonbury now and then.'*
Turn to your Workbook for help.
b. Prepare a short article about Glastonbury for a music magazine.

Help!

'wellies'= gumboots = rain boots
working class / middle class / upper class
bow tie: *noeud papillon*

rich = wealthy = well-off
elegant = smart
formal ≠ casual /ˈkæʒjuəl/
muddy: *boueux*
young / middle-aged / elderly

LANGUAGE AT WORK

+ WORKBOOK
→ Apprendre à apprendre
p. 125 - 126

A Le conseil, la suggestion, la préférence

Précis, p. 268

Observez

Lisez les phrases suivantes.

a. *You should take an umbrella, it is going to rain.*

b. *I'd prefer to go to a sports festival.*

c. *Why don't we go to a music festival?*

Parmi ces phrases, laquelle donne un conseil ? Offre une suggestion ? Exprime la préférence ?

Déduisez

Recopiez ces fiches de rappel sur papier libre et donnez-leur un titre.

…

S + **should** + BV
S + **had/'d better** + BV: *ferait mieux de…*

If I were you, I would + BV

advise sb to + BV: *conseiller à qqn de…*

…

Shall we + BV?

Why don't we/you + BV?
Let's + BV, **shall we**?

What about V-ING?
How about V-ING?
Do you feel like V-ING?
Do you fancy V-ING?

…

S + **would / 'd rather** + BV
S + **would / 'd prefer to** + BV
S + **prefer to** + BV

S + **prefer** V-ING
S + **prefer** sth **to** sth

B Les énoncés exclamatifs

Précis, p. 253

Observez

1 Lisez les phrases suivantes.

What a great festival it was!
What amazing performances!

*He is **such** an incredible artist!*
***Such** shows are unforgettable!*

2 Lisez ces phrases et observez les mots soulignés.

What sunny weather!
*This guidebook offers **such** useful information!*

3 Comparez.

***How** rainy (the day was)!*
***How** brilliantly organised!*
*This festival is (ever) **so** enjoyable!*

Déduisez

Comment sont formés ces énoncés exclamatifs ? Complétez à l'aide de *a / an / Ø*

What / such + … (+ adj) + nom **dénombrable au singulier.**

What / such + … (+ adj) + nom **dénombrable au pluriel.**

Les noms soulignés sont-ils dénombrables ou indénombrables ? Complétez :

What et *such* sont suivis de l'article … si le nom est un nom … .

Voir Précis grammatical p. 259

De quels éléments est suivi *how*?

How + …
How + …

Une exclamation en ***how*** peut être reformulée avec…

Entraînez-vous

1 **Associez ces débuts de phrases à leur fin la plus logique.**

a. *Outdoor festivals are often muddy; …*
b. *Our favourite band is playing tonight; …*
c. *The costumes of the carnival are so colourful; …*
d. *I've always wanted to know more about Edinburgh; …*

1. *shall we take a picture with our camera?*
2. *how about going on the city's website to get some information?*
3. *if I were you I would take my wellies.*
4. *we'd better get close to the stage.*

2 **Complétez les phrases suivantes à l'aide de *prefer* ou *would / 'd rather*.**

a. *They ... camping to going to a hotel but personally I ... choose a more comfortable type of accommodation!*
b. *We … to go to a place where there's a festival. It's such fun!*
c. *Do you really … rap to rock?*
d. *I … spend my money on something else, it's really too expensive.*
e. *If I have the choice, I … go to a sunny place.*

3 **Traduisez ces phrases.**

a. Et si on essayait le wakeboarding ?
b. Si j'étais toi, j'assisterais au festival de Wakestock. Il est absolument spectaculaire !
c. Avez-vous vraiment envie d'aller à Glastonbury en car *(coach)*?
d. Il ferait mieux d'aller voir les spectacles de rues, ils sont fantastiques !
e. L'agence de voyage me conseille de réserver dans une auberge de jeunesse.

4 **Réécrivez ces énoncés à l'aide de *what* et, lorsque c'est possible, de *how*.**

a. *This singer is talented.*
b. *These sports are dangerous.*
c. *This guidebook about festivals gives useful advice.*
d. *Wakeboarding is a physically challenging sport.*

5 **Remettez les phrases suivantes dans l'ordre et rétablissez la ponctuation.**

a. *disappointing / a / was / What / concert / it*
b. *festivals / How / are / some / surprising*
c. *carnival / The / so / ever / was / memorable*
d. *We / there / had / great / a / time / such*
e. *heavy / carried / festival / to / What / luggage / you / the*

ON YOUR OWN!

Observez ce dessin humoristique et imaginez la suite de la conversation.

Utilisez au moins deux énoncés exclamatifs et deux conseils ou suggestions pour un prochain festival (*Next time*,…)

"Hello darling, how was your music festival..?"

IMPROVE YOUR WRITING SKILLS

SAVEZ-VOUS ÉCRIRE UNE LETTRE OU UN EMAIL EN RESPECTANT LES CODES ?

1 Observez cette lettre. Des éléments sont manquants

1 ....

2 ....

3 ....

4 ...., but we have been so busy! We've decided to go to the Notting Hill Carnival this year, and we would be delighted if you could come with us. It will start on 14th August, will you be free by then?

Hope you're all well.

5 ....

Jenifer

6 ....

a 167 Milton Road
London
SE24 0PY

b Sorry for not writing to you earlier

c xxx

e Love,

d Dear all,

f 10th May, 2014

a. Associez les bulles ci dessus aux numéros dans la lettre.
b. Où se trouve la date ? L'adresse ?
c. Que signifie xxx ?
d. Qui est/sont le(s) destinataire(s) de cette lettre? S'agit-il de parents, d'un employeur, d'amis, d'un professeur ?
Quels éléments vous ont aidé(e) à trouver la réponse ?

2 Utilisez la bonne formule

a. Sur papier libre, classez les formules suivantes en deux colonnes: formules d'introduction et formules de conclusion.
b. Pour chacune d'elles indiquez si la situation est formelle ou informelle.

Dear Mrs Johnson, • *Yours Sincerely,* • *My dear Steven,* • *Take care,*
Dear Sir,/Madam • *Regards,* • *Best wishes,* • *Dear Aunt,* • *With love,*

3 Répondez à la lettre ci dessus par un email

a. Quelle formule d'introduction allez-vous utiliser ?
b. Quelle formule de conclusion allez-vous utiliser ?
c. Attention, certains éléments d'une lettre ne seront pas écrits dans un email. Lesquels ?

I love/ enjoy + V-ing
I am not so keen on + V-ing:
je n'aime pas trop

I can't wait to + V
I look forward to + V-ing:
j'ai hâte de ...

Check mail
New
Reply
Forward
Delete
Print

Attach
Send
To: jenifer@yahoo.co.uk
From:
Object:

YOUR TASK

You want to go to one of Britain's famous festivals. Exchange emails with a British travel agency to prepare for your trip.

1. Préparez-vous.
Revoyez ce que vous avez découvert sur les différents festivals dans cette unité, ou renseignez-vous sur d'autres événements (Bestival, Rochester…).

2. Mobilisez les connaissances acquises au cours de l'unité.
- Comment rédiger un email.
- Le lexique et les points grammaticaux de l'unité.
- Comment poser une question.

3. Rédigez votre email à l'agence de voyage.
Posez des questions qui vous permettront de choisir le festival qui vous correspondra le mieux.
N'oubliez pas de donner des indications sur votre personnalité et vos centres d'intérêts.

4. Votre professeur échangera votre email avec celui d'un camarade.

5. Lisez l'email reçu et répondez-y.
Suggérez un festival et expliquez les raisons pour lesquelles vous le recommandez (120-150 mots).

TIPS

You can ask/ give information about:

- accommodation: *hébergement*
- budget
- discount: *réduction*
- student rate
- public transport
- bed and breakfast
- affordable ≠ very expensive
- book: *réserver*
- available: *disponible*

Speaking Corner

To what extent do these cartoons correspond to the festival experience?

"I love it when it's sunny at festivals. It makes the mud so much warmer."

What do festivals mean to you?

"I will not do festivals. The thought of an audience that big frightens the life out of me." Adele

A music festival is just something that helps me escape and be totally free from everything.

If the music is too loud, you're too old.

You are what you listen to.

Unit 15

Masters of Suspense

YOUR TASK AT THE END OF THIS UNIT

Creative writing contest: write a short extract for a detective story or create a short film based on several pictures. Which story or film script will be published in the school newspaper or on the school website? *p. 221*

1 Tune In!

On Thursday James Trudd received a note from his Uncle Tobias. It said: "I didn't want you to marry Helen Reed! You will not get any of my money now. I shall speak to my lawyer about this on Friday."

James decided to kill his uncle immediately, before he could speak to his lawyer. James looked up trains to and from Lowbridge, where Uncle Tobias lived, and set out on his journey.

Soon after he reached the house in Lowbridge, James shot his uncle through the head. For the next three hours he searched his uncle's desk and read every letter in it. There was none to the lawyer.

James then took his uncle's pen and wrote a letter, which said: "Dear James, I do not want to live any longer. I have decided to kill myself. Sorry. Your Uncle Tobias" He put the letter in an envelope and addressed it to himself.

James put the gun into his uncle's hand. He dropped the note of the train times in a basket. Then he left the house.

Before catching the 8.45 train back to his home, James posted the letter to himself in Lowbridge.

▲ David Cobb, *Puzzles for English Practice*, 1979.

1 Case study

a. Read the comic on the opposite page and observe the pictures.
b. Choose one of these scenarios:
• You are a neighbour who lives in the opposite building. You have seen the murder and you report the crime to the police. Imagine the phone conversation. Describe the crime scene briefly (picture 3).
• You are the inspector in charge of the case and start your investigation. You arrive at the crime scene: what can you see? You immediately suspect James Trudd: what clues will help you solve the case? Why did he kill his uncle?

Help!

Victim
pool of blood /blʌd/: *flaque de sang*
a body = a corpse
lie, lay, lain: *être étendu*
commit suicide /'suːɪsaɪd/
shoot oneself
it looks as if ...: *on dirait que*

Clues
murder
weapon /'wepən/ = arm
fingerprints: *empreintes digitales*
handwriting
saliva /sə'laɪvə/
DNA : *ADN*
alibi /'æləbaɪ/
be left-handed ≠ be right-handed
collect the mail
investigate
find evidence of : *trouver des preuves de*

Motive
will: *testament*
an heir /eə/: *un héritier*
be guilty of ...: *être coupable de ...*
be mad at sb
greedy for money: *cupide*
disinherit /dɪsɪn'herɪt/ sb
obey sb
object to sth/sb V-ING: *s'opposer à*

2 Play with words

WB p. 93

Turn to your Workbook to improve your vocabulary.

PREPARE YOUR TASK

3 Police report

Look at the photo. A crime has been committed and the police have just questioned a witness. Write out the report (120 words).

2 A Master of Suspense

PREPARE YOUR TASK

1 On Hitchcock's tracks WB P. 94

Your teacher will give you a role card with some information about Hitchcock's life. Use the chart in your Workbook to ask the other students questions. Then use your notes to write Hitchcock's biography.

2 Get ready

You are going to watch a trailer. To help you understand it, find the words corresponding to the following transcriptions. Then read them aloud.
/sænd/ • /ˈsʌnbɜːn/ • /ˈmaʊntɪn ˈklaɪmɪŋ/ • /dɪˈlaɪts/ • /ˈteɪstfəl/

3

a. Go on the Internet and watch the trailer for *North by Northwest* (Alfred Hitchcock, 1959).

Useful words:
- a charley horse = a muscle cramp
- upper berth: *couchette supérieure*
- bartender: *barman*
- red herring: *fausse piste*

b. In groups, find the following information:
- What is Hitchcock trying to "sell"? • a vacation package? • train tickets? • a film?
- Find the names of two cities. Can you hear any other place names? What monuments can you see?
- What is the main character suspected of? What is he obliged to do? Who does he meet?
- What elements will you find in this film? (adventure, ...)

c. Turn to your worksheet to understand Hitchcock's use of irony in this trailer.

d. Report to the class.

PREPARE YOUR TASK

4 DVD jacket

Look at the stills from the film, below and on the opposite page, and use what, you learnt from the trailer to imagine what happens to the hero. Write a summary for the back cover of the DVD, starting with the sentence below (120 words).

"When New York City advertising executive Roger Thornhill (Cary Grant) is mistaken for a secret government agent by a group of spies, he must flee across the country."

TIPS
- Examine the first sentence, **list the information given**.
- Imagine the **sequence of events**.
- Use the **simple present** for the plot summary.
- Add **link words** (when, but, all of a sudden, later ...)
- Use **relative pronouns** like: the man/woman who ..., the train where ..., a thriller that ... .
- To attract the reader's attention, **ask questions**.
- Don't reveal the end!

Help!

villains = baddies

escape: *(s)échapper*
hide: *(se) cacher*
stab: *poignarder*
be chased by: *être poursuivi par*
climb: *grimper*
flee, fled, fled: *fuire*
manage to + V: *réussir à*

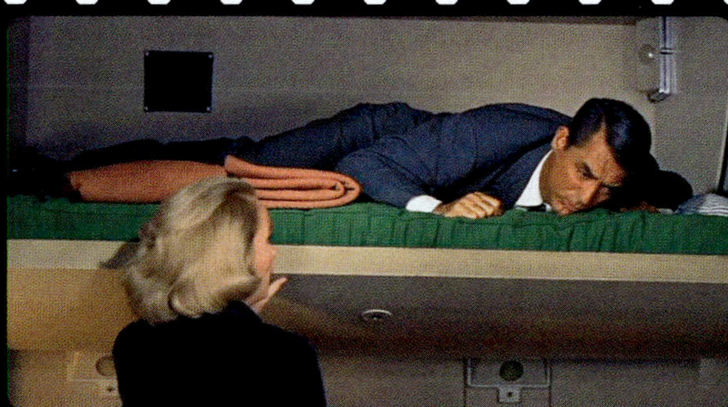

CD 3 PISTE 23

5 How to create suspense WB p. 94

1. Listen to the recording.

a. Who is speaking? Who is the narrator speaking to?

b. What adjectives would you choose to describe:

- The music in the recording?
- The sound effects and their impact on you?

c. Identify the different sounds or noises you can hear.

2. Recap

a. Summarize up the main contents:

- Conditions required to meet ghosts.
- How they can get into a room or a house.

b. What is the narrator going to do at the end of the passage?

c. Sum up Hitchcock's goals in a few sentences.

video

6 Watch a Video

Guilty by Suspicion, Alfred Hitchcock, 1941.
Turn to your worksheet for help.

3 Scream

CD3 PISTE 24

1 Sounds intriguing

a. Listen to the recording and identify the different sounds or noises you can hear.
b. What adjectives would you choose to describe the atmosphere in the recording?

relaxed • tense • creepy /'kri:pi/ = spooky /'spu:ki/: *qui donne la chair de poule* • gloomy: *lugubre* • scary = frightening • weird /wɪəd/ = strange • threatening = menacing • disturbing • joyful

2 Jigsaw reading

Read the beginning of the text (A). The following paragraphs (B to G) have been mixed up. Re-order them with the help of the comic strip on the opposite page.

A. *A few years ago, Helen Stoner's twin sister died mysteriously after her marriage to Doctor Roylott. Now Helen believes her life is threatened too, so she pays Sherlock Holmes a visit. Here is what she tells him about the night her sister died.*
I could not sleep that night. A vague feeling of impending[1] misfortune impressed me. My sister and I, you will recollect, were twins, and you know how subtle are the links which bind[2] two souls which are so closely allied...
1. imminent **2.** connect

B. As I ran down the passage, my sister's door was unlocked, and revolved slowly upon its hinges.

C. I sprang from my bed, wrapped a shawl round me, and rushed into the corridor. As I opened my door, I seemed to hear a low whistle, such as my sister described, and a few moments later a clanging sound, as if a mass of metal had fallen.

D. It was a wild night. The wind was howling outside, and the rain was beating and splashing against the windows. Suddenly, amid all the hubbub of the gale[1], there burst forth the wild scream of a terrified woman. I knew that it was my sister's voice.
1. *tandis que la tempête hurlait au dehors*

E. I rushed out, calling loudly for my stepfather, and I met him hastening from his room in his dressing-gown. When he reached my sister's side she was unconscious, and though he poured brandy down her throat and sent for medical aid from the village, all efforts were in vain, for she slowly sank and died without having recovered her consciousness. Such was the dreadful end of my beloved sister.

F. At first I thought that she had not recognized me, but as I bent over her, she suddenly shrieked out in a voice which I shall never forget: 'Oh, my God! Helen! It was the band! The speckled band!'[1] There was something else which she would fain[2] have said, and she stabbed with her finger into the air in the direction of the doctor's room, but a fresh convulsion seized her and choked her words.
1. *ruban moucheté* **2.** *(archaïque) volontiers*

G. I stared at it horror-stricken, not knowing what was about to issue from it. By the light of the corridor lamp I saw my sister appear at the opening, her face blanched with terror, her hands groping for help, her whole figure swaying to and fro like that of a drunkard. I ran to her and threw my arms round her, but at that moment her knees seemed to give way and she fell to the ground. She writhed[1] as one who is in terrible pain, and her limbs were dreadfully convulsed.
1. *se tordait*

▲ Sir Arthur Conan Doyle, *The Adventure of the Speckled Band*, 1892

3 Key facts WB P.95

Turn to your Workbook for help.

PREPARE YOUR TASK

4 Script writing WB P.97

Sherlock Holmes decides to go and question the stepfather who seems to be the main suspect. He wonders what the speckled band is.
Turn to your Workbook to learn how to correctly write a dialogue, then write their conversation (100 - 150 words).
Be sure to include the following information about the scene between Helen Stoner and her sister:

- The time of the day when the events took place.
- The weather conditions.
- The people present, their actions.
- The emotions and reactions of the different people.

LANGUAGE AT WORK

+ WORKBOOK
→ Apprendre à apprendre
p. 127 - 128

L'interrogation

Précis, p. 256

Observez

1 **Lisez les phrases suivantes.**

a. *Did the burglar break into the room at 10.30 p.m.?*
b. *What time did the burglar break into the room?*
c. *What has the burglar stolen?*
d. *What were you doing at that time?*
e. *Are you sure nothing else was stolen?*

À quelle forme sont les énoncés ci-dessus ?

Déduisez

En anglais, les constructions interrogatives utilisent un … .
Quand la question commence par un mot interrogatif on a l'ordre: interrogatif + … + … + … .

2 **Sujet ou complément ?**

a. *Who saw anything suspicious?*
b. *What did you hear?*
c. *Who do you suspect?*
d. *What happened next?*

À quel temps sont les énoncés ci-dessus ? Classez-les en deux colonnes, pour distinguer ceux où le mot interrogatif est sujet, ceux où le mot interrogatif est complément :
Que remarquez-vous lorsque le mot interrogatif est sujet de la phrase ?

Déduisez

Lorsque *Who* et *What* sont … …il n'y a pas d'auxiliaire ni au … … ni au … … .
La construction est celle de … .

3 **La place de la préposition**

"*What do you suspect this man of?*"
"*I suspect him of being the murderer.*"

Déduisez

Si le verbe se construit avec une préposition, cette préposition est habituellement placée … .

4 **Les mots interrogatifs**

Que cherche à savoir l'énonciateur ?
Associez chaque question à un élément de la liste :

What were you doing yesterday at midnight?
Whose gun is it?
What time did you leave the flat?
How long will it take to have the results?
Where did you go after leaving the flat?
How far was the murderer from his victim?
How is the victim's wife now?
How often did you meet the victim?
How much money was kept in the safe?
What is the kidnapper like?
How many bullets were shot at the victim?
How was the victim killed?

- nombre
- santé
- activité
- possesseur
- demande de description
- lieu
- quantité
- durée
- moyen
- distance
- heure
- fréquence

Entraînez-vous

1 **Mettez les mots suivants dans l'ordre pour obtenir des énoncés interrogatifs.**

a. *you* / *unusual* / *night* / *did* / *last* / *noises* / *hear* / *?*

b. *much* / *has* / *money* / *how* / *stolen* / *been* / *?*

c. *time* / *wife* / *leave* / *flat* / *what* / *his* / *did* / *the* / *?*

d. *were* / *photos* / *by* / *when* / *taken* / *the* / *detective* / *the* / *?*

e. *her* / *know* / *why* / *you* / *he* / *left* / *do* / *?*

f. *work* / *victim* / *morning* / *the* / *to* / *go* / *did* / *yesterday* / *?*

2 **Interrogatoire :** Reconstituez le script ci-dessous. Aidez-vous des réponses suivantes pour compléter chaque question à l'aide d'un mot interrogatif.

The inspector: You saw a suspect. …?
The witness: He was quite tall.
The inspector: …?
The witness: About thirty.
The inspector: …?
The witness: It was dark, short and curly.
The inspector: …?
The witness: No, he didn't. He had a moustache.
The inspector: …?
The witness: It was around ten.
The inspector: …?
The witness: I was walking my dog.
The inspector: …?
The witness: No, never. It's the first time.

ON YOUR OWN!

Un meurtre a été commis. Le commissaire Kate Todd est chargée de l'enquête. Certains élèves joueront le rôle des colocataires et d'autres celui du commissaire ou des experts. Votre professeur distribuera des fiches avec tous les renseignements nécessaires. Interrogez les différents témoins pour compléter les fiches afin de démasquer le coupable.

IMPROVE YOUR WRITING SKILLS

1 Lisez l'extrait suivant

On a December night, I was coming home from school, when suddenly two big, strong, hooded men with dark clothes kidnapped me. I screamed like mad, punched them, called for help again and again, but there was nobody around. They took me to a house in the woods where they locked me in. They tied me to a chair, then left me alone for what seemed like hours. I was desperate and panic-stricken. All of a sudden, I realised my cell phone was in my pocket! I managed to get one hand free and grab it to send an SOS to my parents. A few hours later, I heard police sirens: people were finally coming to my rescue. I was free at last!

2 Identifiez la situation

a. Les circonstances : le lieu, le moment de la journée et personnages présents.
b. Relevez des adjectifs décrivant les sentiments du narrateur.
c. Résumez rapidement en français ce qui se passe dans cet extrait.

3 Repérez ces éléments dans le récit

a. Faites la liste des formes verbales utilisées dans le récit ; nommez le temps grammatical utilisé et indiquez sa valeur.
b. Relevez les termes utilisés pour décrire les deux hommes.
c. Relevez les mots de liaison et les marqueurs de temps.

4 Observez la langue utilisée

Voici le squelette de l'histoire. Comment est-on passé d'une phrase simple à une phrase complexe ?

I was coming home. Two men kidnapped me.	*On a December night, I was coming home from school, when suddenly two big, strong, hooded men with dark clothes kidnapped me.*
They took me to a house.	*They took me to a house in the woods where they locked me in. They tied me to a chair, then left me alone for what seemed like hours.*
I grabbed my cell phone. I sent an SOS to my parents.	*I managed to get one hand free and grab it to send an SOS to my parents.*
People were coming to my rescue.	*A few hours later, I heard police sirens: people were finally coming to my rescue. I was free at last!*

5 Construisez votre récit

Write a story beginning with this sentence: ***"I was lying on the beach, when someone screamed."*** (80 -120 words).
- Utilisez les outils vus ci-dessus ainsi que des :
• mots de liaison : ***when - while - as - because***
• marqueurs chronologiques : ***first - after a while later / eventually*** (plus tard)
- Faites un plan en utilisant le schéma ci-contre.
- Mobilisez le lexique et les structures adaptées à votre contexte.

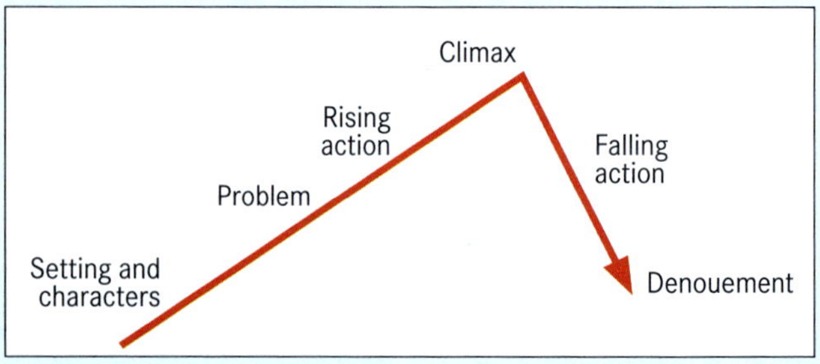

YOUR TASK

Creative writing contest: write a short extract for a detective story or create a short film based on several pictures. Which story or film script will be published in the school newspaper or on the school website?

Scénario 1

1. Observez les images ci-dessous et repérez : le lieu, le moment, les personnages, l'action et les détails importants.
2. Donnez une identité à chacun des protagonistes, quelle relation existe-t-il entre eux ? Nom, prénom, âge, profession, rôle (soyez aussi précis que possible).
3. Imaginez les événements antérieurs : qu'y a-t-il dans l'enveloppe ? Pourquoi se retrouvent-ils au café ? Pourquoi l'homme au chapeau place-t-il la bombe ? Puis inventez une suite. **Appuyez-vous sur les conseils donnés p. 220.**

Scénario 2

Après avoir écrit le scénario correspondant aux images ci-dessus, préparez-vous à jouer, puis filmer votre scénario à la manière d'Hitchcock. Utilisez les pages 228-231 (Commenter une scène de film).

blast-effect: *effet de souffle*
cardboard box: *boîte en carton*
parcel = package: *colis*

track / trail / follow sb: *pister qqn*
blow up = explode
see / watch / observe sb + V-ING
watch from a distance / from the other side of the street
set the timer
plug one's ears: *se boucher les oreilles*

Reading Corner

On arriving in Bath, where he was going to start a new job, Billy Weaver, aged seventeen, took a room at a Bed and Breakfast run by an old landlady[1]*. After he had written his name and address in the guest book, he noticed that there were only two names above his.*

He crossed the room slowly, and sat down on the edge of the sofa. She placed his teacup on the table in front of him.

'There we are,' she said. 'How nice and cosy[2] this is, isn't it?'

Billy started sipping his tea. She did the same. For half a minute or so, neither of them spoke. But Billy knew that she was looking at him. Her body was half-turned towards him, and he could feel her eyes resting on his face, watching him over the rim of her teacup. Now and again, he caught a whiff[3] of a peculiar smell that seemed to emanate directly from her person. It was not in the least unpleasant, and it reminded him – well, he wasn't quite sure what it reminded him of. Pickled walnuts? New leather? Or was it the corridors of a hospital?

'Mr Mulholland was a great one for his tea,' she said at length. 'Never in my life have I seen anyone drink as much tea as dear, sweet Mr Mulholland.'

'I suppose he left fairly recently,' Billy said. He was still puzzling his head about the two names. He was positive now that he had seen them in the newspapers – in the headlines.

'Left?' she said, arching her brows[4]. 'But my dear boy, he never left. He's still here. Mr Temple is also here. They're on the third floor, both of them together.'

Billy set down his cup slowly on the table, and stared at his landlady. She smiled back at him, and then put out one of her white hands and patted him comfortingly on the knee. 'How old are you, my dear?' she asked.

'Seventeen.'

'Seventeen!' she cried. 'Oh, it's the perfect age! Mr Mulholland was also seventeen. But I think he was a trifle shorter than you are, in fact I'm sure he was, and his teeth weren't *quite* so white. You have the most beautiful teeth, Mr Weaver, did you know that?'

'They're not as good as they look,' Billy said. 'They've got simply masses of fillings[5] in them at the back.'

'Mr Temple, of course was a little older,' she said ignoring his remark. 'He was actually twenty-eight. And yet I never would have guessed it if he hadn't told me, never in my whole life. There wasn't a blemish[6] on his body.'

'A what?' Billy said.

'His skin was just like a baby's.'

There was a pause. Billy picked up his teacup and took another sip of tea, then he set it down again gently in its saucer. He waited for her to say something else, but she seemed to have lapsed into another of her silences. He sat there staring straight ahead of him into the far corner of the room, biting his lower lip.

'That parrot,' he said at last. 'You know something? It had me completely fooled when I first saw it through the window from the street. I could have sworn[7] it was alive.'

'Alas, no longer.'

'It's most terribly clever the way it's been done,' he said. It doesn't look in the least bit dead. Who did it?'

'I did.'

'*You* did?'

'Of course,' she said. 'And you have met my little Basil as well?' She nodded towards the dachshund[8] curled up so comfortably in front of the fire. Billy looked at it. And suddenly, he realized that this animal had all the time been just as silent and motionless as the parrot. He put out a hand and touched it gently on the top of its back. The back was hard and cold, and when

1. *logeuse* **2.** *douillet, confortable* **3.** *bouffée* **4.** /braʊz/ *(ici) haussa les sourcils* **5.** *plombages* **6.** *marque/défaut* **7.** *juré* **8.** *teckel*

9. *empaille*
10. die
11. /ɑːməndz/ *amandes amères*

he pushed the hair to one side with his fingers, he could see the skin underneath, greyish-black and dry and perfectly preserved.

'Good gracious me,' he said. 'How absolutely fascinating.' He turned away from the dog and stared with deep admiration at the little woman beside him on the sofa. 'It must be most awfully difficult to do a thing like that.'

'Not in the least,' she said. 'I stuff[9] all my little pets myself when they pass away[10]. Will you have another cup of tea?'

'No, thank you,' Billy said. The tea tasted faintly of bitter almonds[11], and he didn't much care for it.

'You did sign the book, didn't you?'

'Oh, yes.'

That's good. Because later on, if I happen to forget what you were called, then I can always come down here and look it up. I still do that almost every day with Mr Mulholland and Mr...Mr...'

'Temple,' Billy said. 'Gregory Temple. Excuse my asking, but haven't there been any other guests here except them in the last two or three years?'

Holding her teacup high in one hand, inclining her head slightly to the left, she looked up at him out of the corners of her eyes and gave him another gentle smile.

'No, my dear,' she said. 'Only you.'

▲ Roald Dahl, "The Landlady," *Tales of the Unexpected*, 1979

Évaluation sommative
Writing

J'évalue mes progrès

Je revois les stratégies apprises dans les unités précédentes (*Improve Your Writing Skills* p.196, 208 et 220) afin de faire le bilan de mes compétences.

1. Je me prépare

1. You have lost your notes and you need them for a test about *Masters of Suspense*. You write an email to a friend. In your email you need to:
- ask for his/her help.
- explain you will photocopy the notes.
- thank him/her. (40 words)

2. You went to a festival last weekend. You did not enjoy yourself.
Write a comment on the festival's website/on a forum to share your feelings and explain why your experience was so negative. (40 words)

3. On your blog you want to tell your friends what you have been doing recently. Choose one of the following topics:
a. A detective film/story you have just seen/read. Give your opinion about it. (60 words)
b. Your recent trip to New York City. (60 words)

4. Write a story beginning with:
"I was walking home from a friend's house late at night when I heard footsteps behind me."
Don't forget to include your reactions and feelings at that moment. (80 words)

5. Write a story.
You are reading a thrilling detective novel, but discover that most of page 126 has been ripped out. The only words you can read on the page are: *"My heart was pounding. We were together, but where was he?"*
The photo above is on the book cover. Rewrite the missing paragraph. (100 words)

2. Je me corrige

1. Corrigez les erreurs (grammaire ou orthographe) soulignées (cf. Relire son devoir p. 226)

> An old woman <u>was walk</u> in the park <u>push</u> her cart <u>who</u> was full of <u>bag</u>. She <u>sit</u> on a bench next to me and we <u>start</u> talking. She <u>had</u> eighty, her <u>hairs were whites</u>, she <u>looked like</u> very tired. She <u>said</u> me the story of her life. When she was young, she was <u>a</u> actress. A rich man <u>felt</u> in love with her and <u>married to</u> her. Fifteen years later, he <u>leaved</u> her for an other woman. She <u>get</u> a job as a waitress in a restaurant and worked for <u>much</u> years. Then she lost her job and <u>become</u> homeless. She didn't want <u>that I give</u> her any money. She said she didn't need much.

2. **Consultez les corrigés sur le site compagnon et comparez vos productions à celles proposées.**

Je fais le bilan

Analysez vos résultats à l'aide de cette grille d'évaluation où sont définis les différents niveaux de compétence en expression écrite. Le niveau attendu en classe de seconde est B1.

Sujet 1 : Je peux...	Niveaux
... écrire des textes courts et simples, des lettres personnelles simples pour remercier et m'excuser.	**A2**
... rédiger des messages pour demander des informations, communiquer des faits ou exposer des problèmes.	**B1**

Sujets 2 et 3 : Je peux...	Niveaux
... faire une description brève et élémentaire de moi-même, de ma famille, de mes activités, d'événements.	**A2**
... écrire un texte simple et cohérent sur des sujets familiers ou de la vie quotidienne. ... écrire un point de vue personnel (sentiments ou réactions) ou une opinion.	**B1**
... rédiger un compte-rendu portant sur un film, un livre, etc.	**en route vers B2**

Sujet 4 : Je peux...	Niveau
... écrire un texte simple et cohérent sur des sujets familiers ou de la vie quotidienne.	**B1**

Sujet 5 : Je peux...	Niveau
.. décrire un événement, raconter une histoire.	**B1**
.. écrire des descriptions élaborées et relater des événements imaginaires dans un texte articulé.	**en route vers B2**

Évaluation

Votre professeur va vous distribuer un sujet de production écrite sur une des unités travaillées en cours.

Unit 13 City in the Sky

Unit 14 Summer Rocks

Unit 15 Masters of Suspense

Une fois l'évaluation terminée, votre professeur pourra ainsi déterminer à quel niveau vous vous situez par rapport à la grille d'évaluation du Cadre Européen Commun de Référence pour les Langues.

Relire son devoir

Relire

Formes verbales

Auxiliaire modal (*may / must / will / etc.*)
- suivi d'une base verbale (infinitif sans *to*)
- il est invariable
- pas de 's' à la 3ème personne du singulier

He must remember that.

Want / would like sb to do sth

Do you want me to help you?
His parents would like him to work harder.

Formes interrogatives : penser à l'auxiliaire

Do you need anything else?
Did you tell them the truth?

Ordre des mots Attention ! Ne pas calquer

Adjectif devant le nom qualifié

This is a scary story.

COD directement après le verbe

She speaks Chinese very well.

- *He ~~learns English for six years~~*
  *He **has been learning** English for six years.*
- *~~They are married since 2010.~~*
  *They **have been** married since 2010.*

- **Attention à *as soon as* et *when*:** pas de *will* dans une subordonnée de temps.
  *He will take a year off when/ as soon as **he graduates**.*

Ne pas confondre *They are* et *There are*

They are exhausted. Ils sont épuisés.
There are drawbacks. Il y a des inconvénients.

Attention aux verbes irréguliers

p. 271

Accords

***People* + pluriel**

People are worried about the crisis.

***Every / Each* + singulier**

Is everybody ready?

's' à la 3ème personne du singulier au présent

He plays a lot of video games.

Adjectifs invariables :

These books are new.

Emploi de *the*

I love cookies. (en général)
I love the cookies you have bought. (nom défini)

Equivalents anglais de "pour":

***For* + nom / pronom**

*This present is **for you**.*

***(in order) to* + V**

*He stopped **to look** at the map.*

Comprendre les consignes

Repérer

- *In this **excerpt*** (ou ***extract***):
  Dans cet extrait
- ***List the characters** present **in the scene**:*
  Faites la liste des personnages présents dans la scène.
- ***Locate**…/ find **the location**:*
  Situez / trouvez le lieu.
- *Who are the **main characters**?*
  Qui sont les personnages principaux?
- *Who **is mentioned** in this scene?*
  Qui est mentionné /cité dans cette scène?
- *When / Where does the scene **take place**?*
  Quand / Où se passe l'action?
- ***Find** the **key word** / the name of … / one adjective / one verb / a **clue**.*
  Trouvez le mot clé / le nom de … /
  un adjectif / un verbe / un indice.
- *Find the **equivalent** / the **opposite** of / the word **corresponding to the following definition**…:*
  Trouvez l'équivalent / le contraire de / le mot correspondant à la définition suivante.
- ***Choose** / **Pick out** / **Select** the words …:*
  Choisissez / Sélectionnez / Relevez / Repérez les mots …
- ***List** the words which **are connected with** / **are related to** / …:*
  Relevez les mots qui se rapportent à, qui font référence à …

Résumer

- ***Fill in** the **blanks** in the **summary**:*
  Ecrivez les mots qui manquent pour compléter le résumé du texte.
- ***Sum up the story**:*
  Résumez l'histoire.
- ***Sum up** this text **in your own words**:*
  Résumez ce texte en utilisant vos propres mots.

Justifier vos réponses

- ***Give a quote/quotation:***
  Donnez une citation.
- ***Justify** using **key words** from …:*
  Justifiez vos réponses à l'aide de mots clés tirés de … .
- ***Quote** one **sentence**, ⚠ a **phrase:***
  Citez une phrase, groupe de mots / expression

Remettre dans l'ordre

- ***Put** the following words **in the right column**:*
  Classez les mots suivants dans la colonne correspondante.
- ***Reorder** the **events** in **chronological order**.*
  Classez les événements par ordre chronologique.

Associer

- ***Match** the following words **with their definitions**.*
- ***Which** of the following words **apply to** …?*
  Lesquels de ces mots s'appliquent à … ?
- *What do these **figures** refer to?*
  A quoi ces chiffres suivants font-ils référence?
- *Who or what do the **underlined** pronouns **refer to**?*
  A quoi les pronoms soulignés font-ils référence?

Agir

- ***Act** the dialogue /scene **out**:*
  Jouez la scène.
- ***Compare** your results with your neighbour:*
  Confrontez/comparez vos résultats avec votre voisin.
- ***Write down** on a **blank sheet** of paper:*
  Ecrivez sur papier libre
- ***Fill in** the **grid** / **table** / **columns below**:*
  Remplissez la grille/ le tableau/ les colonnes ci-dessous.

Commenter une image

I. Parler d'une image fixe

CD3 PISTE 25 — MP3 PISTE 37

1. Les types d'images

advertisement / advert/ ad: *publicité*	painting
cartoon: *dessin humoristique*	photograph : *une photograhie*
comic strip: *bande dessinée*	⚠ photography: *la photographie (l'art de la photo)*
drawing: *dessin*	poster
map: *carte*	still from a film: *image de film*

2. Situer les différents éléments de l'image

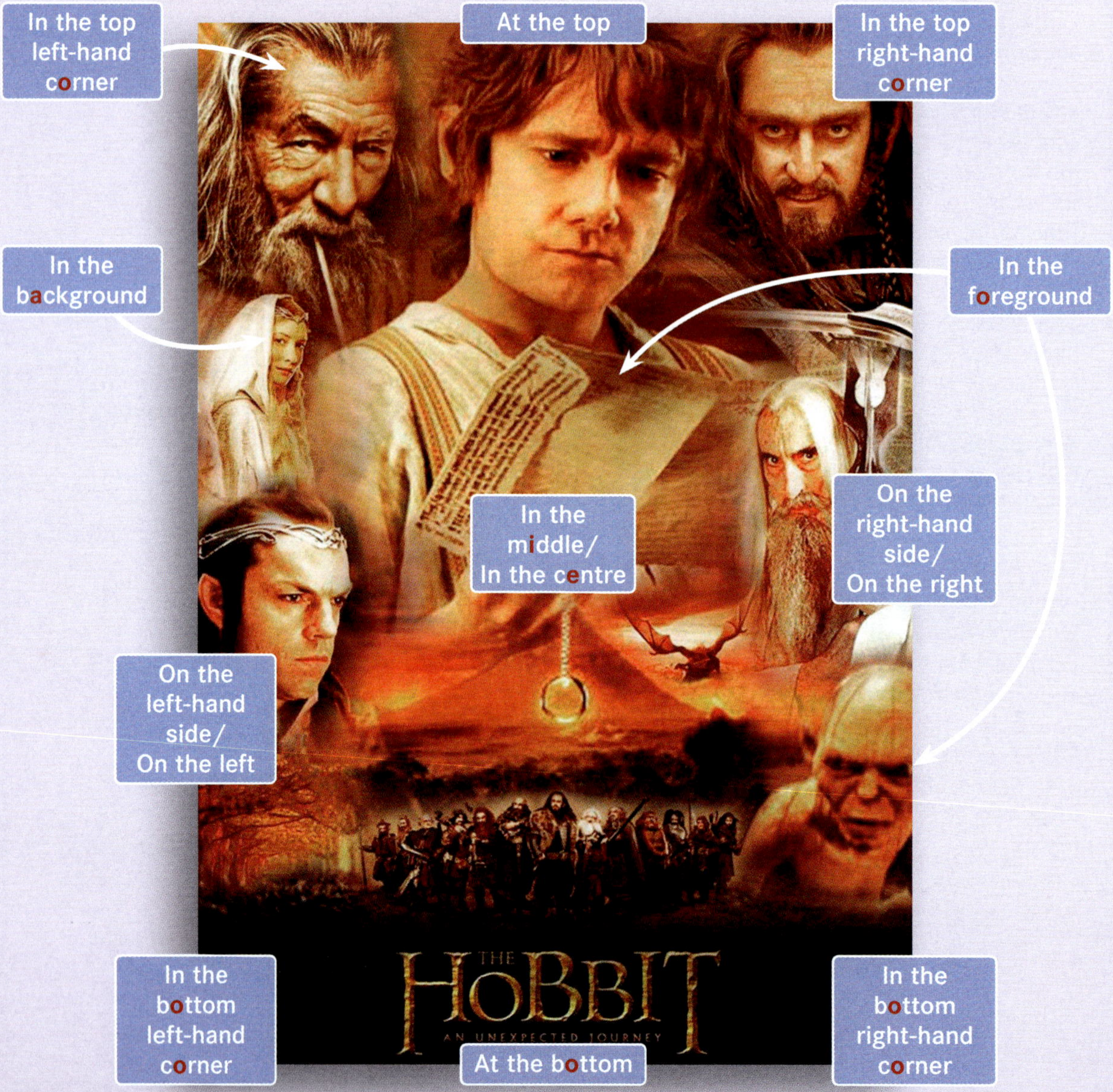

3. Nommer les éléments de l'image

character: *personnage*
⚠ a person / people: *les gens*
setting: *décor*
title, headline
balloon: *bulle*
caption: *légende*

I can see….
There is / are…..
The woman is sleeping (V-ing) and her children are playing.
⚠ *The children* ***look*** *stupid. / They* ***look like*** *monsters.*
The focus is on ...

II. Les prépositions

1. Position

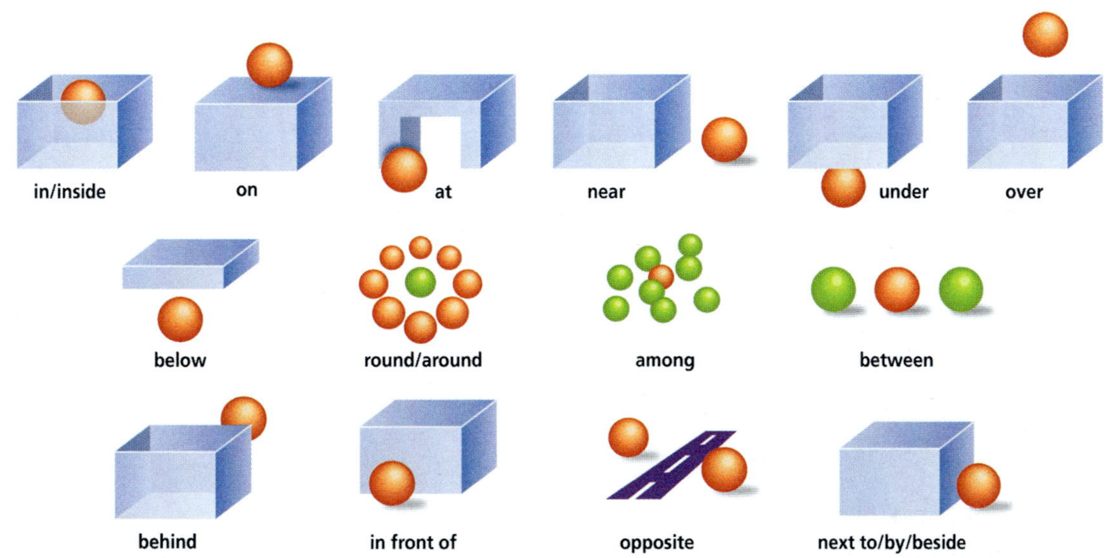

2. Mouvement

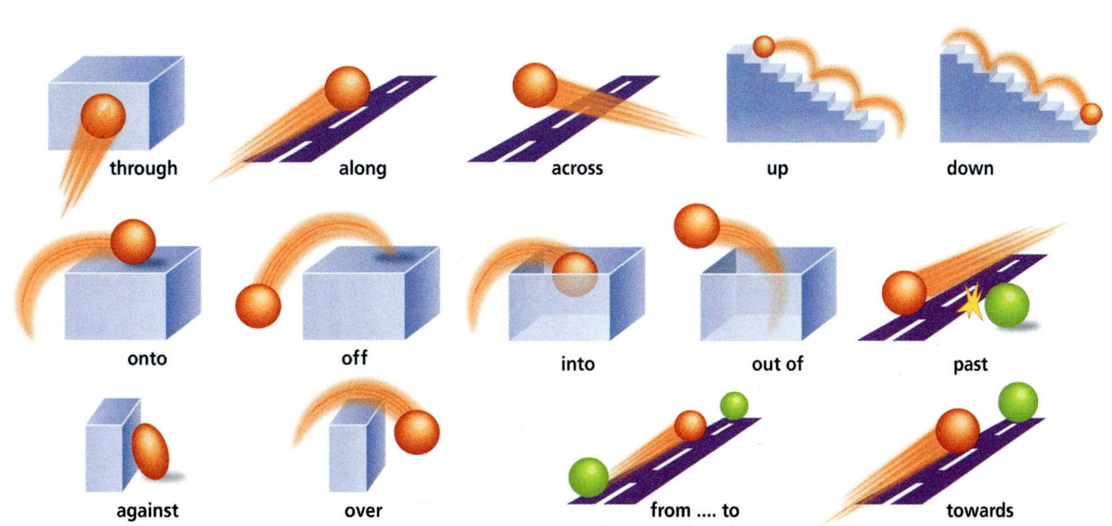

III. Parler d'une image animée

CD3 PISTE 26 MP3 PISTE 38

1. Les plans et les angles

A. Low-angle shot
The character is seen from below and the viewer feels dominated.

B. Long shot
The camera shows a distant object or a landscape.

C. Medium shot
The camera focuses on the character's head and shoulders.

D. Extreme close-up
The viewer can see details on a face or an object. This shot is used to convey / express an emotion.

E. High-angle shot
The shot makes the character look smaller and the viewer dominates the scene.

F. Full shot
The camera shows the characters standing.

2. Les types d'image animée

black and white movie
blockbuster: *film à grand succès*
commercial: *publicité à la TV*
disaster film
detective film
documentary
report: *reportage*

comedy
musical
trailer: *bande annonce*
war / adventure film
thriller
detective film
cartoon

3. Parler d'une scène

Who?
The people involved are ...
What?
The document is about ...
The document deals with ...
Where?
The scene takes place in a station.
The scene is taken from...
The setting is a house, a street, an airport
shoot, shot, shot: *tourner*
It was shot in a studio.
When?
The incident took place during the day / at night

First reactions
What strikes me (the) most in / about this is that ...
I think it is (quite) surprising / funny to see ...
It is incredible: *incroyable*
interesting
ridiculous
impressive
scary: *effrayant*
unusual
disturbing: *troublant / dérangeant*
We get a feeling of suspense / danger / threat: *menace*
moving: *émouvant*
humorous /ˈhjuːmərəs/

4. Les bruits et les sons

soundtrack: *bande son*
sound effect: *bruitage*
film score: *musique*
voice-over: *voix off*
male / female voice

lively /cheerful
dramatic
spooky: *qui fait froid dans le dos*
deafening: *assourdissant*
dull / muffled: *étouffé*

5. Interpréter

The director's aim / goal is to...
The atmosphere is tense / strained: *tendue*
gloomy: *sombre*
It makes me think of...
It reminds me of...: *cela me rappelle*
It illustrates

It is a symbol of ...
It symbolizes
It represents
It is meant to make us aware of...: *on a voulu nous faire prendre conscience de ...*
It criticizes
It denounces

Enrichir sa prise de parole

Get started

- Do you think that…?
- What are the advantages and disadvantages of…?
- Don't you think…?
- Well, to start with…
- First of all, I would like to say that…

How to give yourself time to think

- Well…
- I mean…
- Well, how could I say that…?
- Well, you see… / you know…
- Um…
- What I'm trying to say is that…
- It's an interesting question…

How to check that you have understood correctly

- When you say "…", do you mean "…"?
- I'm not quite sure I understand what you mean here.
- What do you mean by that?
- So, if I understand correctly, you mean that…

How to check somebody has understood you

- Did you get my point?
- Do you see what I mean?
- Does it make sense?

When something is not quite clear

- Could you say that again, please?
- Could you repeat what you said?
- Would you mind repeating, please?
- I'm sorry, what did you say?
- Excuse me, did you say that…?
- Are you saying that…?
- What do you mean by…?

How to introduce your opinion

- To me, …
- In my view, …
- It seems to me that…
- To my mind, …
- In my opinion, …
- I have the feeling that…
- I believe that…

How to present different arguments

- To begin with, …
- Well, first of all…
- Firstly, … Secondly, … Lastly / Finally, …
- I also think that…
- Besides, …
- I'd like to add that…

How to agree strongly

- Exactly!
- Absolutely true!
- That's a very good point.
- Sure!
- That's right!
- That's exactly what I think.

How to half agree

- Yes, I suppose so. However...
- Yes, sure, but...
- Do you really think so?
- Well, in a way, but...
- Well, it depends.
- Well, yes, up to a certain point.
- I've got mixed feelings about that.

How to disagree politely

- Do you really believe that...?
- Yes, but...
- Um, I'm not sure.
- Don't you think that...?
- Well, I think it depends (on)...

How to disagree strongly

- I totally disagree with you.
- I really can't agree.
- You can't be serious!
- No, you're wrong!
- You must be joking / kidding! (informal)
- Nonsense! (informal)

How to counter an argument

- Yes, but remember that...
- That may be true but...
- Don't you think...?
- Contrary to you, I think...
- On the contrary, I believe...

How to give an example

- For example, ...
- Take... for instance, ...
- For instance, ...
- That is to say, ...

How to show different aspects of a question

- Generally, ...
- At first sight, ...
- On the one hand, ... on the other hand, ...
- On second thoughts, ...

How to add something

- What's more, ...
- I'd like to add that...
- On top of that, ...
- By the way, ...
- In addition, ...
- Besides, ...
- I'd also like to say that...
- I'd like to make another point.

How to conclude

- In conclusion, ...
- Lastly, ...
- In that case, ...
- In short, ...
- To sum up, ...
- Finally, ...

Pour mieux parler

1. Se familiariser avec les sons de l'anglais

CD3 PISTE 27 — MP3 PISTE 39

a. Voyelles simples (anglais britannique)

/iː/ /ɪ/ /i/ /e/ /æ/ /ɑː/

/ɒ/ /ɔː/ /ʊ/ /uː/ /ɜː/ /ʌ/ /ə/

b. Diphtongues (anglais britannique)

/eɪ/ /aɪ/ /aʊ/ /əʊ/

/eə/ /ɔɪ/ /ɪə/ /ʊə/

c. Consonnes

/j/	/ð/	/θ/	/ʒ/	/ʃ/	/ŋ/
yes	this	thanks	pleasure	sure	song

1. Observez la liste de symboles des sons des voyelles et des diphtongues.
2. Trouvez les mots repères qui y sont associés. Prononcez-les.
3. Puis écoutez l'enregistrement et vérifiez à l'écoute. Exemple : /iː/ = key

d. Comment prononcer le *th*

CD3 PISTE 28 MP3 PISTE 40

Le *th* anglais ne se prononce ni comme /z/ ou /s/ ni comme /v/ ou /f/. Il se prononce en plaçant la pointe de la langue contre le bord des incisives supérieures.
Différence entre le *th* de *that* (transcrit /ð/) et celui de *thanks* (/θ/) : dans le premier cas, les cordes vocales vibrent, alors qu'elles ne vibrent pas dans le second. (On a la même différence entre /z/ et /s/, ou entre /d/ et /t/.)

How to be British, M. Ford & P. Legon

➲ Écoutez et déduisez

Le *th* des séries suivantes se prononce-t-il comme dans *that* (/ð/) ou comme dans *thanks* (/θ/) ?
- *the* • *this* • *these* • *there* • *that* • *other* • *without*
- *bathe* • *mother* • *clothes*
- *think* • *thousand* • *throw* • *fifth* • *tenth* • *sixteenth* • *twelfth* • *north* • *tooth* • *bath* • *mouth*

➲ Complétez maintenant les phrases suivantes :

- Dans les mots grammaticaux, *th* se prononce en général comme dans … (/…/) ;
- Dans les autres mots, *th* se prononce en général comme dans … (/…/) quand il est à l'intérieur d'un mot, et comme dans … (/…/) quand il est au début ou à la fin d'un mot.

➲ Écrivez les mots qui vont vous être dictés, puis classez-les en deux colonnes selon la prononciation de the: /ð/ (*that*)/ ou /θ/(*thanks*) ?

Tongue twisters

Écoutez puis répétez.

1. I thought a thought. But the thought I thought wasn't the thought you thought I thought.

2. Is this the thing you want?
- Yes, this is the thing.

3. Three thoughtless girls threw thirty thick things and thought they would make a thundering noise.

2. Du son à la graphie

CD3 PISTE 29 — MP3 PISTE 41

Un même son peut correspondre à plusieurs graphies. Pour chaque son ci-dessous voici la liste des graphies les plus courantes.

- « a » + consonne + « e » (late - make) — /eɪ/ — "ai" (mail - pain) ; "ay" (play - say)
- "u" (full) — /ʊ/ — "oo" (good)
- "e" (red - bed) — /e/ — "ea" (bread - read (preterit)) ; "ai" (says - said)
- "oi" (voice - choice) — /ɔɪ/ — "oy" (boy - toy) ; "ay" (play - say)
- "I" + consonne + "e" (nice - bite) — /aɪ/ — "igh" (right - sigh) ; "y" (reply - cry)
- /əʊ/ — "o" (rose)
- "ee" (see - flee) ; "ie" (niece - piece) — /iː/ — "ea" (sea - please) ; "ei" (ceiling - perceive)
- "ue" (clue - blue) ; "oo" (moon - boom) — /uː/ — "ew" (new - few) ; "ui" (fruit - -suit)
- "or" (born - worn) ; "aw" (saw - lawn) — /ɔː/ — "au" (caught - caution) ; "ou" (bought - thought)

Écoutez les phrases suivantes et prenez-les en dictée.
Vérifiez avec votre professeur.

CD3 PISTE 30 — MP3 PISTE 42

3. Accent de mots

a. Apprenez à repérer la syllabe accentuée.

Dans le manuel, les *Help!* en particulier, la voyelle ou la diphtongue de la syllabe portant l'accent principal est en gras et en rouge : sc**a**ry • impr**e**ssive • gener**a**tion

Dans les transcriptions phonétiques des dictionnaires, on utilise le signe /ˈ/ placé avant la syllabe accentuée.
Exemple : *meeting* /ˈmiːtɪŋ/

Il peut y avoir un accent secondaire désigné par /ˌ/ devant la syllabe accentuée.
Exemple : *understanding* /ˌʌndəˈstændɪŋ/

b. Je m'entraîne

CD3 PISTE 31 — MP3 PISTE 44

Recopiez la liste de mots suivants et lors de l'écoute entourez les syllabes accentuées.
Répétez ensuite ces mots à haute voix.

Exemple : *history*
geography • physics • chemistry • English • biology • activity • mathematics • economics

4. Comment trouver la syllabe accentuée ?

a. Les terminaisons contraignantes (imposent une place pour l'accent)

Je repère les indices

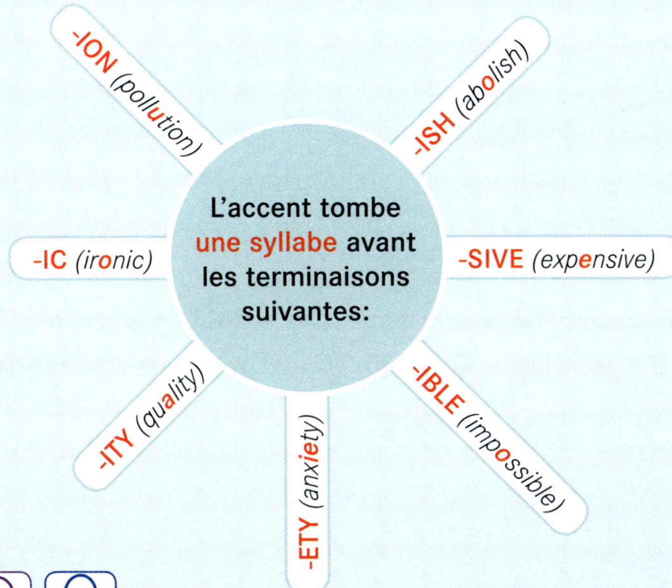

Je m'entraîne CD3 PISTE 32 MP3 PISTE 44

1. Utilisez ce que vous avez appris ci-dessus : recopiez les mots de chaque liste et entourez la syllabe accentuée. Ecoutez l'enregistrement et vérifiez vos réponses :
   - electric • fascination • politician • horrible • simplicity • impressive • discussion
   - pollution • electricity • courageous • geographic • historian • population • artificial • invisible • responsible

2. Entraînez-vous à lire ces mots à haute voix, si possible par groupes de deux.

b. Les mots à suffixe neutre

Un grand nombre de suffixes (dits neutres) ne modifient pas l'accentuation des mots auxquels ils sont ajoutés. Eux-mêmes sont inaccentués, souvent avec une forme réduite.

Exemple : *mother* → *motherless* /ˈmʌðələs/

Notez particulièrement:

-dom /dəm/	*-ful* /fəl/	*-less* /ləs/	*-ness* /nəs/	*-ship* /ʃɪp/	*-hood* /hʊd/	*-ly* /li/
freedom	*hopeful*	*hopeless*	*madness*	*friendship*	*childhood*	*obviously*

Lisez les mots ci-dessous à haute voix et vérifiez à l'écoute :

kingdom • neighbourhood • loneliness • shyly • defenceless • sadness • butcher • dictatorship • revengeful

c. Les voyelles réduites CD3 PISTE 33 MP3 PISTE 45

➲ **L'accent de mot porte sur une syllabe et par conséquent les autres syllabes du mot sont réduites.**

➲ **Certain suffixes qui sont toujours réduits :**

-ous /əs/	*-or* /ə/	*-ar* /ə/	*-er* /ə/	*-ain* /ɪn/	*-ness* /nəs/
ridiculous	*actor*	*particular*	*recorder*	*mountain*	*lightness*

➲ **Lisez les mots ci-dessous à haute voix et vérifiez à l'écoute :**

spectator - dangerous - adventurous - loneliness - fountain

➲ **Qu'ont en commun les lettres soulignées dans les mots suivants ?**

America ago abroad against perhaps
policeman computer probably particularly favourite temperature

➲ **Utilisez ce que vous avez appris pour lire les phrases suivantes :**

- *Do they live in a comfortable house?*
- *I'm afraid I can't give you any other information about it. - That's no problem at all.*
- *I suppose you've heard the news.*
- *This actor is ridiculous.*

d. Mots souvent malmenés par des francophones

CD3 PISTE 34 MP3 PISTE 46

Voici une liste de mots usuels. Trouvez la syllabe accentuée puis vérifiez à l'écoute.

beginning, event, themselves, sometimes, interesting, manage, village, imagine, believe, eleven, police

e. Prononciation de la marque *-ED*

CD3 PISTE 35 MP3 PISTE 47

➲ **Comment se prononce *-ED* dans les verbes suivants ? Recopiez la liste sur papier libre et classez-les en trois colonnes :** *liked • supported • invaded • dominated • launched • destroyed • attached • puzzled • polluted • disappeared • encouraged • asked • reached • robbed • stopped*

/d/	/t/	/id /

➲ **Illustrez chaque règle par des exemples:**

- *ED* se prononce /d/ après la plupart des consonnes sonores : ....
- *ED* se prononce /t/ après /p/ - /f/ - /s/ - /k/ : ....
- *ED* se prononce /.../ uniquement après /t/ et /d/ : ....

Recopiez ce tableau sur papier libre. Combien de syllabes contient chacun des verbes en *-ED* ci-dessous : Une, deux ou trois syllabes ? Classez-les dans un tableau : *needed • played • worked • wanted • opened • watched • decided • moved • missed • laughed • booked*

1 syllabe	2 syllabes	3 syllabes
	needed	

Dans quel cas l'ajout de *-ED* ajoute-t-il une syllabe à la base verbale ?

f. Liaisons consonne - voyelle

CD3 PISTE 36 MP3 PISTE 48

⚠ On fait la liaison entre deux mots lorsque le premier se termine par une consonne ou un e muet et que le second commence par une voyelle inaccentuée.
Exemples : *He lives ↺ in London.* *Come ↺ on ↺ in.* *She has ↺ a lot ↺ of work.*

Recopiez les phrases suivantes et notez les liaisons en couleur. Prononcez chacune d'elles à haute voix, puis vérifiez à l'écoute.

- *They said that I should learn a bit of English.*
- *There has been a lot of violence in our city recently.*
- *These kids are addicted to their Ipads and spend hours on them.*

5. S'entraîner à reproduire la mélodie des phrases

a. Apprenez à repérer les mots porteurs de sens.

CD3 PISTE 37 — MP3 PISTE 49

➲ **Recopiez le poème ci-dessous, écoutez-le et soulignez les mots porteurs de sens.**
Repérez les mots se terminant par *-ion*, entourez la syllabe accentuée. Quelle règle de la page 234 appliquez-vous ?

➲ **Marquez les liaisons consonne - voyelle.**

Référez-vous à la page 238.
Ex : If we stop ↺ and talk ↺ a while

➲ **Vérifiez vos réponses à l'écoute.**

b. Intonation

➲ **Écoutez à nouveau le poème.**

1. A la fin de chaque vers, repérez si l'intonation est montante (➚) ou descendante (➘).
2. Qu'en déduisez-vous?
   - Lorsqu'un message n'est pas terminé, l'intonation reste ...
   - Lorsqu'un message est terminé, l'intonation est ...

➲ **Tous en scène!**

a. Lisez le poème à haute voix. Travaillez en groupes de deux :
   - L'élève A lit les vers impairs.
   - L'élève B lui répond en lisant les vers pairs et les deux vers de conclusion.

b. Mimez la scène ou inventez une mise en scène pour réciter le poème.

Ations by Shel Silverstein

If we meet and I say, "Hi,"
That's a salutation.
If you ask me how I feel,
That's consideration.
If we stop and talk a while,
That's a conversation.
If we understand each other,
That's communication.
If we argue, scream and fight,
That's an altercation.
If later we apologize,
That's reconciliation.
If we help each other home,
That's a cooperation.
And all these actions added up
Make civilization.

(And if I say this is a wonderful poem,
Is that exaggeration?)

Shel Silverstein, *A Light in the Attic*, 1981

Anglais GB et Anglais US

Ecoutez les listes de mots dans les tableaux ci-dessous. Chaque liste sera lue d'abord par un Britannique, puis par un Américain.

I. Prononciation : différences essentielles

A. Voyelles simples

CD3 PISTE 38 — MP3 PISTE 50

Écoutez.

Anglais britannique (GB)			Anglais américain (US)		
pot /pɒt/	rock /rɒk/	boss /bɒs/	pot /pɑːt/	rock /rɑːk/	boss /bɑːs/
thought /θɔːt/	caught /kɔːt/	bought /bɔːt/	thought /θɑːt/	caught /kɑːt/	bought /bɑːt/

Déduisez : Quel est l'équivalent américain habituel des sons britanniques /**ɒ**/ et /**ɔː**/ non suivis de /**r**/ ?

B. Consonnes

Prononciation de la lettre *r* ?

CD3 PISTE 39 — MP3 PISTE 51

Écoutez.

Anglais britannique (GB)			Anglais américain (US)		
car /kɑː/	bird /bɜːd/	four /fɔː/	car /kɑːr/	bird /bɜːrd/	four /fɔːr/

Déduisez et complétez : En anglais britannique, *r* est … devant une consonne *(card)*, ou en fin de syllabe *(car)*, sauf pour liaison devant une voyelle *(the car ↺ industry)*. En anglais américain, *r* n'est jamais …

Prononciation de la lettre *t* ?

CD3 PISTE 40 — MP3 PISTE 52

Écoutez.

Anglais britannique (GB)		Anglais américain (US)	
city /'sɪti/	better /'betə/	city /'sɪt̬i /	better /'bet̬ə/
writing /'raɪtɪŋ/	little /'lɪtl/	writing /'raɪt̬ɪŋ/	little /'lɪt̬l/

Déduisez : En anglais américain, la prononciation du /**t**/ situé entre deux voyelles est dans certains cas proche de celle du /…/.

C. Différences dans la prononciation de certains mots

CD3 PISTE 41 — MP3 PISTE 53

1. Écoutez : /juː/ ou /uː/ ?

Anglais britannique (GB)		Anglais américain (US)	
new /njuː/	tube /tjuːb/	new /nuː/	tube /tuːb/
stupid /'stjuːpɪd/	duty /'djuːti/	stupid /'stuːpɪd/	duty /'duːti/

Déduisez : Sauf en position initiale *(united)* et après certaines consonnes (b, c, f… : *distribution, cube, few*), le /…/ de l'anglais britannique a généralement pour équivalent /…/ en anglais américain.

2. Écoutez : /ɑː/ ou /æ/ ? CD3 PISTE 42 MP3 PISTE 54

Anglais britannique (GB)		Anglais américain (US)	
ask /ɑːsk/	branch /brɑːntʃ/	ask /æsk/	branch /bræntʃ/
half /hɑːf/	past /pɑːst/	half /hæf/	past /pæst/

Déduisez : Dans un grand nombre de mots la lettre ***a*** est prononcée /... / en anglais britannique standard et /... / en anglais américain.

II. Vocabulaire

A. Différences de vocabulaire

Comme le disait Bernard Shaw, un célèbre écrivain irlandais : *"England and America are two countries divided by a common language."* En voici quelques exemples :

Anglais britannique (GB)	Anglais américain (US)	Français
autumn	fall, **au**tumn	*automne*
biscuit /'bɪskɪt/	c**oo**kie /'kʊki/	*gâteau sec*
car park	p**a**rking lot	*parking*
chips	French fries	*frites*
crisps	chips	*chips*
flat	ap**a**rtment	*appartement*
got	gotten	*(participe passé du verbe get)*
ground floor, first floor	first / s**e**cond floor	*rez-de-chaussée, 1er étage*
h**a**ndbag	purse, h**a**ndbag	*sac à main*
h**o**liday	vac**a**tion	*vacances*
l**e**tter box	m**ai**lbox	*boîte aux lettres*
lift	**e**levator	*ascenseur*
l**o**rry	truck	*camion*
m**o**bile phone	cell phone	*téléphone portable*
p**a**vement	s**i**dewalk	*trottoir*
p**e**trol	gas /gæs/	*essence*
r**u**bbish	g**a**rbage /'gɑːrbɪdʒ/	*ordures*
shop	store	*magasin*
town c**e**ntre *(nom)*	downt**ow**n *(nom/ adj./ adverbe)*	*centre ville*
tr**ai**ners	sn**ea**kers	*tennis (chaussures)*
tr**ou**sers	pants, tr**ou**sers	*pantalon*
underground	s**u**bway	*métro*

B. Différences orthographiques

	Anglais britannique (GB)	Anglais américain (US)
Comparez	colour • harbour • neighbour centre • litre • theatre	color • harbor • neighbor center • liter • theater

Déduisez : Les terminaisons ***-our*** et ***-re*** en anglais britannique s'écrivent ... et ... en anglais américain (dans des mots d'origine latine, française ou grecque).

	Anglais britannique (GB)	Anglais américain (US)
Le ***l*** final devant les suffixes *-ed, -ing* et *-er*	travel • travelled • travelling • traveller	travel • traveled • traveling • traveler

Observez et déduisez : En général, on redouble le ***l*** final devant les suffixes *-ed, -ing* et *-er* en anglais britannique et ... en anglais américain.

Utiliser un dictionnaire

A. Préparez-vous !

1. **Allez sur internet pour regarder cette vidéo. De quoi parle-t-elle ? Quels éléments ont retenu votre attention ?** www.howcast.com/videos/368119-How-to-Use-a-Dictionary

2. **Regardez-la à nouveau. Repérez les informations permettant de répondre aux questions suivantes :**

- Quels éléments sont nécessaires pour faire une recherche dans un dictionnaire ?
- Quelles sont les étapes à suivre pour utiliser un dictionnaire ?
- Concluez : quelles informations va-t-on trouver dans un dictionnaire ?

B. Comment utiliser un dictionnaire bilingue ?

1. **Observez cette entrée d'un dictionnaire bilingue papier.**

1 2 3 4

screen [skri:n] **1** *n* **(a)** (*in room*) paravent *m*; (*for fire*) écran *m* de cheminée; (*fig: of troops, trees*) rideau *m*; (*pretence*) masque *m*; V **safety, silk, smoke** *etc*.
(b) (*Cine, TV etc*) écran *m*. **to show sth on a ~** projeter qch; (*TV*) **a 50-cm ~** un écran de 50 cm; (*Cine*) **the ~** l'écran, le cinéma; (*Cine*) **the big** *or* **large ~** le grand écran; (*TV*) **the small ~** le petit écran; **to write for the ~** écrire des scénarios; V **panoramic, television, wide** *etc*.
(c) (*sieve*) crible *m*, claie *f*.
2 *cpd*: **screen actor** acteur *m* de cinéma, vedette *f* de l'écran; **screen door** porte grillagée; **screenplay** scénario *m*; **screen rights** droits *mpl* d'adaptation cinématographique; **screen test** bout *m* d'essai; **to do a screen test** tourner un bout d'essai; (*Brit Aut*) **screen wash(er)** lave-glace(s); **screen writer** scénariste *mf*.
3 *vt* **(a)** (*hide*) masquer, cacher. **the trees ~ed the house** les arbres masquaient *or* cachaient la maison; **to ~ sth from sight** *or* **view** dérober *or* masquer qch aux regards; **he ~ed the book with his hand** il a caché le livre de sa main; **to ~ sth from the wind/sun** protéger qch du vent/du soleil; **in order to ~ our movements from the enemy** pour cacher *or* masquer nos mouvements à l'ennemi.
(b) (*Cine, TV*) *film* projeter.
(c) (*sieve*) *coal* cribler; *candidates, applications* passer au crible. (*fig*) **to ~ sb (for a job)** passer un candidat au crible; (*Med*) **to ~ sb for cancer** faire subir à qn un test de dépistage du cancer.

2. **Principaux repérages**

a. Associez chacun des numéros ci-dessus à l'un des éléments suivants.

- A. La nature / catégorie grammaticale du mot
- B. Un des sens du mot
- C. La prononciation du mot
- D. Le domaine d'utilisation du mot

b. Combien de sens a le mot *screen* ?

c. A quoi correspondent ces abréviations ? *n – vt – fig – sb – sth – cpd – med*

Online Dictionary / Translator Tips

- **Préférez les dictionnaires aux traducteurs en ligne.**
  Les traducteurs donnent souvent des traductions approximatives ou inexactes.
- **Vérifiez bien l'orthographe en français du mot que vous cherchez.**
  Les dictionnaires en ligne ne corrigent pas l'orthographe française et vous pouvez vous retrouver avec une traduction erronée !
- **Ne cherchez pas de verbes conjugués.**
  Trouvez l'infinitif puis conjuguez-le.
- **Vérifiez la prononciation d'un mot si vous devez l'utiliser à l'oral (ou à l'écrit).**
  Certains sites proposent de faire écouter la prononciation du mot. Profitez-en !

Web box

Dictionnaire bilingue:
http://www.wordreference.com

Dictionnaires unilingues:
http://www.merriam-webster.com/
http://dictionary.cambridge.org/

C. C'est à vous !

1. Pour chacune de ces phrases, identifiez la nature du mot *screen*. Aidez-vous de la page ci-contre pour trouver la traduction correspondant au contexte.

a. *He's glued to his **screen**.*
b. *She wore a hat to **screen** her face from the rain.*
c. *They **screened** all the job applicants.*
d. *The patient was **screened** for contagious diseases.*

2. Les mots soulignés peuvent avoir plusieurs significations. Aidez-vous d'un dictionnaire pour trouver leur sens dans ces phrases.

a. *What was his date like? She was fair-haired.*
b. *You need a lot of will and patience to pass this exam.*
c. *I assume he fell into the well.*
d. *He always does things by the book.*

3. Voici un extrait du texte qui présente David Karp (p.105). Observez la traduction en français proposée par un traducteur en ligne.

Karp, of course, is the 26-year-old autodidact who founded Tumblr, the social-networking blog site [...]. Karp isn't your typical Internet entrepreneur. He grew up in New York, on the Upper West Side of Manhattan, and attended the Calhoun School, where his mother was a science teacher. [...]
At Calhoun, Karp drove teachers nuts by trying to hack into the school's computer system. After leaving, he spent a year at the Bronx High School of Science, where he studied Japanese. But he fell in with the wrong crowd and dropped out – besting technology giants such as Jobs, Bill Gates, Larry Ellison and Mark Zuckerberg, who all timidly waited until after entering college to abandon their formal education.

Karp, bien sûr, est l'autodidacte de 26 ans qui a fondé Tumblr, le site de blog de réseau social [...]. Karp n'est pas votre entrepreneur Internet typique. Il a grandi à New York, sur le Côté ouest Supérieur du Manhattan et a assisté à l'École Calhoun, où sa mère était un professeur de sciences. [...]
À Calhoun, Karp a conduit des dingue de professeurs en essayant de tailler dans le système informatique de l'école. Après le départ, il a passé une année au Lycée du Bronx de Science, où il a étudié le japonais. Mais il a accepté la mauvaise foule et a omis – à mieux des géants technologiques comme des Emplois, Bill Gates, Larry Ellison et Mark Zuckerberg, qui tout timidement attendu jusqu'après le collège entrant pour abandonner leur éducation formelle.

a. Que remarquez-vous ?

b. En groupes, essayez d'améliorer la traduction proposée par le traducteur.

c. Que retenez-vous de cet exercice ?

Fast Facts: The United Kingdom

The United Kingdom
Population: 64 million

London: Capital city

10 Downing Street
(Prime Minister's residence)

The City
(financial and commercial district)

Big Ben
by the River Thames

Some Art Museums

National Gallery

British Museum

Tate Modern

Buckingham Palace
(royal residence)

Monarch
(Queen / King)

Government

Prime Minister

The House of Lords

The House of Commons
(MPs)

Westminster
(Houses of Parliament)

Map: See inside cover

National Anthem:
God Save the Queen

The British Flag
The Union Jack

Currency

1 penny

100 pence = £1

The UK: a timeline

43 AD*

Roman invasion of Britain

1066 AD*

William, Duke of Normandy, invaded Britain and became King of England

1509-1547

p.66

During the reign of Henry VIII, the Church of England became independent from the Roman Catholic Church

1558-1603
Elizabeth I (Tudor)

1591

p.62

First performance of a play by William Shakespeare

1805

The Battle of Trafalgar, British Admiral Lord Nelson defeats Napoleon

1837-1901

p.63

Queen Victoria's reign saw the expansion and prosperity of the British Empire

*AD: after Christ (BC: before Christ)

Some British Icons

Novelists

Jane Austen (1775-1817) p.168

J. R. R. Tolkien (1892-1973) p.285

Roald Dahl (1916-1990) p.285

George Orwell (1903-1950) p.62

Charles Dickens (1812-1870)

Sir Arthur Conan Doyle (1859-1930) p.216

Agatha Christie (1890-1976) p.285

Scientists

Alan Turing (1912-1954) Mathematician p.103

Charles Darwin (1809-1882) p.62

Isaac Newton (1643-1727) Physicist

Alexander Fleming (1881-1955) Biologist (discovered the Penicillin)

Playwrights and film directors

Oscar Wilde (1854-1900) p.160

Ken Loach (1936) p.286

Alfred Hitchcock (1899-1980) p.214

William Shakespeare (1564-1616) p.62

Painters

John Constable (1776-1837)

Joseph M. W. Turner (1775-1851)

Francis Bacon (1909-1992)

David Hockney (1937) p.175

Thomas Gainsborough (1727-1788)

1914-1918 World War I

1940-45 and **1951-55** Winston Churchill, Prime Minister

1939-1945 World War II (the Blitz)

1979-1990 Margaret Thatcher, Prime Minister, was nicknamed "The Iron Lady"

1918 Women get the right to vote in the UK p.94

1952

Elizabeth II's coronation

1961

The Beatles' first performance p.46

1973

The UK joined the European Community

1994 The Channel Tunnel is officially inaugurated

2011

Prince William married Kate Middleton

2013 Birth of George, Alexander, Louis of Cambridge, heir to the throne

Fast Facts: The United States of America

The United States
Population: 317 million

Map: See inside cover

Government

The White House, Washington D.C. *(the official residence of the President)*

Congress Capitol Hill, Washington D.C.

The Senate (two senators per state)

The House of Representatives (435 representatives)

Democrats

Republicans

National Anthem: Star Spangled Banner

Uncle Sam personifies the country

Currency

1 cent

Dollar ($) 100 cents (cts)

National Emblems

The **Statue of Liberty,** NYC

Bald Eagle

50 white stars representing the 50 states

13 red and white stripes representing the 13 original colonies

The American Flag: *"The Star Spangled Banner"*

The USA: a timeline

1775-1783 American Revolution (colonists vs. Great Britain) Independence

1804-1806 Lewis and Clark expedition p.116

1861-1865 US Civil War (northern states vs. southern states)

1914-1918 World War I

1492

Discovery of America by Christopher Colombus

1620

The Pilgrims arrive aboard the Mayflower

1776

The Declaration of Independence

1849

The California Gold Rush

1863

President Abraham Lincoln abolishes slavery p.128

1920

Women get the right to vote

1929

Wall Street Crash (Beginning of the Great Depression)

Some American Icons

Political leaders

George Washington
(1732-1799)
1st US President

p.117

Thomas Jefferson
(1743-1826)
3rd US President

p.134

Abraham Lincoln
(1809-1865)
16th US President

John Fitzgerald Kennedy
(1917-1963)
35th US President

Franklin D. Roosevelt
(1882-1945)
32nd US President

Activists

Martin Luther King
(1929-1968)
Civil Rights Activist

Susan B. Anthony
(1820-1906)
Women Civil Rights Activist

Rosa Parks
(1913-2005)
Civil Rights Activist

p.133

Harriet Tubman
(1820-1913)
Abolitionist

Writers

p.131

Langston Hughes
(1902-1967)

Edgar Allan Poe
(1809-1849)

Ernest Hemingway
(1899-1961)

Toni Morrison
(1931)

Scientists

Thomas Edison
(1847-1931)
Physicist, invented light bulb and motion camera

p.103

Bill Gates
(1955)
Computer Scientist, founder of Microsoft

p.103

Steve Jobs
(1955-2011)
Computer Scientist, founder of Apple

Painters

Edward Hopper
(1882-1967)

Andy Warhol
(1928-1987)

p.170

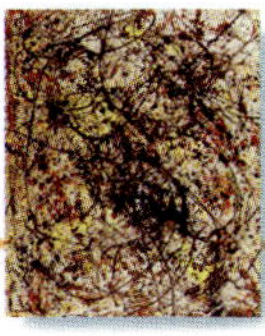

Jackson Pollock
(1912-1956)

Norman Rockwell
(1894-1978)

p.29

1939-1945
World War II

1954-1975
Vietnam War

1941

Attack on Pearl Harbor

1947
Marilyn Monroe appears for the first time on the screen

1954
Beginning of the Civil Rights Movements

1963
Martin Luther King delivers famous speech "*I have a dream*"

1968
Civil Rights Act

1969

First man on the moon (Neil Armstrong)

1977
Elvis Presley's last show

1991
@
The World Wide Web is launched

p.103

9/11/2001
World Trade Center is destroyed by largest terrorist attack in US history

p.198

2009

Barack Obama becomes the 1rst black President of the USA (44th)

Fast Facts: South Africa

11 official languages: Afrikaans, English, Ndebele, Xhosa, Zulu...

Most important cities:
Pretoria
(administrative capital)
Cape Town
(legislative capital)
Johannesburg
(economic centre)

Kruger Park:
a national reserve

Cape Town

'The Rainbow Nation'
Population: 52 million

The springbok:
a national symbol

Apartheid
laws which physically separated different racial groups in South Africa p.72

Nelson Mandela
(1918-2013)
was jailed for opposing apartheid. He remained in prison for 27 years. p.74

F. W. de Klerk
(born 1948)
was the president who ended apartheid in 1990.

Apartheid and its famous icons

Steve Biko
(1946-1977)
an anti-apartheid activist who died in police custody and became a hero.

Bishop Desmond Tutu
(born 1931)
fought against apartheid and has always defended human rights.

ANC
(*African National Congress*):
political party which fought to bring apartheid to an end.

South Africa: a timeline

1652 Dutch farmers ('Boers') settle in Cape Town.

1852 Britain takes control of the Cape Town Province.

1899-1902
The Anglo-Boer War, the Dutch settlers fight the British. Britain wins and gains control of South Africa.

1948 Apartheid is introduced.

1961 South Africa is declared a Republic.

1970s-80s
Active fight against apartheid

1976 The Soweto Riots p.72

1990 Mandela is released from Robben Island Prison. Apartheid is abolished.

1993 De Klerk and Mandela are awarded the Nobel Peace Prize.

1994 Mandela is elected President. A new flag is adopted.

2010 South Africa is the first African nation to host the FIFA World Cup

Précis grammatical
Index p. 270

Adjectifs

- Les adjectifs anglais sont **invariables** :
  *These chairs are very **comfortable**.* Ces chaises sont très confortables.
- Les adjectifs **épithètes** (= rattachés directement au nom) se placent **avant** le nom :
  *He bought six very **comfortable chairs**.* Il a acheté six chaises très confortables.
- En anglais, on emploie les adjectifs comme noms pour désigner **l'ensemble d'une catégorie** :
  ***The poor** are more numerous than **the rich**.* Les pauvres sont plus nombreux que les riches.

  Notez que l'adjectif est précédé de ***the***, qu'il reste invariable, et que le groupe *the* + adjectif a un **sens pluriel**.

> Dans les autres cas, l'adjectif est obligatoirement **associé à un nom ou au pronom *one*** :
> Il y avait deux Français. → *There were two **French people**.*
> Je préfère la bleue. → *I prefer the **blue one**.*

- Certains adjectifs sont formés à partir de **verbes**, auxquels on ajoute :
  - soit la terminaison ***-ing*** (*amuse* → *amusing*, « amusant »),
  - soit la **marque du participe passé** (*amuse* → *amused*, « amusé »).

Attention : la terminaison *-ing* équivaut à la terminaison française « -ant ».

interesting	intéressant	*tiring*	fatigant
interested	intéressé	*tired*	fatigué

Adverbes : leur place dans la phrase

- Les **adverbes de fréquence** usuels (essentiellement *sometimes*, *rarely*, *often*, *always*, *never* et *ever*) se placent **devant le verbe** et, quand il y a un auxiliaire (*BE, HAVE, CAN*, etc.), **après l'auxiliaire** :
  *She **sometimes eats** cornflakes.* Elle mange quelquefois des cornflakes.
  *He **is often** in front of his computer.* Il est souvent devant son ordinateur.
  ***I've never** eaten Jamaican food.* Je n'ai jamais mangé de la nourriture Jamaïcaine.
- **L'adverbe ne doit pas séparer le verbe de son complément d'objet** :
  Il connaît bien le Portugal. → *He knows Portugal **well**.*

All, whole, every, each, both

all = tout(e), tous, toutes	*He ate **all** the bread / **all** the sandwiches.* Il a mangé tout le pain / tous les sandwiches.
the whole /həʊl/ = la totalité (de)	*He drank **the whole bottle**.* Il a bu toute la bouteille.
every = chaque	***Every** problem has its solution.* Chaque problème a sa solution. (= Tous les problèmes ont leur solution.) Notez l'emploi du **singulier** à la suite de *every*.
each = chaque, chacun(e)	***Each** situation is particular.* Chaque situation est particulière.
both /bəʊθ/ = les deux (sous-entendu : pas seulement un/une)	*I've met **both brothers**.* J'ai rencontré les deux frères. (= pas seulement l'un des deux)

Article *a/an*

1. Formes

- ***a*** (/ə/) devant un son « consonne » : ***a** cat*. Attention à certains mots qui, **dans leur forme écrite**, commencent par une voyelle, mais **dans leur prononciation** commencent par une consonne :

  ***a u**niform* (/ˈjuːnɪfɔːm/, consonne transcrite /j/), *a European city* (même chose), ***a o**ne-man show* (/ˌwʌnmænˈʃəʊ/, consonne transcrite /w/).

  Attention aussi au *h* initial, qui est une consonne **prononcée** (***a h**appy day*), sauf dans ***honest***, ***hono(u)r***, ***hour***, ***heir*** (« héritier ») et leurs dérivés : ***an** honest man*, ***an** hour*, ***an** hourly payment*.

- ***an*** (/ən/) devant un son « voyelle » (***an o**range*).

2. Emploi particulier en anglais

- Pour indiquer le métier de quelqu'un, on utilise ***a/an*** + nom de métier :
  *She's **an engineer**.* Elle est ingénieur.

Article *the*

1. Prononciation

- /ðə/ devant un son « consonne » (*the cat* /ðəˈkæt/, *the uniform* /ðəˈjuːnɪfɔːm/, *the one-man show* /ðəˌwʌnmænˈʃəʊ/) ;
- /ði/ devant un son « voyelle » (*the orange* /ðiˈɒrɪndʒ/, *the hour* /ðiˈaʊə/.

2. Emplois

Attention à cette différence avec les articles *le/la/les* du français : on emploie l'article « zéro » (Ø) pour parler de **quelque chose « en général »**, devant les **indénombrables au singulier** et devant les **dénombrables au pluriel** :
***Jazz** was born around 1895 in New Orleans.* Le jazz est né aux alentours de 1895 à la Nouvelle-Orléans.
*He loves **comic strips**.* Il adore les bandes dessinées.

Article « zéro » (Ø)

L'article Ø, ou absence d'article, existe également en français : « Il est sorti de prison. » n'a pas le même sens que « Il est sorti de la prison. ». En anglais, cependant, il est beaucoup plus fréquent qu'en français.

- On utilise l'article Ø quand on veut parler de quelque chose **« en général »**, avec les noms **indénombrables au singulier** et les **dénombrables au pluriel** :
  *He doesn't like **chocolate/oranges**.* Il n'aime pas le chocolat/les oranges.

  En français, on utilise dans ce cas l'article « le/la/les ».

- On utilise l'article Ø pour désigner une chose du point de vue de son **utilisation** ou de sa **fonction sociale** :
  *She's going to **school**.* Elle va à l'école.
  *He'll soon get out of **prison**.* Il va bientôt sortir de prison.

- On utilise l'article Ø devant les noms de pays, continents ou régions : *Germany* (l'Allemagne), *Africa* (l'Afrique), *Alaska* (l'Alaska). Exception pour les noms de pays au pluriel : *the USA, the Netherlands* (les Pays Bas), ou constitués à partir d'un nom commun : *the United Kingdom*.

- On utilise aussi l'article Ø devant les noms de titre suivis d'un nom propre (*President Obama*, *Queen Elizabeth*, etc.).

BE

	Formes affirmatives	Formes négatives	Formes interrogatives
Présent	***I am*** *happy. /* ***I'm*** *happy.* *You* ***are*** *happy. / You'****re*** *happy.* *He/She/It* ***is*** *happy. /* *He/She/It'****s*** *happy.* *We/You/They* ***are*** *happy. /* *We/You/They'****re*** *happy.*	*I* ***am not*** */ I'****m not*** *happy.* *You* ***are*** *not / You* ***aren't*** *happy.* *He/She/It* ***is not*** */* ***isn't*** *happy.* *We/You/They* ***are not*** */* ***aren't*** */ɑːnt/ happy.*	***Am*** *I happy?* ***Are*** *you happy?* ***Is*** *he/she/it happy?* ***Are*** *we/you/they happy?*
Prétérit	*I* ***was*** */wɒz/, /wəz/ happy.* *You* ***were*** */wɜː/,/wə/ happy.* *He/She/It* ***was*** *happy.* *We/You/They* ***were*** *happy.*	*I* ***was not*** */* ***wasn't*** */wɒznt/happy.* *You* ***were not*** */* ***weren't*** */wɜːnt/ happy.* *He/She/It* ***was not*** */* ***wasn't*** *happy.* *We/You/They* ***were not*** */* ***weren't*** *happy.*	***Was*** *I happy?* ***Were*** *you happy?* ***Was*** *he/she/it happy?* ***Were*** *we/you/they happy?*

Participe passé : ***been*** **; forme en -ING :** ***being***

Dans certains cas, l'anglais emploie une construction en BE alors que le français emploie une construction en « avoir » :
*He'****s*** *hungry / thirsty.* Il **a** faim. / Il **a** soif.
*I'****m*** *cold / hot.* J'**ai** froid. / J'**ai** chaud.
*You'****re*** *lucky.* Tu **as** de la chance.
'How old ***is*** *she?' 'She'****s*** *16.'* « Quel âge **a**-t-elle ? » « Elle **a** 16 ans. »

CAN (présent *can*, prétérit *could* - Modaux p. 258)

Le présent ***can*** (forme négative ***cannot/can't***) est l'équivalent habituel du français « je peux » (ou parfois « je sais ») :
Can *I* ***help*** *you?* Je peux vous aider ?
Can *you swim?* Tu sais nager ?
You ***can't*** *vote if you are under 18.* On ne peut pas voter si on a moins de 18 ans.

Pour « je sens » « je peux » = « il se peut que je », on emploie ***may***, et non *can* (p. 257) :
On ne sait jamais, il peut aimer ça. *You never know, he* ***may*** *like it.*

Le prétérit ***could*** (forme négative ***could not / couldn't***) est l'équivalent habituel du français « je pourrais » :
Could you lend me €10? Tu pourrais me prêter 10 € ?

Pour exprimer une possibilité future (« je pourrai »), on emploie ***will be able to*** :
*Next year I'****ll be able to*** *vote.* L'an prochain je pourrai voter.

Comparaison des adjectifs

Adjectifs courts : une syllabe, ou deux syllabes avec terminaison *-y* ou *-er*.
Adjectifs longs : autres adjectifs.

	Adjectifs courts	Adjectifs longs
Comparatif de supériorité (= plus… que…)	*Ella is* ***taller than*** */ðən/ Lucy.* Ella est plus grande que Lucy.	*Nora is* ***more*** *gifted* ***than*** *Lyn.* Nora est plus douée que Lyn.
Comparatif d'infériorité (= moins… que…)	*It's* ***less*** *interesting* ***than*** */ðən/ I thought.* C'est moins intéressant que je croyais. *The book is* ***not as*** */əz/* ***interesting as*** */əz/* ***the film****.* Le livre est moins intéressant que le film.	

	Adjectifs courts	Adjectifs longs
« de plus en plus… »	*It's **easier and easier**.* C'est de plus en plus facile.	*It's **more and more interesting**.* C'est de plus en plus intéressant.
« de moins en moins… »	*It's **less and less easy/interesting**.*	
Comparatif d'égalité (= aussi… que…)	*Jane is **as** /əz/ **tall** / **as gifted as** Lisa.* Jane est aussi grande / aussi douée que Lisa.	
Superlatif de supériorité (= le plus…)	*Ann is **the tallest girl in** the class.* Ann est la fille la plus grande de la classe.	*Liz is **the most gifted girl in** the class.* Liz est la fille la plus douée de la classe.

Le complément du superlatif est introduit par ***in***, sauf s'il désigne un ensemble d'éléments (*the tallest girl **of** all*) ou une période de temps (*the longest day **of** the year*).

Modifications orthographiques avec les terminaisons ***-er*** / ***-est*** :
- *happy* → *happier, happiest* : un *y* qui suit une consonne devient *i*.
- *big* → *bigger, biggest* : une consonne qui suit une voyelle est redoublée.

Comparatifs et superlatifs de supériorité irréguliers

good bon ***well*** bien	***better*** meilleur / mieux	***the best*** le/la/les meilleur(e)(s) / mieux
bad mauvais	***worse*** /wɜːs/ pire	***the worst*** /wɜːst/ le/la/les pire(s)
far loin	***farther/further*** plus loin	***the farthest / the furthest*** le/la/les plus éloigné(e)(s).

Démonstratifs : *this/these* et *that/those*

- ***This*** (+ nom au **singulier**) et ***these*** /ðiːz/ (+ nom au **pluriel**) s'emploient pour désigner ce qui est proche de l'énonciateur dans l'espace ou le temps, ou ressenti comme proche :
  ***This city** is marvellous.* Cette ville [= la ville où nous sommes] est merveilleuse.
  *I love **this song**.* J'adore cette chanson [= la chanson que nous écoutons].
- ***That*** /ðæt/ (+ nom au **singulier**) et ***those*** /ðəʊz/ (+ nom au **pluriel**) s'emploient pour désigner ce qui est éloigné de l'énonciateur (ou ressenti comme éloigné), ou a déjà été mentionné :
  *I hate **that song**.* J'ai horreur de cette chanson.
  *I hate **those songs**.* J'ai horreur de ces chansons.

Discours direct/indirect : rapporter des paroles ou des pensées

Discours direct	Discours indirect
She said, 'I want to go.'	*She said (that) she wanted to go.*
She said, 'I have finished the work.'	*She said (that) she had **finished** the work.*
She said, 'I will help them.'	*She said (that) she would **help** them.*
She said, 'They may be late.' (Ils peuvent être en retard.)	*She said (that) they might **be** late.* (…qu'ils pouvaient être en retard)

1. Caractéristiques du discours indirect

- Il n'utilise pas les guillemets.
- Il peut être introduit par la **conjonction *that*** (**prononcée** /ðət/) ou la **conjonction « zéro »**.
- Certains **pronoms** doivent être modifiés (dans les exemples ci-dessus, *I* devient *she*).
- Il faut respecter les règles dites de **concordance des temps** ; ces règles s'appliquent dans les récits au passé, quand le verbe qui introduit le discours indirect est au **prétérit** (*He said / He thought that*…) :

- Le **présent** du discours direct devient un **prétérit** (voir tous les exemples du tableau).

- Le **prétérit** du discours direct devient généralement un **past perfect** :
*He said, 'I **saw** her on May 1.'* (Je l'ai vue le 1er mai.) → *He said that he **had seen** her on May 1.*

△ Les **adverbes de lieu et de temps** peuvent être modifiés :
*He said, 'I will stay **here** until **tomorrow.**'* (« Je vais rester ici jusqu'à demain. »)
→ *He said that he would stay **there** until **the day after**.*

Autres changements de ce type :
yesterday → *the day before*
last week/month/year → *the week/month/year before*
ago → *before*

2. Le cas particulier des questions

△ Les questions rapportées au style indirect sont à la **forme affirmative** : il n'y a pas d'inversion sujet-auxiliaire, ni d'auxiliaire *do/does/did*, ni de point d'interrogation.
She asked me, 'Where does Susan live?' → *She asked me **where Susan lived**.*

△ Pour rapporter au style indirect une *Yes/No question*, on utilise ***if*** (***whether*** dans un style formel) :
He asked me, 'Do you want some more coffee?' → *He asked me **if** I wanted some more coffee.*

Exclamation : les constructions exclamatives

Selon que l'exclamation porte sur un **nom** ou sur un **adjectif**, ces constructions peuvent être introduites par ***what/such*** ou par ***how/so*** :

***What** a (strange) story!* Quelle histoire (bizarre)!	*It's **such** a strange story!* C'est une histoire tellement bizarre !
***How** strange (it is)!* Comme c'est bizarre !	*It's **so** strange!* C'est tellement bizarre!

Si le nom qui suit *what* ou *such* est un indénombrable, il ne peut pas être précédé de l'article *a/an*, et il faut employer **l'article zéro** : *What strange weather!* (Quel temps bizarre !) *It's such strange weather!* (C'est un temps tellement bizarre !)

« Faire faire »

△ Assez souvent, l'équivalent anglais du français « faire + verbe » est un verbe simple :
Fais-moi **voir** ce que tu as acheté. → ***Show** me what you've bought.*
Il **a fait bouillir** l'eau. → *He **boiled** the water.*

△ Dans les autres cas, « faire » peut avoir pour équivalent *make*, *have* ou *get*, dans des constructions différentes.

- ***Make*** **+ nom/pronom + base verbale** exprime une idée de cause ou de forte contrainte :
*They **made them get off** the plane.* Ils les ont fait descendre de l'avion.
*She **made that poor child cry**.* Elle a fait pleurer ce pauvre enfant. (Notez l'ordre des mots en anglais.)

- ***Have*** **+ nom/pronom + base verbale** exprime une contrainte plus neutre :
*I'll **have him take** your baggage upstairs.* Je vais lui faire monter vos bagages.

△ ***Have/get*** **+ nom/pronom + participe passé :** on s'intéresse au résultat plus qu'à la personne qui accomplit l'action:
*I'll **have** / I'll **get** my hair cut.* Je vais me faire couper les cheveux.

Futur (situer un événement dans le futur)

1.

Pour parler de l'avenir, le français utilise souvent le **présent** : « Demain, il est à Paris ». L'anglais fait de même, mais attention, il faut choisir entre le **présent simple** et le **présent en** *BE* **+ -***ING*.

- On emploie le **présent simple** pour un événement qui fait partie d'un **programme** (planning, horaire de trains, etc.) :
  Tomorrow there ***is*** *a good film on TV.* Demain, il y a un bon film à la télé.
- On emploie le **présent en** *BE* + *-ING* pour exprimer une **intention** :
  Tomorrow evening ***I'm watching*** *the match on TV.* Demain soir je regarde le match à la télé.

2.

L'équivalent anglais du **futur simple** est en général le modal ***will*** (+ base verbale) :
Je m'en **souviendrai**. → ***I'll remember*** *it.*

3.

L'équivalent anglais de **« aller + infinitif »** est souvent ***be going to*** :
Il **va pleuvoir**. → ***It's going to rain.***

Cependant, on emploie ***will*** pour exprimer une **décision prise au moment où l'on parle** :
D'accord, je vais leur demander. → *OK,* ***I'll ask*** *them.*

Habitude

1.

Dans la plupart des cas, l'habitude s'exprime tout simplement en utilisant le **présent** ou le **prétérit** simples associés à un adverbe ou complément de temps :
He ***often visits*** *his grandparents.* Il va souvent voir ses grands-parents.
She ***takes*** *the bus* ***every morning at 8.*** Elle prend le bus tous les matins à 8 h.

2.

Pour exprimer un **comportement habituel**, on peut utiliser ***will*** (présent) ou ***would*** (passé):
*He'****ll*** *listen to that music for hours.* Il écoute cette musique pendant des heures.
*She'****d*** *go jogging in the park every evening.* Elle faisait du jogging dans le parc tous les soirs.

3.

Pour exprimer le sens de **« être habitué à »**, on peut utiliser *BE USED TO* + V-*ING* :
He ***was used to getting up*** *early.* Il était habitué à se lever tôt.

> Ne confondez pas cette construction avec ***used to*** **+ base verbale**, qui n'exprime pas obligatoirement une habitude, et sert simplement à situer un événement ou une série d'événements dans le passé : *There used to be a pub here*. Il y avait un pub ici autrefois.

- Pour exprimer le sens de **« s'habituer à »**, on peut utiliser *GET USED TO* + V-*ING*
  He soon ***got used to*** *getting up at 5 every morning.* Il s'est vite habitué à se lever à 5 heures tous les matins.

HAVE

1.

Have peut exprimer la **possession** au sens large du terme (« avoir un ordinateur / un rhume / des enfants »). On peut alors employer *HAVE* seul, ou suivi de *GOT (HAVE GOT)* :
*He **has** a lot of friends. / He**'s got** (= **has got**) a lot of friends.* Il a beaucoup d'amis.

Have got est employé dans la langue courante ou familière. Les deux formes ne fonctionnent pas de la même façon à la forme interrogative et à la forme négative :

- ***Have*** **employé sans *got*** fonctionne comme un **verbe** ordinaire : il se construit avec les auxiliaires ***do/does/did*** au présent et au prétérit simples **négatif** et **interrogatif**.
  *She **doesn't have** a computer.* Elle n'a pas d'ordinateur.
  ***Did** Alice **have** children?* Est-ce qu'Alice avait des enfants ?
- Dans l'expression ***have got***, l'élément *have* fonctionne comme un **auxiliaire** (il se contruit toujours sans ***do/does/did***) :
  *She **hasn't got** a computer.* Elle n'a pas d'ordinateur.
  ***Has she got** a tablet?* Est-ce qu'elle a une tablette ?

> En anglais US, on dira habituellement *She **doesn't have** a computer. / **Does she have** a tablet?*

2.

Le **verbe *have*** peut être utilisé dans le sens de « prendre », ou dans un sens voisin (manger, boire, etc.) :
***Have** a nice weekend!* Bon week-end !
*They**'re having** lunch.* Ils sont en train de déjeuner.
*We**'ll have** a good time.* On va bien s'amuser.

> *Have* est ici un verbe **d'action**, et il ne peut pas être remplacé par *have got*. La négation et l'interrogation se forment obligatoirement avec *do/does/did* :
> *They **didn't have** a nice weekend.* Ils n'ont pas passé un bon week-end.
> *What time **do you have** dinner?* Vous dînez à quelle heure ?

3.

L'auxiliaire ***have*** est également utilisé pour former le *present perfect* et le *past perfect* : *I **have** / I **had** finished* (« J'ai / J'avais fini » - voir p. 263).

If... et l'hypothèse

Hypothèse **possible** (sur un fait **présent** ou **futur**)	*If it **is** sunny, we **will** go to the seaside.*	S'il fait beau, nous irons au bord de la mer. (Je ne sais pas s'il fait/fera beau.)
Hypothèse **irréelle** (**contraire à la réalité**) portant sur un fait **présent**	*If it **was** sunny [now], we **would** go to the seaside.*	S'il faisait beau [maintenant], nous irions au bord de la mer. (Je sais qu'il **ne fait pas** beau.)
Hypothèse **peu probable**, portant sur un fait **futur**	*If it **was** sunny tomorrow, we **would** go to the seaside.*	Si demain il faisait beau [mais c'est peu probable], nous irions au bord de la mer.
Hypothèse **irréelle** (**contraire à la réalité**) portant sur un fait **passé**	*If it **had been** sunny, we **would have gone** to the seaside.*	S'il avait fait beau [hier], nous serions allés au bord de la mer.

« Il y a un problème » : *There is a problem*

- L'élément conjugué est ***BE*** :
  *There **is** / There**'s** a problem.* Il y a un problème.
  *There **was** a problem.* Il y avait / Il y a eu un problème.
  *There **will be** a problem.* Il y aura un problème.
  *There **must be** a problem.* Il doit y avoir un problème.

- Il y a obligatoirement un accord au **singulier** ou au **pluriel** avec le sujet « réel » (qui est placé après) :
  *There **is** a problem. / There **are** two problems.* Il y a un problème. / Il y a deux problèmes.
  *There **weren't*** /wɜːnt/ *many passengers.* Il n'y avait pas beaucoup de voyageurs.

  En français, on a toujours le singulier (« Il y a … », « Il y avait… »)

- À la forme interrogative, l'inversion se fait avec l'élément ***there*** :
  There is a problem. → ***Is there** a problem?* Est-ce qu'il y a un problème ?

N'utilisez pas la construction *there is / there are* lorsque « il y a » signifie « depuis » :
« Il y a deux mois qu'il est ici. » → *He's been here for two months.* « Il y a trois ans qu'elle est partie. »
→ *She left three years ago.* (voir p. 264) Present Perfect simple

Impératif

2ème personne du singulier ou du pluriel	Base verbale (*don't* + BV pour la négation)	***Be** careful! / **Watch** out!* Fais/Faites attention ! ***Don't ask** him!* Ne lui demande / demandez pas
1ère personne du pluriel	*Let's* + base verbale (*let's not* à la forme négative)	***Let's ask** him!* Demandons-lui ! ***Let's not be** pessimistic!* Ne soyons pas pessimistes !

Infinitif : propositions à l'infinitif en *to* (*to* + V)

Après les verbes qui expriment une volonté ou un souhait, et en particulier après *want*, *prefer* et *would like*, on utilise non pas une proposition en *that* (~~*I want that…*~~), mais une proposition formée avec un infinitif :
*He **wants everybody to keep** silent.* Il veut que tout le monde reste silencieux.
*I **prefer them to stay** here.* Je préfère qu'ils restent ici.
***Would** you **like him to help** you?* Est-ce que tu voudrais qu'il t'aide ?

Quand on utilise un **pronom** dans cette construction, il est à la **forme « complément »** (*me*, *him*, *them*, etc.).

Interrogation (constructions interrogatives)

1.

Ces constructions exigent l'emploi d'un **auxiliaire**, qui est *do/does* pour le présent et *did* pour le prétérit simples : *Did she like the film?*
Elles peuvent être introduites par un mot interrogatif ou une expression interrogative :
***Who** did they contact?* Ils ont contacté qui ?
***Whose** DVD is this?* Il est à qui, ce DVD ?
***How many** people attended the meeting?* Combien de personnes ont assisté à la réunion ?
***How much** money did he want?* Combien d'argent il voulait ?
***How long** did he stay?* Il est resté combien de temps ?
***How tall** is he?* Il mesure combien ?
***How far** did he go?* Il est allé loin/jusqu'où ?

***How often** do you change the batteries?* Tu changes les piles souvent / tous les combien ?
***How** is Sandra?* Comment elle va, Sandra ? (interrogation sur la santé)
***What** is Sandra **like**?* Elle est comment, Sandra ? (interrogation sur l'allure, le caractère, etc.)

> Opposez ***Who** did they see?* (Qui ont-ils vu ?) et ***Who** saw them?* (Qui les a vus ?) : quand le mot interrogatif ou l'expression interrogative est **sujet** du verbe, on emploie une construction affirmative (cf. *John saw them*), sans *do/does/did* au présent/prétérit simples.

2.

Si le verbe se construit avec une **préposition** (voir p. 262), cette préposition se place habituellement **après le verbe** :
*Who did you speak **to**?* Tu as parlé à qui ?
*What were they waiting **for** yesterday?* Qu'est-ce qu'ils attendaient, hier ?

« Laisser faire »

L'équivalent anglais habituel est la construction ***let*** (= autoriser) **+ nom/pronom + base verbale** (attention à l'ordre des mots en anglais) :
*He **let the children go**.* Il a laissé partir les enfants.
*He **let them go**.* Il les a laissés partir.

> Ne confondez pas les verbes *leave* et *let*. L'équivalent du français « laisser = abandonner / ne pas prendre / etc. » est généralement *leave* :
> *He **left** a message on a post-it note.* Il a laissé un message sur un post-it.

Many, much, a lot of, few, little

	Indénombrable (singulier)	**Dénombrable au pluriel**
beaucoup de	*There's **a lot of milk**.* Il y a beaucoup de lait. *Is there **much milk**?* *There isn't **much milk**.*	*There are **a lot of oranges**.* Il y a beaucoup d'oranges. *Are there **many oranges**?* *There aren't **many oranges**.*
peu de, pas beaucoup de	*There's **little milk**.* Il y a peu de lait.	*There are **few oranges**.* Il y a peu d'oranges.
un peu de, quelques	*There's **a little milk** left.* Il reste un peu de lait.	*There are **a few oranges** left.* Il reste quelques oranges.

MAY (présent *may*, prétérit *might* – voir Modaux p. 258)

- L'utilisation essentielle du modal ***may/might*** est l'expression d'une **possibilité logique** (= « il se peut / il se pourrait que… ») :
  *It **may** rain. / It **might** rain.* Il peut pleuvoir. / Il pourrait pleuvoir.
  *He **may not** like it.* Il peut ne pas aimer ça.
  *She **may** have missed her train.* Elle a pu rater son train.
- Dans un style formel, ***may*** peut être utilisé pour demander une permission :
  ***May** I borrow your phone?* Vous permettez que j'emprunte votre téléphone ?

Modaux : généralités

Présent	*can* /kæn/, /kən/	*may* /meɪ/	*must* /mʌst/, /məs(t)/	*shall* /ʃæl/, /ʃəl/	*will* /wɪl/, /wəl/, *'ll*
Prétérit	*could* /kʊd/, /kəd/	*might* /maɪt/		*should* /ʃʊd/, /ʃəd/	*would* /wʊd/, /wəd/, *'d*

> ***Cannot*** s'écrit en un seul mot ; ***can't*** se prononce /kɑːnt/ en anglais GB et /kænt/ en anglais US.
> Notez aussi la prononciation de la forme négative contractée de *will* : ***won't*** /wəʊnt/.

Formes modales simples et composées : exemples avec le modal MAY (présent ***may***, prétérit ***might***)

Modal + base verbale	*He **may/might work.***
Modal + BE + V-ING	*He **may/might be working.***
Modal + *have* + participe passé	*He **may/might have worked.***
Modal + *have been* + V-ING	*He **may/might have been working.***

Caractéristiques de forme des modaux

- Ce sont des auxiliaires : ils forment leur interrogation et leur négation directement (sans *do/does/did*).
- Ils ne prennent pas de *-s* à la troisième personne du singulier.
- Ils ne sont jamais précédés ni suivis de *to*. Ils n'ont pas d'infinitif, ni de forme en -ING, ni de participe passé.
- Dans un groupe verbal, il ne peut y avoir qu'un seul modal, qui est nécessairement le premier élément du groupe verbal.

MUST (voir Modaux p. 258), *HAVE TO, NEED TO*

1. Expression d'une obligation

- Le modal MUST exprime une **forte obligation**, et met en avant le souhait ou l'opinion de l'énonciateur :
  You must see that film! Il faut que tu voies ce film !
- *HAVE TO* (qui est un verbe, et non un modal) exprime également une **forte obligation**, mais de façon plus neutre :
  *On this building site you **have to** wear a helmet.* Sur ce chantier de construction il faut porter un casque.

> Ne confondez pas les formes négatives de MUST et de HAVE TO :
> *You **mustn't** stay here.* Vous ne devez pas rester ici.
> *You **don't have to** stay here.* Vous n'êtes pas obligés de rester ici.

- *NEED TO* (qui est lui aussi un verbe) tend à remplacer MUST, dans un style moins formel :
  *You **need to** be careful when you cross this road.* Il faut faire attention quand vous traversez cette route.

2. Expression d'une forte probabilité

*He **must** be ill.* Il doit être malade.

> Attention aux équivalents anglais du français « il a dû » :
> Sa voiture était en panne, il a dû prendre le bus. → *His car had broken down, he **had to take** the bus.* (Expression d'une **obligation**.)
> Il est en retard. Il a dû manquer son train. → *He's late. He **must have missed** his train.* (Expression d'une **forte probabilité**.)

Nom + 's (ou « génitif », ou « cas possessif »)

La terminaison **'s** ajoutée à un nom exprime la **possession au sens large du terme** (incluant les liens de parenté, etc.)

1. Forme

John's *brother lives in Paris*. Le frère de John vit à Paris.
His parents' house is in the country. La maison de ses parents est à la campagne.

Il n'y a jamais d'article devant le second nom. Il n'y a pas non plus d'article devant le premier nom s'il s'agit d'un **nom propre** : opposez *John's car* à *the doctor's car* (la voiture du docteur).

2. Emplois

- La terminaison *'s* est utilisée notamment avec les noms désignant :
  - des personnes,
  - des animaux familiers (*the cat's legs,* les pattes du chat),
  - des villes/institutions/etc. (*London's most famous monuments*, *UNO's decision*),
  - des repères temporels (*yesterday's paper*).
- Quand le second nom désigne un magasin, un lieu de travail ou une habitation, ce nom est généralement omis : *I have to* ***go to the dentist's / to Claire's***. Je dois aller chez le dentiste / chez Claire.

Noms composés

- Ce sont des noms constitués de plusieurs mots, écrits séparément ou en un seul mot :
  a phone number un numéro de téléphone
  a teacup une tasse à thé
  a ten-dollar bill un billet de dix dollars
  baby milk powder lait en poudre pour bébés
- Le dernier nom est le **nom principal** (*a racehorse* = un cheval de course, *a horse race* = une course de chevaux).
- Les noms qui le précèdent jouent le rôle d'adjectifs, et ils sont invariables : notez la forme singulier de *horse* dans *horse race*, de *dollar* dans *ten-dollar bill*, etc.
- C'est en général le premier nom qui est accentué : *a* ***race****horse*, *a* ***horse*** *race*, *a* ***phone*** *number*, *a* ***tea****cup*, etc.

Noms dénombrables et noms indénombrables

- **Nom dénombrable** (*a cat / two cats, an orange / many oranges*, etc.) : il est possible de **compter des éléments**, et donc de mettre le nom au pluriel.
- **Nom indénombrable** (*milk*, *courage*, etc.) : le nom représente **une « masse » qui ne se subdivise pas en éléments séparés les uns des autres** ; donc, on ne peut pas utiliser l'article *a/an*, ni mettre le nom au pluriel.

En français, il y a également des noms indénombrables (ex. : « courage »), mais il y en a beaucoup moins qu'en anglais. Voici une liste de noms indénombrables anglais courants qui peuvent poser un problème aux francophones :

accommodation	logement	*information*	renseignement(s)
advice	conseils	*knowledge*	connaissances
baggage	bagages	*news*	nouvelles
business	affaires	*progress*	progrès
evidence	preuve(s)	*toast*	toast, pain grillé
furniture	meubles	*traffic*	circulation
garbage	ordures	*weather*	temps (météo)
hair	cheveux	*work*	travail (action de travailler)

Ne mettez pas ces mots au pluriel, et faites l'accord du verbe au singulier :
Ses conseils sont réalistes. → *His/Her advice* ***is*** *realistic.*
Les nouvelles étaient bonnes. → *The news* ***was*** *good.*

N'employez pas l'article *a/an* devant ces noms :
C'est un grand progrès. → *That's great progress.*

Si on veut absolument « dénombrer », on peut dans certains cas utiliser ***a piece of*** :
C'est un renseignement intéressant. → *It's* ***an*** *interesting* ***piece of*** *information.*

Passif : constructions actives et constructions passives

Forme :

Construction active	**Construction passive** (dans le groupe verbal, ajout de BE + marque du **participe passé**)
Tim ***will repair*** *the door.* Tim réparera la porte.	*The door* ***will be repaired*** *by Tim.* La porte sera réparée par Tim.

- Si le complément du verbe se construit avec une **préposition**, cette dernière se place **après le verbe** :
  Le repas avait déjà été payé. → *The meal had already been* ***paid*** *for.*
- Avec certains verbes à deux compléments comme *give*, *ask*, *show*, *tell*, *offer* ou *send*, deux constructions passives sont possibles. Par exemple, partons de la phrase active *They showed me the photos* (Ils m'ont montré les photos). Deux formes passives lui correspondent –la seconde étant de beaucoup la plus courante :
  The photos were shown *to me.* ↔ ***I was shown*** *the photos.* (On m'a montré les photos.)
- On utilise le passif, en particulier, quand on ne peut pas, ou qu'on ne veut pas, dire qui accomplit l'action. Dans ce cas, le français utilise généralement **« on »** :
  On lui a volé ses clés. → *His/Her keys* ***were stolen.***
  On m'a dit qu'il avait eu un accident. → ***I was told*** *he'd had an accident.*

Past perfect (ou *pluperfect*)

- **Forme :** auxiliaire ***had*** (forme contractée : ***'d***) pour toutes les personnes + **participe passé**.
  I/You/He/She/... ***had finished.***

  Pour les verbes réguliers, le participe passé se forme comme le prétérit : on ajoute la terminaison ***-ed*** à la base verbale. (▶ Verbes irréguliers : pp. 271-273, colonne 3.)

Valeur de résultat

*I **had repaired** the TV. So they were able to use it.* J'avais réparé la télé. Donc ils ont pu s'en servir.

Différence avec le *present perfect* : il s'agit d'un résultat **par rapport à un moment du passé**, et non par rapport au moment présent.

Valeur de durée

*I **had known** him for six months / since 2003*. Je le **connaissais** depuis six mois / depuis 2003.

L'événement dure jusqu'à un moment du passé. En français, le temps utilisé est ici l'**imparfait**.

Valeur « imaginaire »

L'élément « prétérit » contenu dans l'auxiliaire *had* peut exprimer un **irréel** (= « contraire à la réalité » – voir p. 265, 2) :
*If I **had finished** I would tell you*. Si j'avais fini je te le dirais.
*I wish I **had listened** to her.* Je regrette de ne pas l'avoir écoutée.

« Pendant »

1.

« Pendant » = « sur une durée de » = *for* :
Il a travaillé pendant deux heures. → *He worked **for** two hours.*

Question correspondante : ***How long** did he work?* (Pendant combien de temps...?)

2.

« Pendant » = « au cours de » = *during* :
Il a travaillé pendant les vacances. → *He worked **during** the holidays.*

Question correspondante : ***When** did you work?* (Quand...?)

Pluriel des noms dénombrables

1.

Pour les **noms réguliers**, on ajoute la terminaison ***-s*** (*one dog → two dog**s***). Les modifications orthographiques sont les mêmes qu'avec la terminaison *-s* des verbes à la 3e personne du singulier du présent (voir p. 264, 2) :
*bus → bus**es***,
*beach → beach**es***,
*party → part**ies***, etc.

Les règles de prononciation sont les mêmes que pour la terminaison *-s* des verbes : *dogs* /dɒgz/, *cats* /kæts/, *buses* /ˈbʌsɪz/, etc.

2. Principaux pluriels irréguliers

child /tʃaɪld/ (enfant) → children /ˈtʃɪldren/
man /mæn/ (homme) → men /men/
woman /ˈwʊmən/ (femme) → women /ˈwɪmɪn/
foot /fʊt/ (pied) → feet /fiːt/
tooth /tuːθ/ (dent) → teeth /tiːθ/
mouse /maʊs/ (souris) → mice /maɪs/

3.

Certains noms qui se terminent par ***-f*** ou ***-fe*** ont un pluriel en ***-ves*** :
half /hɑːf/ → ***halves***

wife → ***wives*** (mais *roof* → *roofs*).

Parmi les plus courants : *life*, *shelf* (étagère), *knife*, *leaf* (feuille), *wolf* (loup).

4.

Avec ***people*** employé dans le sens de « personnes » et ***police***, l'accord au pluriel est **obligatoire** :
*There **were** ten **people** present.* Il y avait dix personnes présentes.
*The police **are** ready to intervene.* La police est prête à intervenir.

Prépositions

Attention aux différences de construction entre le français et l'anglais :
J'attends Tim. ↔ *I'm **waiting** for Tim.* (pas de préposition en français, préposition en anglais)
Il a emprunté l'argent à son frère. ↔ *He **borrowed** the money from his brother.* (préposition « à » en français après « emprunter », *from* en anglais après *borrow*)

Notez aussi : *listen to sb/sth* (écouter qqn/qqch), *look for sb/sth* (chercher qqn/qqch), *prevent sb from doing sth* (empêcher qqn de faire qqch).

Présent en BE + -ING

Le présent en BE + -ING s'oppose au présent simple. Le présent simple voit l'événement **dans son ensemble**. Le présent en BE + -ING réalise un « coup de projecteur » **sur un moment de l'événement** (ou sur plusieurs moments). Ce « coup de projecteur » peut prendre plusieurs formes :

- Il se situe au **moment où on parle** :
  *Look, he**'s trying** to open the door.* Regarde, il essaie (= est en train d'essayer) d'ouvrir la porte.
- Il porte sur un événement **futur** (expression d'une **intention**) :
  *Tomorrow evening **I'm watching** the match on TV.* Demain soir je regarde le match à la télé.
- Avec *always*, l'énonciateur exprime son impatience, sa surprise, etc. :
  *He**'s** always **asking** stupid questions!* Il pose tout le temps des questions stupides !

Certains verbes sont difficilement compatibles avec BE + -ING : ce sont des verbes comme *know* (savoir, connaître) ou *look* (employé dans le sens de « sembler ») ; ces verbes expriment un sentiment ou un état mental vus nécessairement « en bloc » : *I know him.* (Je le connais.) ou *It looks easy.* (Ça a l'air facile.).

Present perfect en BE + -ING

1. Valeur de résultat

	Forme	Valeur
Present perfect simple	*Jenny **has washed** the dog. He doesn't smell any more.* Jenny a lavé le chien. Il ne sent plus mauvais.	**Exprime simplement un résultat** : le chien est propre
***Present perfect* en BE + -ING**	**A:** *There's water everywhere! What's happened?* **B:** *Ted **has been washing** the dog.* **A:** Il y a de l'eau partout. Qu'est-ce qui s'est passé ? **B:** Ted a lavé le chien.	On a constaté un résultat (« Il y a de l'eau partout. »), et la forme verbale en BE + -ING exprime un « coup de projecteur » sur **l'action qui a provoqué le résultat** (sur l'action « Ted a lavé le chien. »)

Notez qu'en français on a la même forme verbale dans les deux cas (« a lavé le chien »).

2. Valeur de durée

Avec les verbes *know*, *look*, *understand*, etc. difficilement compatibles avec BE + -ING (voir p. 262), on utilise obligatoirement le *present perfect* **simple** :
*I've **known** him for ten years.* Je le connais depuis dix ans.

Avec les autres verbes, on utilise généralement le *present perfect* en BE + -ING :
*She**'s been playing** computer games for an hour.* Elle joue à des jeux sur ordinateur depuis une heure.

Present perfect simple

1.

Forme : **auxiliaire** HAVE conjugué au présent + le **participe passé** du verbe.
*I **have finished** my work.* J'ai fini mon travail.

Pour les verbes réguliers, le participe passé se forme comme le prétérit : on ajoute la terminaison ***-ed*** à la base verbale. (Verbes irréguliers : pp. 271-273, colonne 3.)

Forme affirmative	Forme interrogative	Forme négative
*I **have finished.***	***Have** I **finished?***	*I **have not / haven't finished.***
*You **have finished.***	***Have** you **finished?***	*You **have not / haven't finished.***
*He/She/It **has finished.***	***Has** he/she/it **finished?***	*He/She/It **has not / hasn't finished.***
*We/You/They **have finished.***	***Have** we/you/they **finished?***	*We/You/They **have not finished.***

2. Valeur de résultat

- On s'intéresse au résultat présent d'un événement passé :
  *I**'ve fixed** the TV.* J'ai réparé la télé.

  Ce qui importe ici pour l'énonciateur, c'est le résultat : « la télé fonctionne ». Par contre, on utilise le **prétérit** quand on s'intéresse en premier lieu à l'événement passé, ou à ses circonstances :
  *'When **did** you **fix** it?' '[I **fixed** it] This morning.'* « Quand est-ce que tu l'as réparée? » « Ce matin. »

  Pour le même événement passé, on peut donc choisir, **en fonction du point de vue qu'on adopte**, soit le *present perfect* soit le prétérit.

- Avec le *present perfect*, on emploie souvent des adverbes ou compléments de temps comme *already*, *ever/never*, *not... yet*, *over the past few weeks/months*, qui font implicitement référence au moment présent :
  *He has **already** finished his work.* Il a déjà fini son travail.
  *I have sent six SMS messages **so far**.* J'ai envoyé six SMS jusqu'à maintenant.

  Par contre, certains adverbes, ainsi que les indications de date, d'heure, etc., sont **incompatibles avec le *present perfect***, et exigent l'emploi du **prétérit** :
  *I **sent** six SMS messages **yesterday / on February 7th / two weeks ago**.*

3. Passé récent

Associé à l'adverbe ***just***, le *present perfect* exprime un passé récent :
*I**'ve just seen** her.* Je viens de la voir.

En anglais US, on emploie le **prétérit** pour exprimer un passé récent : *I **just saw** her.*

4. Valeur de durée

On emploie le *present perfect* pour une action ou un état qui a commencé dans le passé et qui **dure encore au moment présent**. *I **have known** him <u>for six months</u>.* Je le **connais** depuis six mois / Il y a six mois que je le **connais**.
*I **have known** him <u>since last year</u>.* Je les **connais** depuis l'an dernier.

Notez les deux **équivalents du français « depuis »** :
- ***for*** + indication d'une **durée** (*for six months*, *for ten years*, etc.)
- ***since*** + indication du **point de départ** de l'événement (*since June 5th*, *since 2 o'clock*, etc.)

For peut aussi indiquer la durée d'un événement qui est **entièrement coupé du présent**, et donc est exprimé avec un **prétérit**. Opposez :

Il habite New-York **depuis** dix ans.
(il y habite encore)

Il a habité New-York **pendant** dix ans.
(il n'y habite plus)

L'emploi du prétérit est normal dans le second cas : l'événement est séparé du présent.

Présent simple

1. Conjugaison

Forme affirmative	Forme interrogative	Forme négative
I ***work.***	***Do*** *I* ***work?***	*I* ***do not / don't*** /dəʊnt/ ***work.***
You ***work.***	***Do*** *you* ***work?***	*You* ***do not work / don't work.***
He/She/It ***works.***	***Does*** /dʌz/ *he/she/it* ***work?***	*He/She/It* ***does not work / doesn't*** /ˈdʌznt/ ***work.***
We/You/They ***work.***	***Do*** *we/you/they* ***work?***	*We/You/They* ***do not work / don't work.***

2.

Terminaison -*s* à la 3ème personne du singulier : **modifications orthographiques**

- Quand la base verbale se termine par *-s, -x, -z, -ch, -sh* ou *-o*, on ajoute ***-es*** :
  pass → *pass**es***, *fix* → *fix**es***, *watch* → *watch**es***, *wash* → *wash**es***, *go* → *go**es***.
- Quand la base verbale se termine par un **-*y* précédé d'une consonne**, ce *y* devient ***-i***, et on ajoute ***-es*** :
  try → ***tries***, *marry* → *marr**ies*** (mais dans *play*, le *y* est précédé d'une voyelle, donc *play* → *plays*).

3.

Terminaison -*s* à la 3ème personne du singulier : **prononciation**

- La terminaison écrite ***-es*** se prononce /ɪz/ lorsqu'elle **suit une consonne** : *passes* /ˈpɑːsɪz/ *fixes* /ˈfɪksɪz/, *judges* /ˈdʒʌdʒɪz/, etc.
- Dans tous les autres cas, la terminaison écrite ***-s*** / ***-es*** se prononce soit /**z**/ (*plays* /pleɪz/, *knows* /nəʊz/, *goes* /gəʊz/, *lies* /laɪz/), soit /s/ (*looks* /lʊks/, *sits* /sɪts/).

Deux cas particuliers : ***does*** se prononce /dʌz/, et ***says*** se prononce /sez/.

4. Emplois du présent simple

Le présent simple est utilisé pour parler d'un fait, ou d'une série de faits, considérés au moment présent et **vus dans leur totalité**.

- On parle d'une **caractéristique du sujet** :
  Laura ***plays*** *the piano* (= *Laura is a pianist*). Laura joue du piano.
  Ted ***likes*** *hip hop.* Ted aime le hip hop.
- On parle d'un **comportement habituel** :
  Ted ***plays*** *football every Saturday.* Ted joue au foot tous les samedis.
- On parle d'une **action** qui est située au moment présent, et qui est **considérée dans sa totalité** :
  I ***click*** *on this icon, and the menu* ***opens****.* Je clique sur cet icone, et le menu s'ouvre.
  And now Ricardo ***gets*** *the ball, he* ***shoots****, and he* ***scores****!* Maintenant Ricardo prend la balle, il shoote, et il marque !

Prétérit en *BE* + *-ING*

Forme : auxiliaire ***was / were*** + forme en ***-ing*** du verbe.
'What ***were*** *you* ***doing*** *yesterday at 8 pm?' 'I* ***was watching*** *TV.'*
« Qu'est-ce que tu faisais / vous faisiez hier à 8 heures du soir ? » « Je regardais la télé. »

Le repère dans le temps est ici un **moment du passé**. Dans l'exemple ci-dessus, le moment-repère est *yesterday at 8 pm*. Le prétérit en *BE* + *-ING* désigne une action qui était en cours de déroulement à ce moment-repère.

Le moment-repère peut être constitué par un **autre événement** :
When I entered the room, he ***was watching*** *TV.* Quand je suis entré dans la pièce, il regardait la télé.

Prétérit simple : emplois

1. Le prétérit de récit

Le prétérit est utilisé dans le récit d'événements passés, vus comme **nettement séparés du présent** :
Marilyn Monroe ***was*** *a great actress. She* ***played*** *in about 30 movies.*
Marilyn Monroe était une grande actrice. Elle a joué dans environ 30 films.

L'événement passé est **repéré dans le temps** par un adverbe (*yesterday*, etc.), par une date, par l'indication d'une période ou d'une heure (*last year*, *at 5 p.m.*...) :
He arrived in London yesterday / at 5. Il est arrivé à Londres hier / à 5 heures.

Il peut également être repéré dans le temps par une construction formée avec ***ago*** :
He ***arrived*** *in London* ***two years ago / one week ago****.* Il est arrivé à Londres il y a deux ans / une semaine.

2. Le prétérit imaginaire

- Dans une proposition en ***if***..., le verbe au prétérit peut renvoyer à un événement « contraire à la réalité » :
  If I ***knew*** *her phone number I could call her.* Si je connaissais son numéro de téléphone je pourrais l'appeler. (sous-entendu : je ne le connais pas)

  Pour *BE*, il existe une forme pour exprimer ce prétérit imaginaire : ***were*** utilisé à toutes les personnes.
  If I were rich...(« Si j'étais riche... »). Dans la langue courante, on dit *If I was rich*...

△ On trouve aussi ce prétérit après :

- le verbe ***wish*** (« souhaiter », « regretter de ... ne ... pas / que ... ne ... pas ») :
*I wish I **knew** her phone number!* Je regrette de ne pas connaître son numéro de téléphone.

- ***If only...!***
*If only I **knew** her telephone number!* Si seulement je connaissais son numéro de téléphone !

- ***It's time...***
*It's time the children **went** to bed.* Il est temps que les enfants aillent se coucher.

Prétérit simple : formes

1. Affirmation

À toutes les personnes, on ajoute la terminaison ***-ed*** :
*I **worked** /wɜːkt/ from 9 to 5.* Je travaillais de 9 h à 17 heures.

Attention au cas particulier des **verbes irréguliers** (voir p. 271-273, colonne 2) : *begin* → prétérit *began*, *break* → prétérit *broke*, etc.

2. Interrogation et négation.

À toutes les personnes, on utilise l'auxiliaire ***did*** et la **base verbale** :
***Did** her brother **work** in a bank?* Est-ce que son frère travaillait dans une banque ?
*They **did not / didn't work** very much.* Ils/Elles ne travaillaient pas beaucoup.

3. Terminaison *-ed* du prétérit : modifications orthographiques

- *try* → *tr**ied***, *marry* → *marr**ied*** : ***y*** qui suit une consonne **devient *i***.
- *stop* → *stop**ped*** : une consonne finale qui suit une voyelle est **redoublée** dans les verbes d'une seule syllabe *(stop)*, ou si la syllabe finale est **accentuée** : *preˈ**fer*** → *preˈ**ferred*** (mais *ˈoffer* → *ˈoffered*).

4. Terminaison *-ed* du prétérit : prononciation

- On prononce /ɪd/ après ***t*** ou ***d*** : *star**ted*** /ˈstɑːtɪd/, *nee**ded*** /ˈniːdɪd/.
- Dans les autres cas, on prononce soit /d/ (*play**ed*** /pleɪd/, *lov**ed*** /lʌvd/), soit /t/ (*look**ed*** /lʊkt/, *stopp**ed*** /stɒpt/, *miss**ed*** /mɪst/).

Pronoms personnels et possessifs

Pronoms sujets	Pronoms compléments	Déterminants possessifs	Pronoms possessifs	Pronoms réfléchis (voir 34)
I	*me*	*my* (mon/ma/mes)	*mine* (le mien / la mienne / les miennes)	*myself* (accentuation sur *self*)
you	*you*	*your*	*yours*	*yourself*
he	*him*	*his*	*his*	*himself*
she	*her*	*her*	*hers*	*herself*
it	*it*	*its*	*its own*	*itself*
we	*us*	*our* /aʊə/	*ours* /aʊəz/	*ourselves*
you	*you*	*your* /jɔː/	*yours* /jɔːz/	*yourselves*
they	*them*	*their*	*theirs*	*themselves*

Les **possessifs** (série *my*, *your* etc. et série *mine*, *yours* etc.) s'accordent uniquement avec le « possesseur » :

He introduced me to ***his*** *sister /* ***his*** *brother.* Il m'a présenté à sa sœur / son frère.

She introduced me to ***her*** *sister /* ***her*** *brother.* Elle m'a présenté à sa sœur / son frère.

Propositions relatives

Les propositions relatives sont introduites par des **pronoms relatifs**, qui sont :

- les pronoms relatifs en *wh-* (***who*** /huː/, ***which***, ***whose*** /huːz/ ;

- ***that*** (prononcé /ðət/) ;

- le relatif « zéro » (Ø), c'est-à-dire un vide.
The girl I met is Irish. La fille que j'ai rencontrée est irlandaise.

Le choix entre ces relatifs est déterminé par :

- le type d'**antécédent** (c'est-à-dire de nom que le pronom relatif remplace) ;

- la **fonction** du pronom relatif (est-il sujet du verbe, ou complément du verbe, ou complément d'un nom ?).

Il y a souvent plusieurs possibilités de choix. Dans la pratique, les relatifs sont utilisés comme indiqué dans le tableau ci-dessous.

Règles à appliquer absolument :

- ***who*** uniquement pour les « personnes », et ***which*** uniquement pour les « choses » ;

- Ø n'est **jamais utilisé en fonction sujet** : il ne peut pas remplacer *who/which/that* dans des phrases comme *The girl who called yesterday is my sister.* (La fille qui a appelé hier est ma sœur.) ou comme *The book which/that is on the top shelf is a dictionary.* (Le livre qui est sur l'étagère du haut est un dictionnaire.).

	Antécédent humain	Antécédent non humain
Sujet	*The girl* ***who*** *called yesterday …*	*The book* ***which/that*** *is on the top shelf…*
Complément direct	*The girl Ø I met…* (La fille que j'ai rencontrée…)	*The book Ø you bought…* (Le livre que tu as acheté…)
Complément indirect	*The girl Ø I told you about yesterday…* (La fille dont je t'ai parlé hier…)	*The book Ø I told you about yesterday…* (Le livre dont je t'ai parlé hier…)
Complément de nom	*The girl* ***whose*** *father…* (La fille dont le père…)	*The book* ***whose*** *title…* (Le livre dont le titre…)

Si le verbe se construit avec une **préposition** (voir ci-dessus, préposition *about*) : avec le **relatif Ø**, la préposition est obligatoirement **placée après le verbe.** Exemple :
The book I told you about yesterday. Cf. **passif** et **constructions interrogatives** (voir p. 260 et 256).

Should (voir aussi Modaux p.258)

- Le modal ***should*** permet d'exprimer **un conseil** ou **une suggestion** (sens du français « tu devrais ») :
  *You **should** be more careful.* Tu devrais être plus prudent.
- Suivi de ***have* + participe passé**, ***should*** permet d'exprimer **un reproche** :
  *You **should have been** more careful.* Tu aurais dû être plus prudent.

Some, any, no et leurs composés (*somebody*, etc.)

1. *Some* /səm/ ou *any* /'eni/ : « une certaine quantité / un certain nombre de… »

	Indénombrable (singulier)	Dénombrable au pluriel
Affirmations : *some*	*There's **some milk** in the fridge.* Il y a du lait dans le frigo.	*There are **some tomatoes** in the fridge.* Il y a des tomates dans le frigo.
Questions pour offrir/ demander qqch. : *some*	*Would you like **some more coffee?*** Tu veux un peu plus de café ?	*Would you like **some more sandwiches?*** Tu veux d'autres sandwiches ?
Autres interrogations : *any*	*Is there **any milk** left?* Est-ce qu'il reste du lait ?	*Are there **any tomatoes** left?* Est-ce qu'il reste des tomates ?

Les articles français « du / de la / des » ont pour équivalent *some/any* quand ils signifient « un certain nombre / une certaine quantité de… ». Toutefois, s'ils servent à indiquer la **nature** de quelque chose, sans idée de quantité, comme dans « Tu veux du thé ou du café ? », ils ont pour équivalent l'article zéro : *Would you like tea or coffee?*

Any est souvent utilisé dans des énoncés affirmatifs avec le sens de « n'importe quel(s) / n'importe quelle(s) » : *Just take a card – **any** card.* (Prends simplement une carte. N'importe quelle carte).

2. *Not any* ou *no* : quantité nulle (= « pas de… », « aucun… », etc.)

	Indénombrable (singulier)	Dénombrable au pluriel
Construction négative + *any*	*There isn't **any milk**.* Il n'y a pas de lait.	*There aren't **any tomatoes**.* Il n'y a pas de tomates.
Construction affirmative + *no*	*There is **no milk**.* Il n'y a pas de lait.	*There are **no tomatoes**.* Il n'y a aucune tomate.

Le pronom qui correspond à *no* est ***none*** /nʌn/ : *I wanted some milk / some tomatoes but there was / there were **none**.* (… il n'y en avait pas / il n'y en avait aucune.) Ne pas confondre avec *no one* (= personne, voir ci-dessous).

3. Composés de *some* /sʌm/, *any* /'eni/, no /nəʊ/ et *every* /'evri/ :

Dans ces composés, *some*, *any*, *no* et *every* gardent leur valeur habituelle (voir ci-dessus), qui détermine le choix entre *somebody* et *anybody*, *something* et *anything*, etc.

somebody /'sʌmbədi/, ***someone*** /'sʌmwʌn/ quelqu'un	***anybody, anyone*** quelqu'un	***nobody*** /'nəʊbədi/, ***no one*** personne	***everybody*** /'evri,bɒdi/, ***everyone*** (+ singulier) tout le monde
something quelque chose	***anything*** quelque chose	***nothing*** /'nʌθɪŋ/ rien	***everything*** (+ singulier) tout
somewhere quelque part	***anywhere*** quelque part	***nowhere*** nulle part	***everywhere*** partout

En anglais (≠ français), on emploie **une seule négation par proposition** :
Il ne parle jamais à personne → *He* ***never*** *speaks to* ***anybody****.*

Subordonnées de but

1.

So (that) peut exprimer le but :
Speak up ***so (that) I can hear you****.* Parle plus fort pour que je t'entende.

2.

Le but peut également être exprimé par ***to***, ou (dans style formel) par ***in order to*** / ***so as to*** :
He got up early ***to*** / ***in order to*** / ***so as to*** *catch the 7:15 train.* Il s'est levé de bonne heure pour avoir / afin d'avoir le train de 7 h 15.

V-*ing* (verbe + terminaison -*ing*)

- **V-*ING*** peut avoir notamment une fonction d'**adjectif** (*It's an* ***amusing*** *story.*) ou de **nom** (*He loves* ***skateboarding****.* Il aime beaucoup le skateboard). L'emploi de V-ing avec une valeur de nom est appelé le **gérondif**.
- L'emploi de V-*ING* est obligatoire :

  - après une **préposition** (*about, after, at, before, of, ...*) :
  Before opening *the window, she turned the heating off.* Avant d'ouvrir la fenêtre, elle a coupé le chauffage.
  He took the DVD ***without asking*** *permission.* Il a pris le DVD sans demander la permission.

  - après les verbes qui expriment une **appréciation**, un **jugement**, un **sentiment** :
  He ***can't stand seeing*** *such poverty.* Il ne peut pas supporter de voir une telle pauvreté.
  I ***enjoyed working*** *with them.* J'ai eu plaisir à travailler avec eux.
  I don't feel like ***going*** *out tonight.* Je n'ai pas envie de sortir ce soir.

  - après la plupart des verbes qui indiquent la **continuation** ou la **fin** d'une action, notamment *carry on* / *keep (on)* / *go on* (continuer à) / *stop* / *quit* (arrêter de) :
  He ***gave up*** / *He* ***quit smoking*** *last year.* Il a arrêté de fumer l'an dernier.

Verbes pronominaux (« se regarder », etc.)

Le français utilise la même forme pour le sens **réfléchi** (« Ils **se sont vus** dans la vidéo. », = chacun a vu lui-même) et pour le sens **réciproque** (« Ils **se sont vus** [= rencontrés] hier. »).

- En anglais

  - pour le **sens réfléchi**, on utilise un **pronom réfléchi** (*myself, yourself*, etc. - voir p. 266) :
  They ***saw themselves*** *in the video.*

  - pour le **sens réciproque**, on utilise l'un des deux **pronoms réciproques** ***each other*** / ***one another*** (le choix étant libre) :
  They ***saw each other*** / *They* ***saw one another*** *yesterday.*

Les verbes comme *get up*, *shave*, *wash*, *meet* ou *quarrel* se construisent seuls, sans pronom réfléchi ou réciproque, quand leur sens réfléchi ou réciproque est évident :
*He **got up** at seven, **shaved**, and **dressed** carefully.* Il **s'est levé** à 7 heures, s'est rasé, et **s'est habillé** avec soin.
*They often **meet** and **quarrel**.* Ils **se rencontrent et se disputent** souvent.

When

(a) *I don't know **when we'll see** them again.* Je ne sais pas quand nous les reverrons.

(b) *I'll tell them **when I see them**.* Je le leur dirai quand je les verrai.

Dans l'énoncé **(a)**, la proposition introduite par *when* est une **subordonnée interrogative** (cf. *When will we see them again?* Quand est-ce qu'on les reverra ?). Dans ces subordonnées, on peut utiliser *will* pour exprimer un futur.

Dans l'énoncé **(b)**, la proposition introduite par *when* est une **subordonnée de temps** (qui pourrait être remplacée par *tomorrow* ou *next time*). Dans les subordonnées de temps, on ne peut pas employer *will* pour exprimer un futur : on utilise le **présent simple**.

Index

Les verbes irréguliers

Groupe 1 : CD3 PISTE 43 MP3 PISTE 55
les trois formes verbales sont identiques.

Base verbale	Prétérit	Participe Passé	Traduction
bet /e/	bet /e/	bet /e/	*parier*
burst /ɜː/	burst /ɜː/	burst /ɜː/	*éclater*
cast /ɑː/	cast /ɑː/	cast /ɑː/	*lancer*
cost /ɒ/	cost /ɒ/	cost /ɒ/	*coûter*
cut /ʌ/	cut /ʌ/	cut /ʌ/	*couper*
hit /ɪ/	hit /ɪ/	hit /ɪ/	*frapper*
hurt /ɜː/	hurt /ɜː/	hurt /ɜː/	*blesser*
let /e/	let /e/	let /e/	*laisser*
put /ʊ/	put /ʊ/	put /ʊ/	*mettre*
set /e/	set /e/	set /e/	*placer*
shut /ʌ/	shut /ʌ/	shut /ʌ/	*fermer*
split /ɪ/	split /ɪ/	split /ɪ/	*fendre*
spread /e/	spread /e/	spread /e/	*répandre, étaler*

Groupe 2 : CD3 PISTE 44 MP3 PISTE 56
deux formes verbales sont identiques.

	Base verbale	Prétérit	Participe Passé	Traduction
Formes en D	bleed /iː/	bled /e/	bled /e/	*saigner*
	feed /iː/	fed /e/	fed /e/	*nourrir*
	find /aɪ/	found /aʊ/	found /aʊ/	*trouver*
	have /æ/	had /æ/	had /æ/	*avoir*
	hear /ɪə/	heard /ɜː/	heard /ɜː/	*entendre*
	hold /əʊ/	held /e/	held /e/	*tenir*
	lay /eɪ/	laid /eɪ/	laid /eɪ/	*poser à plat*
	lead /iː/	led /e/	led /e/	*mener*
	make /eɪ/	made /eɪ/	made /eɪ/	*faire*
	pay /eɪ/	paid /eɪ/	paid /eɪ/	*payer*
	say /eɪ/	said /e/	said /e/	*dire*
	sell /e/	sold /əʊ/	sold /əʊ/	*vendre*
	stand /æ/	stood /ʊ/	stood /ʊ/	*être debout*
	tell /e/	told /əʊ/	told /əʊ/	*dire*
	understand /æ/	understood /ʊ/	understood /ʊ/	*comprendre*

	Base verbale	Prétérit	Participe Passé	Traduction
Formes en T	bend /e/	bent /e/	bent /e/	*courber*
	build /ɪ/	built /ɪ/	built /ɪ/	*construire*
	burn /ɜ:/	burnt, burned /ɜ:/	burnt, burned /ɜ:/	*brûler*
	deal /i:/	dealt /e/	dealt /e/	*distribuer*
	dream /i:/	dreamt /e/, dreamed /i:/	dreamt /e/, dreamed /i:/	*rêver*
	feel /i:/	felt /e/	felt /e/	*(res)sentir*
	get /e/	got /ɒ/	got /ɒ/, gotten /ɒ/ (US)	*obtenir*
	keep /i:/	kept /e/	kept /e/	*garder*
	leap /i:/	leapt /e/	leapt /e/	*sauter*
	learn /ɜ:/	learnt, learned /ɜ:/	learnt, learned /ɜ:/	*apprendre*
	leave /i:/	left /e/	left /e/	*quitter*
	lend /e/	lent /e/	lent /e/	*prêter*
	light /aɪ/	lit /ɪ/	lit /ɪ/	*allumer*
	lose /u:/	lost /ɒ/	lost /ɒ/	*perdre*
	mean /i:/	meant /e/	meant /e/	*signifier*
	meet /i:/	met /e/	met /e/	*rencontrer*
	send /e/	sent /e/	sent /e/	*envoyer*
	shoot /u:/	shot /ɒ/	shot /ɒ/	*faire feu, tirer*
	sit /ɪ/	sat /æ/	sat /æ/	*être assis*
	sleep /i:/	slept /e/	slept /e/	*dormir*
	smell /e/	smelt /e/	smelt /e/	*sentir*
	spell /e/	spelt /e/	spelt /e/	*épeler*
	spend /e/	spent /e/	spent /e/	*dépenser*
	spill /ɪ/	spilt /ɪ/	spilt /ɪ/	*répandre*
	spoil /ɔɪ/	spoilt /ɔɪ/	spoilt /ɔɪ/	*gâter*
	sweep /i:/	swept /e/	swept /e/	*balayer*
Formes en GHT	bring /ɪ/	brought /ɔ:/	brought /ɔ:/	*apporter*
	buy /aɪ/	bought /ɔ:/	bought /ɔ:/	*acheter*
	catch /æ/	caught /ɔ:/	caught /ɔ:/	*attraper*
	fight /aɪ/	fought /ɔ:/	fought /ɔ:/	*combattre*
	read* /i:/	read /e/	read /e/	*lire*
	teach /i:/	taught /ɔ:/	taught /ɔ:/	*enseigner*
	think /ɪ/	thought /ɔ:/	thought /ɔ:/	*penser*

** Attention : prononciation différente des formes verbales au prétérit et au participe passé.*

	Base verbale	Prétérit	Participe Passé	Traduction
2 formes verbales identiques	become /ʌ/	became /eɪ/	become /ʌ/	*devenir*
	come /ʌ/	came /eɪ/	come /ʌ/	*venir*
	hang /æ/	hung /ʌ/	hung /ʌ/	*pendre, suspendre*
	run /ʌ/	ran /æ/	run /ʌ/	*courir*
	stick /ɪ/	stuck /ʌ/	stuck /ʌ/	*coller*
	strike /aɪ/	struck /ʌ/	struck /ʌ/	*frapper*
	swing /ɪ/	swung /ʌ/	swung /ʌ/	*(se) balancer*
	win /ɪ/	won /ʌ/	won /ʌ/	*gagner*

Groupe 3 : CD3 PISTE 45 MP3 PISTE 57
les trois formes verbales sont différentes.

	Base Verbale	Prétérit	Participe Passé	Traduction
Participe passé en EN	be	was /wɒz/, were /wɜ:/	been /bi:n/	*être*
	bite /aɪ/	bit /ɪ/	bitten /ɪ/	*mordre*
	break /eɪ/	broke /əʊ/	broken /əʊ/	*casser*
	choose /u:/	chose /əʊ/	chosen /əʊ/	*choisir*
	drive /aɪ/	drove /əʊ/	driven /ɪ/	*conduire*
	eat /i:/	ate /e/	eaten /i:/	*manger*
	fall /ɔ:/	fell /e/	fallen /ɔ:/	*tomber*
	forbid /ɪ/	forbad(e) /eɪ/	forbidden/ɪ/	*interdire*
	forgive /ɪ/	forgave /eɪ/	forgiven/ɪ/	*pardonner*
	forget /ə/	forgot /ɒ/	forgotten/ɒ/	*oublier*
	freeze /i:/	froze /əʊ/	frozen /əʊ/	*geler*
	give /ɪ/	gave /eɪ/	given /ɪ/	*donner*
	hide /aɪ/	hid /ɪ/	hidden /ɪ/	*cacher*
	ride /aɪ/	rode /əʊ/	ridden /ɪ/	*aller à cheval*
	rise /aɪ/	rose /əʊ/	risen /ɪ/	*s'élever*
	see /i:/	saw /ɔ:/	seen /i:/	*voir*
	shake /eɪ/	shook /ʊ/	shaken /eɪ/	*secouer*
	speak /i:/	spoke /əʊ/	spoken /əʊ/	*parler*
	steal /i:/	stole /əʊ/	stolen /əʊ/	*voler (qqch)*
	take /eɪ/	took /ʊ/	taken /eɪ/	*prendre*
	wake /eɪ/	woke /əʊ/	woken /əʊ/	*réveiller*
	write /aɪ/	wrote /əʊ/	written /ɪ/	*écrire*
Participe passé en N ou NE	blow /əʊ/	blew /u:/	blown /əʊ/	*souffler*
	do /u:/	did /ɪ/	done /ʌ/	*faire*
	draw /ɔ:/	drew /u:/	drawn /ɔ:/	*dessiner*
	fly /aɪ/	flew /u:/	flown /əʊ/	*voler*
	go /əʊ/	went /e/	gone /ɒ/	*aller*
	grow /əʊ/	grew /u:/	grown /əʊ/	*pousser (= croître)*
	know /əʊ/	knew /u:/	known /əʊ/	*connaître*
	lie /aɪ/	lay /eɪ/	lain /eɪ/	*être couché*
	show /əʊ/	showed /əʊ/	shown /əʊ/	*montrer*
	swear /ɜə/	swore /ɔ:/	sworn /ɔ:/	*jurer*
	tear /ɜə/	tore /ɔ:/	torn /ɔ:/	*déchirer*
	throw /əʊ/	threw /u:/	thrown /əʊ/	*lancer*
	wear /ɜə/	wore /ɔ:/	worn /ɔ:/	*porter (un vêtement)*
I-A-U	begin /ɪ/	began /æ/	begun /ʌ/	*commencer*
	drink /ɪ/	drank /æ/	drunk /ʌ/	*boire*
	ring /ɪ/	rang /æ/	rung /ʌ/	*sonner*
	sing /ɪ/	sang /æ/	sung /ʌ/	*chanter*
	sink /ɪ/	sank /æ/	sunk /ʌ/	*couler*
	swim /ɪ/	swam /æ/	swum /ʌ/	*nager*

Entraînez-vous

1 Vous pensez connaître vos verbes irréguliers, alors testez-vous ! Recopiez la grille ci-dessous sur un papier libre. Si vous mettez plus de 2 minutes pour la compléter, c'est que vous n'êtes pas encore prêts et qu'il faut réapprendre vos verbes par cœur.

Base verbale	Prétérit	Participe passé	Traduction
lay			
		dealt	
spoil			
	flew		
			répandre, étaler
show			
	swept		
		sworn	
			souffler
	cast		
spill			

2 Conjuguez les verbes entre parenthèses au prétérit. Attention, tous ne sont pas des verbes irréguliers !

Barack Obama (be born) on August 4, 1961 in Hawaii. Soon after his birth, his father (leave) his wife and his son. Barack Obama only (see) his father a couple of times in his lifetime. His mother later (remarry) an Indonesian man and the family (move) to Jakarta. Barack Obama (grow up) there but at the age of 10, his mother (send) him back to live with his grandparents in Hawaii. As he (be) one of the three African-American students enrolled at the school, he (begin) to realize what it (mean) to be black. Barack Obama (graduate) with honors from high school. After high school, Barack Obama (study) political science at Columbia University and then (go) to Harvard Law School. After his studies, he (move) to Chicago where he (meet) Michelle Robinson. They quickly (fall) in love and (get) married four years later. They (have) two daughters after their marriage. Barack Obama soon (get) involved in politics. He (win) the 2008 and 2012 presidential elections and he (become) the very first black president of the United States.

3 Traduisez les phrases suivantes.

a. J'ai lu un très bon roman pendant les vacances et je l'ai prêté à ma meilleure amie. Elle l'a trouvé très intéressant.
b. Cette nuit-là, Amy dormit très mal car elle entendit des bruits étranges *(strange)* dehors. Elle ferma alors la fenêtre de sa chambre.
c. Elle a eu un accident de vélo : elle s'est fait mal et a beaucoup saigné.
d. Il n'a pas de chance : il a perdu son portefeuille il y a une semaine, il en a alors acheté un nouveau mais il l'a oublié dans le bus.

4 Faites un cadavre exquis avec vos camarades. Prenez chacun une feuille de papier libre. Faites une phrase avec le premier verbe de la liste ci-dessous, commencez votre phrase par *Last Halloween*. Ensuite, repliez votre feuille de façon à cacher votre phrase et passez votre feuille à votre camarade de droite. Continuez votre histoire sur la feuille qui vous a été donnée en faisant une deuxième phrase avec le deuxième verbe de la liste, cachez votre phrase et passez la feuille à votre voisin de droite et ainsi de suite jusqu'au dernier verbe. Dépliez alors la feuille et lisez l'histoire ainsi créée !

1. go – 2. choose – 3. bring – 4. eat – 5. run – 6. hear – 7. hide – 8. feel – 9. strike – 10. wake up

Corrigés des pages Apprendre à apprendre WB

Unit 1 Me, Myself and I WB P. 99-100

► **1. a.** tomboy • *personalité* • *candidat* • quote/quotation • *l'aviron*
serviable, aimable • frightened, scared • *contrarié(e)* • ill at ease, uncomfortable • *bon(ne) en + nom* • *qui a réussi* • talented, gifted • *joyeux(se), gai(e)* • miserable
réussir à • *habituellement, d'habitude* • I can't stand + V-*ing* • *se hisser au sommet* • start from scratch • I don't mind + V-*ing* • enjoy • *s'entraîner, pratiquer*

b.

☹ 👎	☺	☺ 👍	☺ 👌
hate + V-ing dislike + V-ing I can't stand + V-ing	I don't mind + V-ing	like + V-ing enjoy + V-ing	love + V-ing be crazy about+ V-ing be fond of + V-ing

c. **a)** miserable **b)** frightened **c)** talented **d)** comfortable **e)** angry **f)** ecstatic **g)** scared
Mot mystère : *annoyed* (contrarié)

► **2. a.** **Qualités que vous appréciez chez un ami :** helpful • reliable • trustworthy • truthful • honest • sincere • funny…
Vos réactions : I agree ≠ I disagree with this quote. • I think that… / I believe that… • In my opinion… • To my mind…

b. A good friend must be **reliable, truthful**, and **funny**. He / She should also **know me very well.** I usually enjoy **doing sports / activities and going outside** with my best friend but I dislike **fighting** with him / her.

c. **1.** I love playing and I want to win this competition.
2. I know the other contestants are very gifted / talented but I am very sporty / athletic because I go rock-climbing and do archery.
3. I don't mind going shopping with you but I can't stand queueing for hours.

Unit 2 Choose Your School WB P. 101-102

► **1. a.** co-ed school • *pensionnat* • motto • *désordre*
lay • *riche, fortuné(e)* • severe, strict • messy • *public/que* • lenient • *sens dessus dessous*
Fais-moi confiance. • Are you kidding? • I don't agree / I disagree with you. • *Je ne vois pas les choses ainsi.* • spill • scattered / lying all over the floor • *faire une sieste* • get rid of

b. **a)** private **b)** religious **c)** formal **d)** tolerant **e)** headmaster **f)** unruly **g)** mischief **h)** obedient **i)** subject **j)** library **k)** schoolmate

► **2. a.** **Picture 1 :** library, study, hard-working, uniform, formal clothes, obedient, enthusiastic, dedicated…
Picture 2 : classroom, unruly, brat, be up to some mischief, throw chairs, disobey, have fun…

b. The students in the first picture are certainly in the **school library** while the students in the second picture are obviously in a **classroom**. The students on the left look quite **serious** and **obedient / hard-**

working compared to the **unruly** teenagers who are **up to some mischief**. They seem to be real **brats**! The students on the left are wearing **uniforms** whereas the teenagers on the right are wearing **casual** clothes. I think that the students on the left are more likely *(ont plus de chances)* to **pass** their exam!

c. **1.** Bart Simpson does not like going to school whereas his sister Lisa is a very hard-working student. **2.** I know for sure that the rules are stricter in English boarding schools than in French high schools. **3.** I can assure you that American students wear more casual clothes than English students.

Unit 3 Change the World

WB P. 103-104

1. a. *frontière* • the rich and the poor • firm / corporation
thrilling / exciting • *intrépide, audacieux(euse)* • *qui s'ennuie* • *démuni(e)* • weak • fearless • powerful • take measures • take risks • *être sur un pied d'égalité* • denounce • criticize • urge sb to do sth

b. **1.** He is fed up with inequalities. **2.** He can't stand jealousy. **3.** He managed to start a new life. **4.** We must respect one another. **5.** They find it hard to bridge the gap between the two countries.

d. /iː/ weak - peace - dream - eager • /e/ measure - jealousy

2. a. **Personnages ? Situation? Pourquoi ?** men and women, build a bridge, people, live in different worlds, countries, continents, help one another...
Message: symbolize, gap, the divide between the North and South, developed and developing countries, ethnic or religious groups, enemies, overcome prejudices, have relations, contacts...

b. The **gap** may symbolize the limit between developing and developed countries, **the rich and poor**, different ethnic or religious groups, people who are enemies, **borders** between countries. Everyone is participating. They are trying to **bridge** the **gap**, that is to say to have relations, contacts, exchanges with people on the other side. The message is quite **optimistic** and **hopeful** because it means that everything is possible when we make an effort. The artist is **committed** to promoting peace between people. I believe this dream could **come true** if everybody tried.

c. **1.** He wishes he could fly. **2.** He wishes he were a hero. **3.** He wishes he could have any adventures. **4.** He wishes he could live differently. **5.** If only he could be somewhere else.

d. **1.** If he takes risks Calvin will crash. **2.** He knew that if he took risks, he would crash. **3.** It is time women had equal opportunities with men / the same opportunities as men.

Unit 4 Destination UK

WB P. 105-106

1. a. **Ireland** / Irish / the Irish • **England** / English / the English • **Scotland** / Scottish / the Scots • **Wales** / Welsh / the Welsh • **Europe** / European / the Europeans

b. **1.** bacon and eggs **2.** chips **3.** strawberries **4.** meat **5.** scone **6.** pie **7.** sausages **8.** roast potatoes **9.** jam **10.** baked beans **11.** mushrooms

c. The thistle is the emblem of Scotland. • The red rose is the emblem of England. • The daffodil is the emblem of Wales. • The shamrock is the emblem of Ireland.

d. generous ≠ stingy • relaxed ≠ stiff • sober ≠ drunk • polite ≠ rude • intelligible ≠ incomprehensible • sunny ≠ rainy

e. – The cook is **awful**. So the food is **tasteless** / **inedible** /**disgusting**. – This woman feels superior. She is **contemptuous** / **arrogant**. – This apple pie **tastes** good. – I'm **fond** of hiking, but I'm not so **keen** on sailing.

f. /iː/ beans - cream - people - beef • /ɪ/ chicken - chips - pudding • /aɪ/ rice - pie - Marmite

2. **1.** The Scots are said to be stingy. It's a prejudice. **2.** The Brits are often considered bad cooks.

3. Hadrian's Wall is worth visiting. **4.** "Would you like / Do you want some Marmite?" "Yes, I'd like to have a try." **5.** "What is his job?" "He is a judge." **6.** The chime of Big Ben is famous all around the world.

Unit 5 Over the Rainbow

WB p. 107-108

▶ **1.** a. landscape / scenery • *protestation / manifestation* • despair • *libération* • prejudice
breathtaking • *émouvant(e)* • determined / strong-minded • *amer (amère)* • on an equal footing • *engagé(e)* • rebellious
be discriminated against • *écraser une émeute* • threaten • *lutter* • promote • *sensibiliser / alerter qqn au sujet de* • make sb aware of sth • *combler le fossé* • overcome • *manifester contre*

b. Black South Africans were discriminated **against** but they rebelled **against** white domination. Nelson Mandela acted **for** peace and wanted all people to be **on** an equal footing. He was deeply involved **in** the struggle **against** apartheid and fought **for** justice and equal rights. He succeeded **in** bridging the gap between Blacks and Whites thanks to rugby. Johnny Clegg alerts people **to** racial problems in South Africa and urges them **to** overcome the barriers. All his life, he has been fighting **against** prejudices.

c. discriminated • rebelled • domination • involved • apartheid • justice • succeeded • alerts • overcome • barriers • prejudices

e. **a)** youth **b)** demonstrations **c)** wilful **d)** threatened **e)** injured **f)** crush

▶ **2.** a. **Description:** Mandela and the captain of the South African rugby team shake hands, support, congratulate sb for, respect one another…
Message: act for peace and reconciliation, overcome prejudices, barriers, bridge the gap between two communities, determined to fight for equality…
Réactions: optimistic, hope for the future, bright future, moving…

b. In *Invictus*, Clint Eastwood shows that Mandela was **determined** to fight for equality and act for **peace**. In this still from the film, the two characters are shaking hands. It shows that they **respect** each other, and proves that sport was also a way to **bridge** the gap in South Africa. I find this film **brilliant** and **moving** and on top of that it has a happy **ending**.

c. **1.** There have been many problems since the end of apartheid. **2.** Nelson Mandela left his prison cell in 1990. **3.** Robben Island prison has been a museum since 1996.

Unit 6 Beyond Limits

WB p. 109-110

▶ **1.** a. standard of living • *produits de base* • below the poverty line
misérable, démuni(e), dans le besoin • *audacieux(euse)* • determined • smart, clever • *téméraire* • weak • *maltraité(e)*
become, became, become • *interdire* • *parler au nom de qqn* • overcome obstacles • *être récompensé* • give up • *mourir de faim* • improve • *fournir qqch à qqn* • win, won, won • fulfil one's dreams

b. poverty • suffer • pioneer • success • have access • obstacle • clever • intelligent • phenomenon

c. adventurous • daring • courageous • skillful • energetic • inventive

d. ***Present perfect*** **a.** *He's just read a book on Shackleton.*
Verbe être b. *Shackleton's an explorer.*
Cas possessif c. *Shackleton's ship was called the Endurance.*

e. William lives in a remote village. The locals had no access to water or electricity. Their standard of living is low. William designed a mill to provide them with electricity. He dreamt of improving the situation and he succeeded.

▶ **2.** a. **Problèmes rencontrés :** difficulties, problems, obstacles…

Ce qu'il ne faut pas faire : give up, be discouraged…
Ce qu'il faut faire : qualités nécessaires : be determined, have a goal, courageous, brave, strength, overcome obstacles, be persevering, be energetic, go ahead *(aller de l'avant),* achieve our goal, take up the challenge *(relever le défi)...*

b. We are often **confronted with** difficulties. Yet, we must never **give up**, we must take up the **challenge** and go on **fighting**. To **overcome obstacles** we must be **determined**. We will **manage to** achieve success only if we are courageous and **persevering**. To **reach** our **goals** we must be brave and **energetic**. The message is **positive**.

c. **1.** The most famous • the most courageous **2.** the best • the greatest **3.** the bravest • the most daring **4.** the most amazing • the scariest • the most fantastic

d. **1.** Shackelton was twenty-eight (years old) when he went to / left for Antarctica. **2.** He was lucky to explore the South Pole with Scott. **3.** There was a lot of snow. There were many dangers / risks. **4.** He was very cold but he was not scared / frightened. **5.** He was forty-eight (years old) when he died in Antarctica.

Unit 7 Geeks

WB P. 111-112

► 1. a. *informatique* • engineer • *lecteur numérique de musique* • lack of • *percée* • turning point • private life • *carrière (professionnelle)* • device
time-consuming • *travailleur(euse)* • *qui créé une dépendance (addictif)* • innovative • *qualifié(e)* • determined / strong-willed • *intelligent(e)* • brand new • shocked
posséder un téléphone portable • *encourager* • *se passer de quelque chose* • warn sb against / alert sb to • *se débarrasser de* • criticize sb for • *fabriquer* • hire • keep in touch with • *espionner*

b. **1.** I'm going to stop / quit / give up watching films online. **2.** He is dependent on / addicted to / hooked on screens. **3.** This young woman is gifted / talented. **4.** The company / firm / corporation has just released / launched a new product.

c. **a)** software **b)** virtual **c)** harmful **d)** convenient **e)** rebellious **f)** outdated **g)** usually **h)** time-saving
Mot mystère : *wireless* (sans fil)

► 2. a. **Description de la situation :** laptop, desk, typing on his keyboard, surfing the Internet, two characters, hacker, geeks, addicted to / dependent on, do without…
Messages / Buts : make fun of, computer-friendly, denounce addiction, intelligent / clever, get caught out at his own game…
Vos réactions : funny / hilarious / amusing, concerned, experience the same problems…

b. I find this cartoon **funny / amusing / hilarious** and **interesting** because it is obviously making **fun** of this boy who wants to be a **hacker**. He wanted to **change** his grades but he can't be **more intelligent** than the school computer. Apparently, he is completely **addicted** to his own computer and couldn't **do / live** without **going / playing / surfing** online.

c. **1.** Instead of doing his homework, he can't help playing online. **2.** I can't stand arguing with my parents, I would like them to stop criticizing me for staying up late. **3.** They are used to having quick access to information, they hate searching for hours.

Unit 8 Go West!

WB P. 113-114

► 1. a. *paysage* • income • *perspectives d'avenir* • opportunities • standard of living
needy • jobless • miserable • *disponible* • enormous, huge • disillusioned
succeed • realize • fulfil one's dreams • *vivre une expérience* • attract visitors • *être bloqué*

b. - This park is worth visiting. - He spends his time watching westerns. - He urges him to leave the reservation. - He expects him to succeed. - When he got lost in the blizzard, he realized that the journey was going to de difficult.

c. /d/ followed, travelled • /t/ pushed, asked, stretched, helped, walked, cooked • /ɪd/ wanted, ended, loaded, decided, started, expected

► 2. a. **Personnages : qui ? Groupes en présence ? À quelle occasion ?** Lewis and Clark's arrival, group of Native Americans, friendly, peaceful, welcoming, curious to meet the newcomers, during the expedition… **Buts de la rencontre ? Résultats ?** explore the new territory, find a direct route to the Pacific, collect information about plants, animals, the climate, meet the tribes, find help through unknown territories and support…

b. Lewis and Clark returned to St. Louis as **heroes**. They were the first United States citizens to **see** and **describe** the West, and they had made **maps** that would guide future **pioneers / travellers**, described hundreds of **animals** and **plants**, and created new opportunities for **trade**. Their **journey / expedition** could not have happened without the generous cooperation and contributions of numerous Native Americans. They faced many difficult **challenges**, as the territory through which they **travelled** was largely unknown. The expedition **succeeded**, because Native Americans generously **shared** their **knowledge** and resources.

c. **1.** Dr. Whitman was one of the most famous guides. He was able to help the pioneers because he had already been to the West. **2.** No one had crossed the Rockies before. The pioneers trusted him and they made it. **3.** The settlers knew that they could find food and medicine at the Whitmans' house. **4.** The Indians killed Dr. Whitman and his wife because the doctor hadn't been able to save an Indian chief.

Unit 9 Free at Last

WB p. 115-116

► 1. a. human being • slave • *vente aux enchères* • reward • cabin • *propriétaire* • *navire négrier*
obedient • desperate • *impitoyable* • *impuissant(e)* • inhumane • *terrible*
souffrir de • flee, run away, escape • *se plaindre de* • rebel • *récolter* • obey • hide, hid, hidden • save sb from • *enchaîner*

b. **1.** be considered as cattle **2.** transport below deck **3.** She died of despair. **4.** a runaway slave **5.** feel threatened **6.** a heart-rending moment **7.** split up / tear apart families

c. humiliated • captured • punished • terrified • abolished • plantation • violence • tobacco • cruel • cotton • admire • resolute

d. **Down 1.** determined **2.** courageous **3.** plantation **4.** escape
Across 5. slavery **6.** naked **7.** abolitionist **8.** cotton **9.** freedom **10.** sunrise **11.** inhumane

► 2. a. **Personnages :** family, slave, mother, child, young, tired, worn out, for sale, to be sold, auction, slave market…
Sentiments : anxious, desperate, terrified, scared to death, horrified, powerless, heartbroken…
Obligations / interdictions : obey, accept the master's decision, do as they are told, rebel, refuse an order, complain about sth…

b. We can see two **slaves**, a mother and her **son**, waiting to be sold on the **auction block / market**. They certainly felt **anxious / desperate** and **terrified / scared to death**. This drawing reminds us of the **heart-rending / awful/ dreadful** moment slaves feared the most: when families were **torn apart / split up**. Slaves in this situation could not **disobey** nor **refuse their master's decision**. They had to **do as they were told / obey** so as to stay alive.

c. **1.** The mother wanted her son to stay with her. **2.** The slaves expected their owners to sell them. **3.** The young boy intended to escape/ flee / run away to the north.

Unit 10 Green Art

WB p. 117-118

► 1. a. *cheminée d'usine* • waste • factory / plant • *gaz à effet de serre* • endangered species • *rivage* • sustainable development

scary • *troublant(e)* • *perplexe* • *étrange* • humorous • effective • useless • *très sale*
realise • *déverser* • prevent from • *prendre conscience de* • threaten • *disparaître* • destroy • *fondre* • use up / exhaust (resources) • cope with a problem

b. **1.** live closer to nature **2.** upset nature's balance **3.** I find this ad surprising. **4.** To my mind, this advertisement is useless. **5.** The goal / purpose is to...

c. pollution • deforestation • sustainable • development • humorous • efficient • disappear • endangered species • puzzled • realistic

d. **1.** sewage **2.** careless **3.** rubbish **4.** threatens **5.** spill **6.** dustbin **7.** global warming

► 2. a. **Buts :** impact on the environment, endangered species, responsible for...
Problèmes soulevés : ice melting, global warming, rising level, flood...
Vos réactions : make people aware of the problem, shock the viewer, device to alert people, we are all concerned...

b. It deals with **global warming** and its impact on the **environment**. The ice cap has melted; that's why bears have become an **endangered species**. Man is **responsible** for pollution. Our careless attitude is **threatening** our planet. The photographer's **goal** is to make us **aware** of the situation, to **warn** us about the risks we are running if we **upset** nature's balance. The scene does not look very realistic but the photomontage is **clever** and the situation is **scary** / **alarming**.

c. **1.** This advertisement doesn't make me laugh because it is weird. **2.** If governments don't do anything / do nothing, the situation will get worse. **3.** We mustn't / can't let factories spill their waste in the rivers.

Unit 11 On Stage

WB P. 119-120

► 1. a. self-confident / self-assured • *abasourdi(e)* • *sérieux(euse)* • obedient • submissive • authoritative • *vaniteux(euse), superficiel(le)*
defy / challenge sb • *soutenir, encourager qqn* • disappoint • *prévenir qqn de* • prevent from

b. - polite: well-mannered - careful: cautious - direct: straightforward - rich: wealthy / well-off - very unhappy: miserable - very surprised: amazed / astonished - shocked: outraged - angry: cross

c. Does Jack belong **to** the aristocracy? Lady Bracknell is prejudiced **against** Jack. She doesn't approve **of** her daughter's engagement. She disapproves **of** the young man. She is worried **about** her daughter's fortune. She will inquire **into** the man's past. She would like to impose the man she has chosen **on** Gwendolen.

d. - répondit-il en hésitant : *he replied / answered hesitatingly* - répondirent-ils avec mépris : *they answered / replied contemptuously* - dit-elle fièrement : *she said proudly* - dit-elle plein d'espoir : *she said hopefully* - dit-elle avec impatience : *she said impatiently* - dit-il sincèrement : *He said sincerely*

e. Phrase 1 : surprise • Phrase 2 : ironie • Phrase 3 : colère

► 2. a. **Personnages, situation :** parents, girl and her future husband, introduce sb to, propose, open a huge box, full of / filled with money, discover, a huge fortune...
Critiques : judge sb on, greedy for money, interested in, care about, girl's happiness...
Réactions ? Pourquoi ? delighted, approve of, marriage, wealthy...

b. The parents **seem** to be **amazed** / **astonished** at seeing such a fortune. The parents **look** impressed by the young man's fortune. Before, they were **prejudiced against** him. They **disapproved of** their daughter's choice, but now he will gain the parents' **approval** because he is **wealthy** / **well-off**. I'm **outraged** because they don't care about their daughter's feelings.

c. Brad asked Angie if she would marry him. She answered / replied she would, she had been waiting for that moment for years. Angie added they would tell her mother the following / next day. She announced she was in love with Brad and that they wanted to marry. The mother replied that she couldn't believe what her daughter had just told her. She asked if Angie was out of her mind. She added she was too young. She asked where they would live and if they would have enough money. She asked if Brad had a job and where he worked. She ordered her to listen to her.

Unit 12 Pop Goes My Art

WB p. 121-122

► 1. a. *bande dessinée* • advertising • *renommée* • icon • print • *marque*
fashionable / state-of-the-art • similar • *attiré(e) par* • *coloré(e) / vif (vive)* • pitiless • average • *impuissant(e)*
expose / denounce • *incarner* • get rid of • sack / fire • crush • *agrandir* • *être intéressé(e) par*

b. **1.** It leaves me cold. **2.** be bored to death **3.** be considered an object **4.** show off **5.** be brainwashed into + V-ing **6.** be haunted by

c. **1re syllabe accentuée :** photograph • public • figure • icon • contrast • popular
2e syllabe accentuée : success • ideal

d. **a)** everyday life **b)** device **c)** materialistic **d)** geometrical **e)** icon **f)** wealthy **g)** advertising **h)** trendy **i)** bold **j)** luxurious **k)** superficial **l)** replicate

► 2. a. **Description :** silkscreen, identical bottles of Coke, brand name in red, recognizable, realism, advertising…
Interprétation : icon mass consumption, consumer society, embody, symbolize, everyday life…
Impressions / réactions : uniformity, standardization, expose / denounce…

b. We can see five bottles of Coca-Cola in a **row** and they all look **similar / identical**. The famous **brand name** stands out in red, which is a **vivid** colour that attracts the attention. This object of our **everyday life** is immediately **recognisable**. Coke is the most **popular** soft drink in the USA: It is what can be called a cultural **icon**. Warhol painted bottles of Coke because they **embody** mass consumption and are **symbols** of the American way of life and of our **consumer** society. But it also suggests **uniformity** and the standardisation of tastes.

c. **1.** The MoMA must be the most interesting museum in New York City. **2.** She may go and see the Keith Haring exhibition. **3.** This painting is a copy, it can't be a real Warhol.

Unit 13 City in the Sky

WB p. 123-124

► 1. a. skyscraper • *maladie*
moved • impressive • *soulagé(e)* • impressed • *surpeuplé(e) / bondé(e)* • frightened • *étouffant*
subir • *débarquer (ici)* • *faire l'éloge de* • expect to • fear • *atteindre ses buts / ses objectifs* • fulfil one's dreams

b. **1.** start from scratch **2.** I disapprove of this idea. **3.** I disagree / I don't agree with you. **4.** The singer refers to...

c. immigrant • opportunities • fascinated • control • disease • glamorous • overcrowded • excited • for instance = for example • fulfil

d. **1.** Ellis Island **2.** Giovanni da Verrazzano

► 2. a. **Personnages, situation :** immigrants, Ellis Island, Europe, poor countries, Greece, Italy...
Sentiments et impressions des personnages, espoirs : tired, frightened, puzzled, moved, worried, anxious, impressed, lost, better education, job opportunities, go up the social ladder…

b. They have travelled **below deck**, the boat was **overcrowded**. The atmosphere was **stifling**. They are **moved** because they have just arrived. They were **impressed** by the Statue of Liberty. They are **relieved** because they **got through** customs. They are **frightened** because they don't know what is going to happen to them. They are also **excited** because they are going to start from scratch. They **expect** to **fulfil** their dreams.

c. **1.** Among the New York skyscrapers, the Chrysler Building is / can be admired. **2.** The Freedom Tower is situated / located (in the place) where the World Trade Center stood. **3.** Many buildings have been renovated in Brooklyn. **4.** Every year, the Statue of Liberty is visited by millions of tourists.

Unit 14 Summer Rocks WB p. 125-126

► 1. a. line-up • dressed up as • steel band • stage • drum

b. *hébergement* • campsite • *gare* • discount • performance • suit • *déguisement / costume*
thrilled / overjoyed • affordable • *disponible*
acclamer • *réserver* • I'm looking forward to +V-ing • *défiler* • *jouer (une pièce de théâtre)*

c. enthusiastic • hysterical • overcrowded • impressive • experience • casual • clothes • overjoyed • exciting • elegant

d. The fans were so enthusiastic and overjoyed that they screamed and jumped on the stage. Some of them were hysterical. It was impressive. What an exciting experience! You shouldn't wear smart clothes, just dress casual! You don't need to look so elegant.

e. **a)** stage **b)** mud **c)** muddy **d)** scream **e)** festival **f)** weather

► 2. a. **Description :** rain, wet, mud, muddy, experience, rain boots, unusual, fine weather, lost, live the real thing…
Vos réactions : humorous, funny, weird…
Buts : make money out of, essential, festival experience…

b. Rainy **weather** is part of the Glastonbury experience and festival-goers should never forget their **wellies / rain boots / gumboots** because when it rains it gets very **muddy**. The visitor seems a bit lost and wonders if he should buy a bucket of **mud** to make the experience more authentic. I find this cartoon humorous because people usually **prefer** sunny **weather** to rain, but here the cartoonist shows that **mud** really is a part of the festival experience. He makes fun of the visitors who **attend** concerts in the rain and of the organisers who try to make money out of everything.

c. **1.** I'd prefer to go / going to a festival in England because I prefer British bands to French bands. **2.** How expensive! How about looking for a campsite instead of a bed and breakfast? **3.** You should ask Natalia to come with us.

Unit 15 Masters of Suspense WB p. 127-128

► 1. a. *menace* • evidence • fingerprints
weird • *effrayant (e)* • *lugubre* • *effrayant (e)*
hide • être poursuivi par • flee • *signaler un crime* • escape • *enquêter sur* • climb • commit a crime • *be lying down*

b. **1.** will **2.** disinherit **3.** weapon **4.** greedy **5.** murderer **6.** handwriting **7.** DNA **8.** suicide **9.** guilty

c. The man was found lying in a pool of blood. • The police have just found a weapon. • Are they the suspects? • He suspects his neighbour. • Sherlock Holmes is a fictional detective who uses his skills of observation and deduction to solve the most difficult crimes.

► 2. a. **Situation :** woman, man, hide, stalk sb, be chased by, flee, meet, manage to, shadow, hold a gun, ready to shoot, in the middle of the night…
Émotions : scary, suspense, tense, frightening, threatening, gloomy…

b. The atmosphere is **gloomy** and **scary**. She **is holding a gun** in her hand. She has seen the **shadow** of a man who is ready to **shoot** her. He **is** now **hiding** behind the building. But she heard footsteps and realized he was following her and wanted to **kill** her. She is **tense** because she knows her life is in danger. She doesn't want to **flee**, she wants to confront him.

c. **1.** What were you doing at midnight last night? Where were you going? **2.** How many people were with you? **3.** How long did you wait for the bus? **4.** Who saw you? Who did you meet on the way? **5.** How far away was the car? **6.** What did the man look like? **7.** Whose gun is this? **8.** How long were you together?

Classroom English Survival kit

Habituez-vous à utiliser ces expressions pour communiquer et exprimer vos besoins en cours d'anglais sans repasser par le français.

1. Accueil, début et fin de cours

a. Trouvez au moins deux expressions en anglais pour :
- dire bonjour.
- deux autres pour quitter le cours en fin d'heure.

b. Vous souvenez-vous de ce qu'il convient de dire dans ces situations?
- Vous arrivez en retard et expliquez pourquoi (retard du bus, réveil qui n'a pas sonné ...).
- Vous avez oublié votre matériel (cahier, classeur, stylo...).
- Vous n'avez pas fait vos devoirs et vous vous en excusez.

c. Comment répondez-vous présent à l'appel ?
Comment signalez-vous un(e) élève absent, un(e) élève malade ?

2. Besoins immédiats

a. Observez ces images et faites la liste de toutes les expressions qui vous viennent à l'esprit.

b. Complétez vos listes grâce aux expressions que vous allez entendre. CD3 PISTE 46 MP3 PISTE 58

c. Trouvez à quoi servent ces expressions :
- *Can you switch on / off the lights, please?*
- *Do you mind if / May I go to the medical room?*
- *Can you play the recording again, please?*
- *Could you explain the instructions for exercise 1, please?*

3. Être plus efficace

a. **Lisez ces expressions et trouvez dans quelles situations de classe elles peuvent être utiles.**

Pour ...
- *How do you spell this word?*
- *Could you write it on the board, please?*
- *I didn't understand this word, could you spell it, please?*

Quand ...
- *I'm not so sure of the answer.*
- *Sorry, I can't remember what's next.*
- *May I have a few minutes to think about it?*

Quand ...
- *You should have said...*
- *I think there's / I think you made a mistake.*
- *Instead of saying... you should say...*

Pour ...
- *How do you pronounce this word?*
- *Is that the right way to say it?*
- *Is that correct?*

Quand ...
- *Could you step aside, please?*
- *I can't see the board.*

Quand ...
- *I'm afraid I don't know.*
- *I haven't a clue /klu:/.*
- *I'm sorry, but I haven't understood the question.*
- *Sorry, I don't know what you mean.*
- *I am not sure I can answer.*
- *I'm sorry, but I don't know what to say.*

b. **Écoutez l'enregistrement et entraînez-vous à répéter ces phrases.** CD3 PISTE 46 MP3 PISTE 58

c. **Pensez à varier vos expressions et à améliorer l'anglais de vos demandes (A2 → B1)**
- *Sorry I'm late.* → *I apologize for being late.*
- *What's the English for...?* → *How do you say...?*
- *What's the French for...?* → *What does the word "..." mean in French?*
- *Repeat, please.* → *Would you mind repeating, please?*
- *I don't understand, I'm sorry.* → *I'm not sure I understand what you mean.*

4. Nommer les objets utiles en classe

a. **Observez ce nuage de mots. Quels mots vous sont familiers ? Chercher la traduction des mots inconnus dans le dictionnaire.**

b. **Votre professeur va vous distribuer une fiche à compléter à l'aide des mots ci-dessus. Combien d'objets pouvez-vous nommer rapidement ?** (Attention à l'orthographe, certains mots sont des noms composés.)

Good reads, good films: why not enjoy English outside school?

Fancy reading in English but too shy for the real thing?

Try reading simplified versions of famous classics. Choose, for example, the **intermediate level** in the **Macmillan Readers** collection or **Easy Readers (Longman)**.

Here are a few examples of classics you could read:

Pride and Prejudice, Jane Austen, 1813
Jane Eyre, Charlotte Brontë, 1847
Wuthering Heights, Emily Brontë, 1847
Alice's Adventures in Wonderland, Lewis Carroll, 1865
The Great Gatsby, F. Scott Fitzgerald, 1925
The Murder of Roger Ackroyd, Agatha Christie, 1926
Of Mice and Men, John Steinbeck, 1937
Rebecca, Daphne du Maurier, 1938
The Big Sleep, Raymond Chandler, 1939
Black Boy, Richard Wright, 1945
Animal Farm, George Orwell, 1945
1984, George Orwell, 1949
Fahrenheit 451, Ray Bradbury, 1953
The Lord of the Rings, J.R.R. Tolkien, 1954-55
A Wrinkle in Time, Madeleine L'Engle, 1962
Tales of the Unexpected, Roald Dahl, 1979

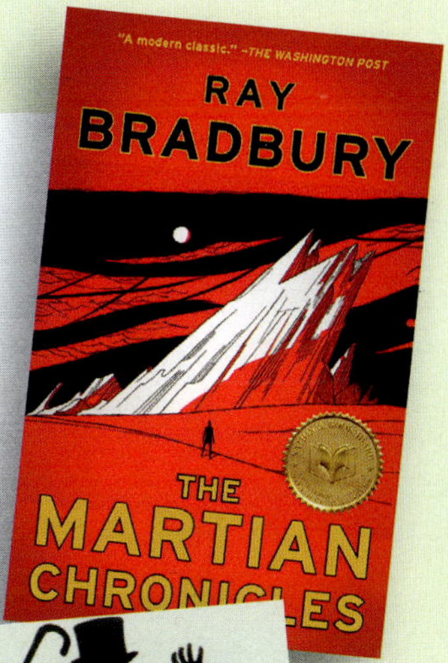

Some entertaining modern reads:

The Host, Stephenie Meyer, 2008
Ender's Game, Orson Scott Card, 1985
The Hunger Games Trilogy, Susan Collins, 2008-10
The Girl Who Loved Tom Gordon, Stephen King, 1999
The Book Thief, Markus Zusak, 2006
The Boy in the Striped Pyjamas, John Boyne, 2006

You can also listen to many books online and it's free!
Go to : openculture.com/freeaudiobooks

Train your ear outside school, go to the following sites:

rea.ccdmd.qc.ca/ri/listening/
www.elllo.org
If you want to watch the news you can go to: www.bbc.co.uk/news/video_and_audio
Or edition.cnn.com/US/studentnews/quick.guide/archive/

Looking for a good old film? Here are a few ideas:

Frank Capra, 1946
As George Bailey prepares to jump from a bridge, his guardian angel intercedes.

Elia Kazan, 1955
Cal Trask is a particularly unhappy young man. When his father rejects a gift from him, he sends Cal into an act of revenge that will have tragic consequences.

Billy Wilder, 1959
A legendary comedy about two musicians who witness the St. Valentine's Day Massacre and try to elude their pursuers by joining an all-girl band.

Stanley Kubrick, 1968
HAL, the computer that runs a spaceship, takes on a life of his own and starts controlling the humans.

John Boorman, 1987
The story of a boy called Bill as he grows up in London during the blitz of World War 2

- *Gandhi* (1982) • *Cry Freedom* (1987), Richard Attenborough
- *The Gold Rush* (1925) • *Modern Times* (1936), Charlie Chaplin
- *The Deer Hunter* (1978), Michael Cimino
- *The Man Who Shot Liberty Valance* (1962), John Ford
- *Rear Window* (1954) • *North by Northwest* (1959) • *Psycho* (1960), Alfred Hitchcock
- *A Room With a View* (1985), James Ivory
- *Dances With Wolves* (1990), Kevin Kostner
- *Barry Lyndon* (1975), Stanley Kubrick
- *Kes* (1969) • *Raining Stones* (1993) • *Land and Freedom* (1995) • *Bread and Roses* (2000) • *Ae Fond Kiss* (2004) • *The Wind That Shakes the Barley* (2006) • *The Angels' Share* (2012), Ken Loach
- *The Last of the Mohicans* (1992), Michael Mann
- *Little Big Man* (1970), Arthur Penn
- *Jeremiah Johnson* (1972), Sydney Pollack
- *River of No Return* (1954), Otto Preminger
- *Rebel Without a Cause* (1955), Norman Ray
- *Taxi Driver* (1976), Martin Scorsese
- *West Side Story* (1961), Robert Wise
- *Forrest Gump* (1994), Robert Zemeckis